D1035571

The Rise of the Student Estate in Britain

By Eric Ashby

Challenge to Education
Scientist in Russia
Technology and the Academics
Community of Universities
African Universities and Western Tradition

By Eric Ashby and Mary Anderson

Universities: British, Indian, African
Adam Sedgwick's Discourse on the Studies of the
University (edited, with introductory essay)

The Rise of the
Student Estate in Britain

ERIC ASHBY AND MARY ANDERSON

Harvard University Press
Cambridge, Massachusetts
1970

© Sir Eric Ashby and Mary Anderson 1970

First published 1970

SBN 674-77290-3

Printed in Great Britain

Contents

Acknowledgements   vii

Introduction   ix

1 The Latent Estate: 1815–50
   Contrasts of north and south   1
   Patterns of paternalism and discipline   4
   Student response   10
   Verdicts of the royal commission of 1826–30   16

2 The Scottish Example
   The students' representative council   20
   Participation and recognition   27

3 Student Awakening in the South
   Student organisation and statutory recognition   40
   Student participation in university government   51
   A false start in cohesion   57

4 National Co-ordination
   The National Union of Students   61
   In search of an identity   70
   Blueprint for the future   86

5 The Flowering of the Student Estate
   Post-war readjustment   91
   Corporate opinion   97
   Participation   103
   Partnership with the Establishment   108

6 The Conscience of the Student Estate
   'A conscience of society'   121
   Categories of the student conscience   123

The strategy of protest   129
Abuse of the student conscience   130
'Aggressive tolerance'   136
Power and participation   138
Authority in the university   149

Documents

Memorial of the students' representative councils of the
Universities of St Andrews, Glasgow, Aberdeen and
Edinburgh to members of H.M.G. on the Universities
(Scotland) bill, 1888   156
Statement by the students' representative council of the
University of Edinburgh to the Scottish Universities Com-
mission, February 1890   162
Charter of student rights and responsibilities, 1940   166

References   168

Index   181

Acknowledgements

The research on which this book is based was supported by a grant from the Leverhulme Trust Fund. It is a pleasure to acknowledge our debt to the Trustees and the Director. In collecting material for the book we have had help from many sources. We would especially like to record our thanks to Mr Geoffrey Martin, who, when he was president of the National Union of Students, allowed us to consult the archives of the union, and to Mrs Stella Greenall, research officer of the union, for her unfailing help. We were privileged to be able to consult Sir Ivison Macadam, the first president of the National Union of Students, who read the draft of Chapters 1–4 and made many very valuable comments and suggestions. We are grateful to Mr Charles Parkin, fellow of Clare College, who wrote for us a paper on authority and participation in universities, which we have drawn upon for one part of the discussion in Chapter 6. Sir James Mountford, the Scottish Record Office, and the libraries of the Universities of Edinburgh and Cambridge generously helped to trace documents for us. We wish to thank also Mrs C. Durant-Lewis for typing the book from an untidy manuscript and Mrs M. M. Anderson for reading the proofs and arresting many small errors.

E. A.
M. A.

December 1969

Introduction

In the autumn of 1968 the Committee of Vice-Chancellors and Principals of the British universities and the National Union of Students issued a joint statement about the part students should play in the management of universities. Opinions differ about the merits of this document. What is beyond dispute is that it symbolises the recognition of a 'student estate' in Britain. The origins and rise of this estate is the theme of this book.

The estate did not emerge suddenly. For a generation official bodies have sought the views of the National Union of Students, or have received unsolicited memoranda from them, on many questions concerning higher education. At first there was a touch of reluctance, not to say condescension, about the consultations; but in recent years it has come to be recognised that the corporate opinion among students on matters of close concern to them is important, and ought to be influential, and it has been assumed that statements by the National Union of Students are a fair expression of this corporate opinion. Moreover, the statements themselves are for the most part shrewd and perceptive and often coincide (as they did, for instance, in evidence given to the Robbins Committee on higher education) with what subsequently becomes adopted policy.[1]

The surprise is not so much that a student estate has emerged as a power to be reckoned with, as that it has taken so long to emerge. For, on paper at any rate, students are *members* of the university; they differ from pupils in a school or patients in a hospital or passengers on a ship. Although there is a medieval ambiguity about the meaning of the word 'scholar',[2] it is nevertheless significant that the University of Cambridge, for instance, is defined as a corporation of three constituents: chancellor, masters and scholars; when the university enters into a contract it is signed on behalf of all three of these constituents. In the University of Glasgow, when a student has matriculated, he becomes *civis universitatis*. This right of membership is reasserted in the charters of the civic universities, including the most recent ones; in the University of East Anglia, for instance, undergraduate students are reckoned, along with the officers, the academic staff, and the graduates, as 'Members of the University'.

The response of universities, and even of parliament, to the claims of students to exercise their membership, leaves no doubt that the student estate is a reality. This reality has received further support from the Family Law Reform Act 1969, which lowers the age of majority from twenty-one to eighteen. But there is confusion about the activities and purposes and rights of this new estate. A narrow concern with educational procedures inside the university is mixed up with a world-wide protest about the values of society. Demands to take part in decision-making in faculties and senates are inflamed by a world-wide rejection of traditional deference to authority. A great deal has been written about the anatomy of protest and we attempt to analyse some of it at the conclusion of this book.

But although so much has been written about contemporary student activity in Britain, it has not been put into its historical setting. One consequence of this is that the influence which students are now exerting on universities is not seen in perspective. To supply this historical setting, and to interpret contemporary events in the light of the history of student participation in British universities, is the purpose of this book.

Universities exist in a continuum of time and space. They are inseparable from their past and from one another. Since the time of Abelard students have felt themselves to belong to a supra-national community. As recent events demonstrate only too clearly, student life in London cannot be disengaged from student life in Paris and Berlin and Berkeley. Nor can student life in 1970 be disengaged from the life students led even as long ago as in the middle ages; indeed the student-controlled universities of medieval Italy are often cited today in arguments for student power. We therefore had a frustrating choice: either to draw an impressionistic cartoon over an enormous canvas, or to select certain episodes which illuminate the path which has led to the student estate. We have chosen the second course. In time we restrict the chronicle to the nineteenth and twentieth centuries. In space we restrict it to Britain. Our theme is not the familiar one of the influence of universities upon students, of the masters upon the scholars; it is the less familiar one of the influence of students upon universities, of the scholars upon the masters.

1 The Latent Estate: 1815–50

Contrasts of north and south

I regard, then, the academical institutions of England and Scotland, as things specifically distinct. . . . I please myself in thinking that the two institutions have different objects, and that they are both excellent in their different ways. That each system might borrow something with advantage from the other is very possible, but I respect both of them too much to be fond of hasty and rash experiments.[1]

Such was the complacent conclusion of the young J. G. Lockhart, writing under an assumed name in 1819. His complacency was misconceived but his opinion – that the two institutions had different objects – was indisputable, and this difference was vividly reflected in the lives led by students north and south of the border.

The contrast has often been described. The two English universities were monastic institutions adapted to the secular purpose of keeping up 'the race of English gentlemen' (as Lockhart put it) and the scarcely less secular purpose of providing a non-vocational and largely irrelevant education for those destined to occupy England's rectories and deaneries and bishops' palaces. The common age of entry for a student was eighteen. Three-quarters of the students came from public schools. They had to subscribe, on matriculation at Oxford and on graduation at Cambridge, to the tenets of the anglican church. Their fathers were predominantly anglican clergy or professional men or landowners.[2] Apart from examining those who chose to read for degrees, the university played little part in the students' lives; they were housed in colleges under the care of fellows who had to be celibate, and taught by fellows or, more commonly, by private tutors they themselves hired. There was no obligation to be studious and throughout the first half of the nineteenth century the majority of students who were sent to Oxford or Cambridge went (as one of the witnesses to the 1850 commission on Oxford put it) 'for the same reason that, at certain periods of their life they were breeched, then put into a jacket, then into a coat. . .'.[3] It was the respectable thing to do; it provided 'a last polish to their education, and . . . the opportunity of forming connexions in the world. . .'.[4]

But this description was not true of a minority of English students. In unreformed Cambridge, for instance, some third of the undergraduates were 'reading men', who had voluntarily entered the savage competition for honours. Success could lead to a fellowship, preferment in the church, a headship in a public school. The curriculum was narrow and severe: classics and mathematics, culminating in the struggle for a place as a wrangler. The ambitious student, with no assured job awaiting him, had to accept this unhealthy obsession with an examination in subjects of dubious educational value. Some of the self-appointed victims of this system complained bitterly about it afterwards. One disenchanted senior wrangler, in the *London Magazine and Review* in 1825, wrote that the course had 'dried up the fountains of the imagination and the fancy', and T. B. Macaulay, who revelled in the friendships, the conversation, the leisure to read, the intellectual hierarchy of Trinity, never reconciled himself to mathematics. Writing to his mother, he complained: 'I feel myself becoming a personification of Algebra. . . . All my perceptions of elegance and beauty gone, or at least going' – though it would have taken more than Cambridge mathematics to blunt Macaulay's perceptions: his taste for literature was so strong that he found time to walk miles out of Cambridge to meet the coach bringing the last new Waverley novel.

The English student 150 years ago could, according to his circumstances, choose at Cambridge a life of elegant idleness or rich intellectual enjoyment or desperate competition, in surroundings of magical beauty, at a financial outlay, if he wished to be comfortable and to hire a private tutor, of about £300 a year. Or he could travel north and enrol in a Scottish university.

Over two centuries had passed since James the sixth of Scotland had come with his court from Holyrood to Whitehall to become James the first of England. Yet in 1815, when our story begins, the Union had led to no integration between the universities of Scotland and the universities of England. They were kept apart by barriers of religion, endowments, and social purpose. The Scottish universities – though they required no religious subscription from their students – were as beholden to the kirk as Oxford was to the bishops. They were pitifully poor compared with the richer colleges in the south. The student body, instead of being drawn predominantly from gentlemanly families, covered the whole spectrum of society, from the sons of crofters to the sons of affluent Edinburgh lawyers. The purpose of the Scottish universities was (as the royal commission of 1826 was told by one of its witnesses) that of diffusing throughout the lower classes of society 'that degree of various knowledge and sound sentiments on moral and religious subjects, which has brought forward the people of this country to a condition much beyond what has been reached by any other'.[5]

The regime of the universities was geared to this purpose. The academic year began in November after the potatoes were lifted and ended in May in time for the student to walk home for the haymaking; it was the prototype of the modern sandwich course. There was no entrance examination. Boys came to the university at the age of fourteen or even younger. Lodgings might cost less than £5 for the whole academic year[6] and a boy content to live on porridge and herrings could get by on £30 a year: a tenth of the cost of study at Cambridge. There was none of the exclusive, cosy cohesion of college life in the south. Students preferred the solitude and independence of lodgings; when the University of Edinburgh offered students chambers to live in, the offer was not accepted and the chambers were turned into classrooms.[7] Except for its professional teaching in medicine, law, and theology, the Scottish university served the purpose of a grammar school. Few of the students took degrees: the class certificate issued by the professor was the qualification they took back to farm and village.

As in England, so in Scotland, the universities, though not insisting on high academic standards, did offer opportunities and inducements, though modest ones, to the genuine scholar; and one gets the impression that 'learning for its own sake' was more common than in England. Side by side with the ragged urchin laboriously construing his Latin were men in their sixties attending classes as earnestly as the W.E.A. student three generations later in the cotton towns of Lancashire.

One important consequence of this difference in student life between north and south was that attendance at the university was much more widespread in Scotland than in England. In 1825, when the population of England was six times that of Scotland, the English universities had only 3000 students compared with 4000 in the Scottish universities.[8] Teaching in universities as big as Edinburgh and Glasgow took the form of the professor's lecture, to an audience of two or three hundred. After the lectures the students dispersed to their lodgings, their homes, or to taverns in the city.

Since Lockhart's day, and by a process as leisurely as he could have wished, the universities of the north and the south have borrowed

3

something from one another. The first impact of Scotland on student life in the south was not through England's ancient universities (which still remained stubbornly immune from Scottish influence) but through the two colleges, University and King's, which became part of the University of London. These colleges offered to students of the middle classes a cheap, non-residential higher education and did not prescribe any religious tests. Lectures in University College were held from 8 a.m. to 4 p.m. There was, as in Scotland, some flexibility in choice of courses, not the *table d'hôte* of Oxford or Cambridge. Student life, in the first two decades at any rate, was gloomy and drab; commuting to Gower Street or the Strand, attending too many lectures and swotting for too many examinations: altogether a mean and modest beginning to a movement, inspired by the universities of Scotland and Germany, which transformed English higher education. But there was created in London a student life with some similarities to student life in Scotland. The London students were younger than those in Oxford and Cambridge, they had (to use the modern jargon) a stronger motivation, and this was reinforced, as in Edinburgh and Glasgow, by the high proportion of medical students among them.[9]

Patterns of paternalism and discipline

In the days we are writing about there was no organised student estate, but it is interesting that the first traces of one were to be found, not among the sophisticated gentlemen in Trinity or Christ Church, but among the adolescent pupils of Glasgow and Aberdeen. There are two reasons for this: the contrast between the concepts of paternalism held by the masters in Scottish and English universities, and the tradition in Scotland which gave students a right to participate in university government denied to their brothers in the south.

It is commonly supposed that on the one hand the Scottish professor was indifferent to the moral and spiritual welfare of his pupils, and that on the other hand the tutor at Oxford and Cambridge exerted a solicitous supervision over the whole of his pupils' private lives. These suppositions are wrong. The contrast between south and north was not in the presence or absence of concern on the part of the masters toward the scholars: it was in the way the masters interpreted the meaning and purpose of higher education.

To illustrate this contrast we can do no better than compare the views of two distinguished academics, both of whom flourished in the first half of the nineteenth century: Whewell in Cambridge and Jardine in Glasgow. Their writings are personal and subjective, but there is good evidence from the comments of their contemporaries that they were paradigms of what was regarded as the best academic thought of their time.

Whewell's small book *On the principles of English university education*, published in 1837, is a frankly tendentious essay, for he was deeply committed to the system he described and he was defending it against assault. Discipline, for Whewell, began with the content of the curriculum and the manner of teaching it. One can, he said, follow a 'respectful' system in which students are required to familiarise themselves with subjects of indisputable truth, such as classics and mathematics, where the superiority of the teacher is assured. Or one can follow a 'speculative' system, such as philosophy, in which students are invited to think for themselves and are placed 'in the position of critics instead of pupils'. Whewell came down emphatically in favour of the respectful system, which leads the scholar 'to entertain a docile and confiding disposition toward his instructor'. He vindicated his choice by reference to the vehement hostility which students in Germany and France were at that time displaying towards the institutions of their country – a consequence which 'may naturally flow from an education which invokes the critical spirit, and invites it to employ itself on the comparison between the realities of society and the dreams of system-makers'. There could be no greater contrast between this view of the purpose of education and Jardine's view, namely that the education of his Scottish pupils of fourteen should begin, as Bacon taught, 'by divesting the pompous teacher of nearly all his acquirements and by impressing upon the mind of the pupil that his own senses and reflection were the only sure guides to knowledge'.[10]

But before we discuss Jardine's concept of higher education, we must consider some consequences of Whewell's views. For discipline inside the curriculum he depended upon a willing subjection to the teacher's authority. Outside the classroom there must be a similar willing subjection. The custom in continental universities, where the student's private life and social conduct were his own affair and did not fall under the university's jurisdiction, was anathema to Whewell. Academic freedom, he said, has never been the system of English universities. For the 'Free University', as Whewell (happily innocent of its present meaning) described the continental system, had led (how topical his words sound!) to tumults in France and Germany and, nearer home, among medical students in London. No such disturbances had ruffled

Cambridge. This was Whewell's vindication of university and college discipline in Cambridge: compulsory chapel, modesty and purity of manners in college, gate hours, obedience to those set in authority over their pupils, and so on.

That this spirit of paternalism at Cambridge was not peculiar to Whewell is evident from other pronouncements of that time. Thomas Thorp, for example, in a commemoration sermon preached to freshmen in 1840, urged his congregation that we (the members of the university) should walk together 'in entire subordination of our individual inclinations and conduct to the principles of the Institution into which we are admitted';[11] and Thomas Whytehead, in a small treatise published for the edification of undergraduates in 1845, asserted that it was an essential part of a college student's character 'to regard superiors . . . with reverence and honour, and to pay a glad and graceful obedience to discipline and law'.[12]

The corollary of filial submission on the part of the scholars is parental care on the part of the masters: indeed the statutes of colleges enjoined tutors to act *in loco parentis*. But, with exceptions of course, it appears that neither side observed these principles very conscientiously. There is a lively account of Cambridge by an American, C. A. Bristed, who was there in the early 1840s.[13] He was struck by the adolescent behaviour of the undergraduates: 'youths of eighteen or nineteen . . . precocious enough in vice, but the veriest schoolboys in everything else – making a noise and throwing about pens and paper in the lecture-room, waxing uproarious at night over the worst liquors. . . .' Bristed's impression was that many undergraduates, thrown into a condition of almost entire freedom 'in which they can go where they like, order what they please, and do almost anything they please . . . provided they do not openly outrage public decorum', were anything but respectful and obedient; even some of those destined for the church (he went on to say) appeared at divinity lectures after undergraduate lives 'marked by drunkenness and debauchery'.

For the fact was that despite all this talk about the fatherly care of masters for scholars at Oxford and Cambridge – and with exceptions which were gratefully acknowledged in the recollections of alumni from these universities – most of the dons wanted a quiet life, and the way to ensure one was to avoid trouble with undergraduates. They were prepared to help the earnest and diligent student, but real companionship between the two generations was rare enough to merit special mention. J. Venn, who was at Gonville and Caius College in 1853, wrote: '. . . I never received a single word of advice during my

6

whole time from the tutor unless it were as to what church I had better attend or avoid. . . . In all respects we were left very much to ourselves in the matter of our studies. The tutor, Mr Clayton, never lectured. We saw him for a few minutes at the beginning and end of term; that is to report our arrival and to secure our exeats.' (He went on to say that Mr Clayton was a kind-hearted man who would certainly have helped an undergraduate who went to him in a difficulty: 'But that was not the custom.') 'I feel', Venn went on to write, 'as certain as one can be that during my first two years I never had a word of private conversation with any authority of the College as to my studies, and equally sure that I never paid an informal visit to any Fellow's rooms. We selected our coaches by mutual advice and comparison; we decided for ourselves what line of studies we would follow.'[14]

Some of the masters were equally frank. 'College life', said Mark Pattison, tutor at Lincoln College, to the Oxford commission of 1850, 'has ceased to be the life in common . . . as between the Fellows as a body and the students it creates no society whatever. . . . The relation between the student and the College official is, in general, as distant and technical as that between the officer and the private in our army . . . .'[15] Another witness, Henry Wall, fellow of Balliol, was more emphatic: '. . . if any parent thinks that when he enters his son at a College he *necessarily* puts him where his moral and intellectual training will be carefully watched over by a Tutor, – I can only assure him that he is under a pleasing delusion.'[16]

It was the private tutor, the coach, hired by the student anxious to pass his examinations, a man living in the town but not a member of the college or university hierarchy, who often became the undergraduate's confidant and friend. But the notion of 'affectionate tutelage on the one side, grateful and respectful deference on the other',[17] though true for a few individual masters and scholars in early nineteenth-century Oxford and Cambridge, was not the typical pattern of student life in those universities; a mutual policy of non-intervention would be a better summary. There was in fact a diversity of view among the dons themselves. Adam Sedgwick, a contemporary of Whewell, was more realistic in his attitude to the young, probably because he was one of the few fellows of Trinity who took the trouble to understand them. When the students of Cambridge were abused in the press, Sedgwick wrote four letters to the *Leeds Mercury* defending them.[18] A sentence from one of these letters could well serve as a warning to some over-censorious dons today: he wrote that to carry into effect a discipline severe enough to prevent the commission of licentious acts 'would require a degree of personal restraint at once incompatible with the spirit of English law, and fatal to the formation of manly character, and to the germination of manly virtue'. And the Oxford commissioners of 1850 agreed with him. 'Men', they wrote, 'cannot be governed like boys. . . .'[19]

I 'affectionate tutelage' and 'respectful deference' at Oxford and Cambridge were largely mythical, so was the belief that Scottish professors took no pastoral interest in their pupils. Jardine, who held the chair of logic and rhetoric in Glasgow, published in 1818 his *Outlines of philosophical education*.[20] One cannot put it beside Whewell's essay without being impressed by its superiority in quality of thought and its absence of cant. 'The experience of the perplexities which assail the juvenile mind', he wrote, 'in its first endeavours to discover materials and to find expressions, has induced me to lay aside the authority of the teacher, and to place myself as the companion or friend of the student, in those moments when his difficulties are most formidable.'

There was no skimping of moral education in Jardine's teaching. Every Saturday morning was devoted to the contemplation of a First Cause and the necessity of a divine revelation. Students – even the boys who attended Jardine's lectures on logic and rhetoric – should be 'treated like men' and taught to act from reasonable motives. His criterion for the content of his teaching was *relevance*, not in the spurious sense in which some modern students use that word, but relevance to the business of living. He was critical of the preoccupation with classics in English universities, not through any disrespect for these subjects, but (one suspects) for the way they were commonly taught: didactically, not speculatively. The object of the teacher must be to train 'his students 'to reason, to inquire, to arrange their thoughts clearly, and to clothe them with ease in a suitable form of expression . . .'. In brief, Jardine was willing to do with boys what Whewell was unwilling to do with young men: teach them not only a corpus of orthodoxy, but the art of rational and cautious dissent from orthodoxy.

This is not to say that Scottish students escaped some of the impositions laid upon students in England. In St Andrews attendance at chapel was compulsory for students and they were at one time prohibited from sailing in boats, or 'from the amusement of foot-ball', because of its dangers.[21] And in Edinburgh the professor of humanity, James Pillans, issued class certifiactes classified into the virtues of regularity of attendance, propriety of behaviour and proficiency in studies, with proficiency third on the list.[22]

So paternalism from the masters toward the scholars existed in both

8

English and Scottish universities; but in Scotland it was more liberal for it allowed, even encouraged, the student to become (as Lockhart described him) a keen doubter and disputer, and it made no effort – as it did in Oxford and Cambridge – to constrain him into a style of life and pattern of behaviour becoming to a gentleman. The first ingredients for a student estate are that students should feel the minimum obligation to convention and the maximum encouragement to individuality. Scottish universities did not supply these ingredients as generously as they were to be found in Germany or France, but they supplied them much more generously than they were supplied in England.

There was another ingredient supplied in Scotland and altogether absent from English universities, namely a tradition of rudimentary student participation. It is significant, for instance, that students presented petitions to the royal commission on Scottish universities in 1826–30; they were invited also to give oral evidence, and there is a vivid record of exchanges between the commissioners with William Lamond and James Jarvis, students in Glasgow, and with David Rintoul, student in St Andrews: complaints about the library, compulsory chapel, and abuse in the award of bursaries.[23] Nearly a generation later, the commissioners for Oxford and Cambridge neither received memoranda from the students nor called them to give evidence, and in their reports there is not more than one reference to student opinion, and that a casual one.[24] Another kind of student participation was to be found in Scotland but not in England. The award of prizes was put into the hands of students, apparently to most people's satisfaction, and some professors, notably Jardine in Glasgow, enlisted student help for the correction of class exercises.[25]

The chief tradition of participation was the part students played, with other members of the university, in electing the rector. But in 1826, when the commission began its work, this vestigial remnant of medieval practice had indeed atrophied. In Edinburgh, where the town had gained control of the university, the office was a perquisite for the lord provost. In St Andrews all students were eligible to vote (the franchise had recently been restored to first- and second-year students) but it had been decreed that the only eligible candidates were the principals of the two colleges or the two professors of divinity and ecclesiastical history, known as the four *viri rectorales*. In Aberdeen the students at King's College took no part in the election of their rector; those at Marischal College did vote, but had been accustomed to accepting as their candidate a man nominated by the senatus of professors. Only in Glasgow

9

had students remained in full possession of their electoral rights, and although greatly outnumbering senior members of the university and effectively controlling the elections, they nullified their opportunity by choosing non-residents to represent them.

The royal commission of 1826 heard a great deal of evidence about this curious practice. Most professors, not surprisingly, were against it. It led to 'insubordination and tumult'; it had fallen, in Glasgow, into the hands of smooth-tongued 'gentlemen' from England in the moral and natural philosophy classes, dissenters, of course, whose principles 'inclined to the democratic side of the constitution' (the Georgian equivalent, in its threat to security, of American Maoists at the London School of Economics); it was inconsistent with the dignity of the university that boys of twelve should elect the chief magistrate of their society; it saddled the university with some totally inappropriate 'idol of the day'.[26] Clearly the rector was – indeed he occasionally still is today – a potential embarrassment to the principal and the professors. But the rectorship remained, and the act of 1858 confirmed (or, where it had atrophied, restored) the right of 'the Matriculated Students' to vote either in accordance with the usage of the time or in a manner to be determined by the commissioners.

Student response

The fact that the undergraduates of Oxford and Cambridge gave no evidence before the commissions in 1850-2 can be interpreted in two ways. It might be a sign that the commissioners had no interest in eliciting student opinion; or that the students had nothing much to complain about. Both these interpretations are correct.

The Cambridge undergraduate grumbled: about compulsory mathematics, about gate hours, about the food. But the very aloofness of the dons meant that no one seriously interfered with his behaviour, provided he did not 'openly outrage public decorum' – a trait of hypocrisy which irritates the modern undergraduate but which in the early nineteenth century was accepted with satisfaction; nothing so satisfying as to have a high moral standard to which one is not obliged to attain. This blend of liberty and restraint, the *esprit de corps* based on the intimacy of college, the undoubted elevation of morals during Victoria's reign and, as Whewell smugly observed, the stratum of society from which students came: all these conferred a stability on the student body of Oxford and Cambridge. Their indiscipline took the form of horseplay, lightly tinged with politics: a hubbub in the gallery of the senate house at congregations or during voting for a high steward; three groans for the proctors and pleasantries howled at distinguished men on ceremonial occasions; a protest (one of the rare university ones of this period) when the vice-chancellor and proctors dissolved the Union in 1817.[27] Like an African tribe, the unit of cohesion was a sort of extended family – the college – with, no doubt, frequent domestic tiffs (there is on record a charming protest about the food from the undergraduates of Clare Hall – in Latin); but the students did not feel themselves to belong to a student class, with class interests to cultivate. They were temporarily detached, but still belonging to the class to which their parents belonged.

In Scotland it was otherwise. Unruly behaviour in lectures could easily get out of hand, for the numbers attending lectures were far greater than in the south. There were genuine grievances, such as the exclusion of students from the library or methods of giving out books which the commissioners of 1826 described as 'offensive and illiberal'; some bad teaching (one of the problems set before the commissioners was how to pension off professors who were 'bordering on imbecility') and, of course, rectorial elections. These grievances produced some outspoken manifestations of student protest. For those who imagine that student protest in Britain began in 1967 it is instructive to recall these early occasions, especially as some of them, too, had political overtones; not surprising, in the wake of the Napoleonic wars, with revolutionary ideas stirring in Europe (for Scottish intellectuals had at that time close links with France and Holland), and with the early symptoms of the social consequences of the industrial revolution – the Luddites – still fresh in the memories of middle-aged men.

Details of one example must suffice. Up to 1823 the students at Marischal College, Aberdeen, were accustomed to accept as rector a man nominated by the senatus. The professors had usurped the students' rights. In 1823 the students awakened to their rights under the charter and a movement among them was started to secure the election of Joseph Hume (the man who helped to secure recognition of trade unions), who was then a radical member of parliament for Aberdeen. The movement failed, evidently due partly to intimidation from the professors. ('How could I', complained one of the younger students, 'divide in favour of Mr Hume when the Professors were just looking at me?')[28] But in the following year Hume was elected, and re-elected in 1825.

The professors' fears were justified. Mr Hume was evidently willing to act as a rector in the medieval manner, and to support the students in their grievances against the college. But (as the chronicler of the episode wryly remarked): 'The undergraduates had got a Rector, but they had not got a grievance!'[29] The modern student-left sometimes finds itself in a similar embarrassment; but, like the modern student-left, the students of Marischal did not have to wait long. Up to 1825 the examination for the degree of M.A. was singularly agreeable. The custom was to dictate to the candidates both the questions and the answers. No one ever failed. In 1825 'the spirit of reform seized the authorities, and they insisted upon an actual examination'. Hume could hardly do anything about that, but in April five candidates who 'could not answer the simplest question' were failed and prohibited from graduating:

> As no undergraduate protest had been made when the examinations were announced, it was difficult to find any ground for objection now. But a bright thought occurred to one of their number, a certain Francis Henderson. The professors were not in the habit of lecturing for a full hour; hence, he had been unable to obtain sufficient knowledge to pass the examinations. As the fault lay, thus, at the professor's door, he ought to have his degree. On this ground he appealed to the Rector.[29]

Hume held a rectorial court of inquiry, for the first time since 1738, to consider this and other grievances, viz, 'that the Professors were not regular in their attendance; that the state of the Bursaries required to be looked into; that the Students had been deprived of the use of the Library; that the Charter had in different respects been infringed. . .'.[30] The court was in public and was attended by large numbers of students. Hume did not come to a finding in Henderson's favour, but he did reprove the professors for unpunctuality. In his third term (he was re-elected again in 1828) he discharged his office by writing a public letter to the students, denouncing the senatus.

For four years these events harried the principal and the professors in a most unseemly way, familiar to their successors in some universities today. Inflammatory handbills were posted on the gates and circulated among the students:

> How to choose a RECTOR – *Fit Via Vi* – Gentlemen, if you wish to regain your infringed rights – if you think that another RECTORIAL COURT would do any good – if you wish to keep up the character of the University – if you wish to make the Professors redeem that

12

pledge which they gave in the Rectorial Court and which they have since refused to fulfil – if you wish well to the cause of learning – if you would evince the same spirit which has been done for these last two years – and if you would banish dogmatism and supercilious pedantry from MARISCHAL COLLEGE, then re-elect MR HUME.[31]

And during one of the stormy elections of this time the undergraduates tried to burst in upon the senatus in session and the professors were 'on the point of sending for the civil power to protect us'.[32]

Marischal College was not the only trouble spot. In 1834 a group of students in King's College, Aberdeen, considering themselves 'entitled to certain rights and privileges' demanded to see the college charters.[33] In 1825 the students of St Andrews rebelled against the restriction of the rectorship to four *viri rectorales* (see p. 9) by electing Walter Scott as rector; but the election was disallowed and in March 1826 a student committee, mandated by a general meeting of students, petitioned the rector, principals and professors for a relaxation of this restriction.[34] In Edinburgh students met on one occasion in the natural philosophy classroom in an attempt to influence the election of a new professor in this subject;[35] and (as an illustration of the suspicions current at the time) the town-and-gown riot there in 1838 was so savage that Louis Philippe's ministers are said to have suspected that it was 'part of a general revolutionary insurrection among the university students of Europe'.[36]

Student turbulence was not a monopoly of the Scots. Although students at the ancient universities did not go beyond adolescent horseplay in the senate house or on the Broad, the medical students in London (as Whewell complacently noted), deprived of the benefits of compulsory chapel and college gate hours, were liable to behave in an outrageous fashion, not – as in Whewell's Cambridge – merely out of pardonable youthful exuberance, but for serious purposes which interfered with the work of the colleges. (The contrast is noteworthy, for it still persists in the disposition to condone a destructive carousal after the May races, but to condemn a demonstration against chemical warfare.)

One such incident is well documented and is worth a place in this chapter, if only as an instructive example of a strategy of protest recently used, in a refined form, at the London School of Economics.

It took place among the medical students at the college, in Gower Street. It began in the session 1828–9. An essential background to the story is that in those days there was no strong tradition of academic freedom for the professors. The college council ran the college. 'It regarded the professors in the same light as any other of its employees, and all its employees with suspicion.'[37] If the teaching staff had few rights, the students had even fewer. So the college council was not accustomed to entertaining grievances from undergraduates.

In the session 1828–9 there were complaints about the incompetence of Professor Pattison, who held the chair of anatomy. The complaints were anonymous and dismissed as unfounded. More anonymous charges were made in the following session, and in April 1830 there was a signed complaint from one of the medical students, N. Eisdell. The council declined to investigate the charge of a single pupil, whereupon a month later it received a memorial signed by seventeen students, which was to say the least of it unambiguous: 'We charge him [Professor Pattison] with *unusual ignorance* of old notions, and *total ignorance of* and *disgusting indifference* to new anatomical views and researches . . . he is ignorant, or, if not ignorant, indolent, careless, and slovenly, and above all, indifferent to the interests of the science.'[38] This the council could hardly ignore. On 29 June it appointed a committee of inquiry, and subsequently reached what must have seemed to potential patients of that day an alarming conclusion: that Professor Pattison should be relieved of a part of his duties in anatomy, and appointed to the chair of surgery!

The matter was by no means over. Before dispersing for the vacation, the students entrusted their affairs to a certain Dr A. Thomson. Thomson was described in *The London Medical Gazette* as 'an ex-student, wholly unconnected with the establishment',[39] but he appears to have worked in the college dispensary. With the concurrence of Eisdell and two other students, he submitted a further memorial, urging the dismissal of Pattison, at the beginning of August. By this time the scandal had broken in the press. Already *The Lancet*, notoriously radical in its sympathies, had published a letter from a fellow-student of Eisdell, supporting him and drawing attention to the distinction of some of those who had signed the earlier memorial (several of them were medallists or prize-winners).[40] It now published a letter from Thomson explaining (in terms all too familiar) how he had fulfilled his 'trust' to the protesting students.[41] The college council responded by dismissing Thomson from the dispensary, and all was set for trouble at the beginning of the autumn term.

There was trouble. Early in October, the warden of the college allowed Thomson, despite his dismissal, to enter college premises to harangue an assembly of students about Pattison's incompetence.

Meanwhile Pattison tried to lecture in conditions of such chaos that they would – if only they had occurred 140 years later – have attracted TV cameras like wasps over a honey pot. Dissecting rooms and cloisters became the scene of a determined student campaign, and (again, how familiar to modern academics!) the grievance enlarged: tricolour emblems with slogans 'Thomson and truth!' were scattered round the college and there were demands that Thomson should be reinstated.[42] The council confirmed his dismissal.

In episodes like these (and in 1970 similar episodes are fresh in the memories of a dozen British universities) one false step can make matters worse. Hitherto it was not the man's character, it was his ignorance which was under attack. In fact, in a further memorial complaining about him, students had gone out of their way to praise his 'kindly bearing . . . his urbanity of manner and disposition'.[43] He must have been a colourful character. His hobby was fox-hunting and he occasionally appeared in the lecture theatre in scarlet coat and top boots, temporarily sobered under the fustian of his black academic gown: the sort of eccentricity dear to the hearts of the young.[44] But Pattison jettisoned all this goodwill by beginning (as a student wrote in *The Lancet*) 'to evince irritation'.[45] Incensed by the preparation of this fresh memorial, he suddenly decided to grant no certificates of attendance unless students actually attended and submitted themselves to weekly examinations. He refused a certificate to the student who had organised the memorial, and finally he made the disastrous error of ordering the students (who, as every professor knows, like to sit at the back of a lecture theatre) to sit where he wanted them to, in the front. In doing this (the student added in his letter) 'he had committed a gross and unwarrantable outrage upon their liberty . . . he had broken through that bond of courtesy which ought to exist between the lecturer and his pupil . . .'.[45] (One would have thought that the bond of courtesy might have been broken already by the students; it is a nice example of the use of counter-accusation so familiar in modern confrontations.)

The students now had a new cause for protest. Must they submit to the insult of being ordered about by a man 'who has pocketed large fees for the purpose of instructing them'?[46] They set up (again the strategy is familiar) a 'committee of 24' elected by a general meeting of the class (it would today be called an 'action' or an 'ad hoc' committee). Three students were ordered to appear before the college council. They were not allowed to call witnesses; two were found guilty of insubordination and excluded from the lectures of anatomy and surgery for the rest of the session. This, of course, is the classical

15

recipe for escalation of a 'happening'. Student grievance rose to new heights: now there had been victimisation. An indignant protest against the expulsion, signed by 119 students, was sent to the council; and Pattison's next attempt to lecture was defeated by 'the indignant voice of the class'.[47] By now the situation had become more confused than ever by the polarisation which always accompanies such episodes as these. Some students sided with the professor and deplored the lack of deference to him. The rebels shouted them down.

Here, for the theme of this book, the story must end. But it was not the end of the story. For months the press correspondence and comment continued. Eventually Pattison was ousted from his chair, and this precipitated a protest from the professors (against infringement of academic freedom) and the resignation of three of them, including the distinguished mathematician Augustus de Morgan. The ripples of the 'battle of Gower Street' continued for years. Like some modern student uprisings, there were good effects as well as bad; the troubles of 1830-1 hastened the provision of hostel accommodation for medical students in London, but they also strengthened Whewell's prejudices.

Verdicts of the royal commission of 1826–30

It is a lamentable confession for an academic to make, but it is true that British universities have not evolved in step with British society without periodic prodding from governments. In the early nineteenth century both the Scottish and English universities were in need of reform, but the resistance put up by professors and dons was massive, cunning and tenacious. A royal commission laboured over the Scottish universities from 1826 to 1830 and embodied its findings and evidence in thousands of pages of print.[48] The resistance of the professors and the kirk postponed any legislation on these findings for twenty-eight years. A royal commission on Oxford, and another on Cambridge were appointed in 1850, after years of lobbying by reformers in these universities.[49] The hysterical hostility from some dons toward the Oxford commission is well known. Cambridge was more amenable; but, again, there was successful dragging of feet for a generation before some of the recommendations were adopted in these universities.

For the purpose of this book the great value of royal commissions is that they are moments of academic stocktaking. All persons with views about the university have an opportunity to ventilate their views in public. The commissioners can examine witnesses and assess their reliability. The recommendations of the commission are the resultant of the thrust of progressives moderated by the brake of traditionalists, the utopian flights of reformers reconciled with the hard realities of politics.

The Scottish commissioners were predominantly conservative by persuasion and non-academic by profession: politicians, lawyers, divines, or simply members of the aristocracy. Their aim was not innovation but restoration of efficiency. They had to rescue the universities from the exclusive despotism of professors and to ensure that the public interest was represented. (In Edinburgh they had a peculiar task: to rescue the professors from the town council.)

The commissioners received petitions from students and clearly took them seriously. At the end of their oral evidence representatives of the students were specifically asked whether there was any other matter of complaint or representation which they wished to bring before the commissioners and they replied no. We cannot assume, however, that the students' case is adequately on record, for (as the Glasgow students put it) there was 'a certain dread of offending those in authority' which may have muted their voices.

It was a modest case, respectfully, but quite frankly, presented; more modest than the claims to be found in some student magazines of the period. There was (from Glasgow) an 'openly avowed' angry feeling and prejudice among some students against professors.[50] Edinburgh petitions, by contrast, disclosed no such ill feeling. Even the recently graduated students did not wish to 'make a reflection on any one of the individuals comprising the present body of professors'; indeed students and professors there were allied in their opposition to the town council.[51] The substance of the petitions was access to libraries and museums, the proper management of bursaries, accommodation in church (though in St Andrews it was objection to a compulsory place of worship) and, of course, concern over students' rights in rectorial elections. The omissions are more noteworthy than the inclusions: nothing about direct participation themselves in the administration of the university; nothing about the provision of lodgings or other amenities (except for recreational facilities in Edinburgh); no great concern over what was taught or how it was taught or over examinations. But in these courteously – almost obsequiously – worded petitions are the beginnings of a student estate. The petitioners were aware of their traditional rights and sensitive to them. The most vivid illustration of this comes from the petition of the Edinburgh students. In the autumn of 1825, during vacation, the magistrates of the town had entered the college gates to instal the lord provost as *ex officio* rector. Commenting on this the students wrote to the commissioners:

> The petitioners are unwilling to say anything disrespectful to the Patrons, but they must take the liberty to say, that it was a proceeding apparently uncalled for, and not consistent with their respectability, that a measure ostensibly tending to introduce a new domination into the University should be made at a time when the essential members, for whom the University was created and subsists, viz., the students, were necessarily absent. . . .[52]

In some respects the commissioners recognised that students were 'essential members'. Their recommendations fully supported the students' petitions over libraries and bursaries. But over the crucial issue of the rectorship – was the rector to represent the body corporate of the university, including its junior members? – they were curiously evasive. They confirmed the long-standing rights of students at Glasgow (though diluting them, as elsewhere, by the addition of graduates to the suffrage). They admitted students at King's College, Aberdeen, to the rights already existing at Marischal. But at St Andrews they withdrew the franchise that had recently been extended to first- and second-year students. And at Edinburgh, despite the student submission that if a rector were to be elected there 'the right of election ought to be . . . vested in the members of the University at large including the petitioners'[53] the commissioners actually proposed to debar students from the suffrage altogether – presumably on the optimistic assumption that what they had never had, they would never miss. It was not till 1858 that voting rights were restored to all students in all Scottish universities.

But steps had been taken toward a student estate. The students of Scotland had, through their evidence to the commission, undoubtedly influenced their universities. And they had champions among their seniors, not all as mischievous as Joseph Hume. In 1834 the solicitor-general, Henry Cockburn, who was lord rector of Glasgow University, gave evidence before another commission, on municipal corporations in Scotland. He was asked what interests ought to be represented on the new supreme governing bodies, the courts, proposed for Scottish universities. He replied:

> The voice of the students ought to be very distinctly heard in it. It should contain one person, at the very least, directly elected by them. . . . I am not, at present, prepared to specify the exact par-

ticulars in which I think it [the court] defective, except that, in general, I think that the students have too little say in it, and the *ex-officio* members rather too much.[54]

The first section of this chapter is entitled *Contrasts of north and south*; there could be no more telling illustration of the contrast than Cockburn's evidence. Even today, 135 years later, his views would not be widely accepted in Oxford or Cambridge.

2 The Scottish Example

The students' representative council

The *Act to make Provision for the better Government and Discipline of the Universities of Scotland* received the royal assent in 1858. It gave parliamentary recognition to the student estate by including, for all four universities of Scotland, two representatives of the undergraduates – a rector elected by them and an assessor nominated by the rector – on the courts, which were the newly created governing body for each university. The courts were small bodies (only six members for St Andrews and Aberdeen, seven for Glasgow, and eight for Edinburgh); so this was no token recognition. But in none of the universities did the students make as much use of this opportunity as might have been expected: they continued, for the most part, to elect distinguished members of the Establishment who appeared only to deliver a rectorial address. Yet this recognition was a privilege the students greatly prized, and when their elections were frustrated they could, and did, cause trouble. One cause of frustration was that in two of the universities (Glasgow and Aberdeen) voting was not by simple majority but by 'nations' – a survival of the medieval Italian custom which divided the students according to where they were domiciled, and gave one composite vote to each 'nation'. This sometimes caused a tie in the votes and the principal or the chancellor could determine the election by a casting vote.

This happened in 1860 in Aberdeen. The students wanted Sir Andrew Leith Hay, the 'local candidate', and there was in fact a numerical majority for him, since the numbers in the 'nation' which comprised the Aberdeen constituency were greater than those in the 'nations' which came from outside Aberdeen. Reckoned by 'nations' and not by numbers, there was a tie between Hay and Maitland, the solicitor-general. The principal gave a casting vote in favour of Maitland. This was taken as a deliberate move to back the professors against the students. In March 1861 Maitland came to deliver his rectorial address. The academic procession, along with the magistrates and the town

20

council, entered the hall. Cheering, hooting and yelling greeted their appearance; this was to be expected: it was the traditional accompaniment to every rectorial address. But then the scene became ugly. Chunks of splintered wood hurtled across the hall. The audience were, of course, expected to come unarmed, but some of them had brought in hammers and other instruments with which they uprooted the seats and smashed them into sizes suitable for projectiles.

The principal took his place at the rostrum and called on the meeting to join him in prayer. Out of respect for the kirk there was a temporary lull. But the uproar resumed as soon as the oath was administered to Maitland, and he stood at the lectern to give his address. At this point some of the professors left the platform to 'remonstrate personally with those taking a leading part in the row'. The rector kept smiling and endeavoured to proceed with his address, but at this stage blood was trickling down his face. The more respectable students were ashamed, and added to the pandemonium by hissing. There were cries of 'Call in the police'. After ineffectual intervention by the principal, several police were 'brought up to the hall door, but no force was used by them. . .'. The rector calmly and impressively completed his oration, the principal pronounced a benediction, and the proceedings, 'which had lasted upwards of two hours', were brought to a close.[1]

This occasion demonstrated what the protesting students of the 1960s would call 'concern' for their rights in rectorial elections. But in the early nineteenth century the student estate in Scottish universities manifested itself mainly through such episodes of occasional and spasmodic unity as the rectorial elections of Hume and Maitland; mainly but not entirely, for there was a quieter and much more significant manifestation; the noisiest revolutions are not the most effective ones. More effective than catcalls and the throwing of broken seats, peasemeal, flour and shell-fish was the coalescence, in 1834, of five student societies in Edinburgh.

The student societies of Edinburgh were small but important points of cohesion for student life. Four of them were founded in the eighteenth century: the Royal Medical Society (founded in 1737 and granted a charter in 1778), the Speculative Society (founded by six students in 1764), the Theological Society (1776) and the Dialectic Society (1787). Most of the early societies met in taverns, though some acquired halls of their own and some were allocated rooms in the university. On completion of the new buildings, they were excluded from meeting on university premises for fear of 'impropriety'. But in 1833, with the help of Henry Cockburn, who was then rector of Glasgow, five student societies secured permission to meet in the precincts of the university. And in the next year these five (the Dialectic, the Scots Law, the Diagnostic, the Hunterian Medical and the Plinian) decided to coalesce into a body called the Associated Societies.[2] The affairs of the body were managed by a council of two delegates from each society. It was the pioneer of organised student representation in Scotland. Fitzroy Bell, who was president of one of its constituent societies, the Dialectic, was later on to establish the first students' representative council (S.R.C.). He deserves a place in history as the founder of student representative government in Britain.

For fifty years the Associated Societies in Edinburgh remained the sole organised expression of the student estate. Rectorial elections, of course, brought the student body together, but after they were over most of the students dispersed again into their own individual lives, like so many solitary bees. Then, in 1883, there began the movement which led to the student estate of today.

Its genesis is well described in a letter written to *The Scotsman* years afterwards, on 9 February 1905, by Otto Schlapp, who was a student in 1883 and who subsequently held the chair of German. At the coming-of-age of the Edinburgh S.R.C. there were festivities and reminiscent letters to the press. The founder, Fitzroy Bell, had recalled his part in the events of 1883, and this elicited the letter from Otto Schlapp:

Sir – The letter of Mr R. F. Bell in to-day's issue of your paper reminds me vividly of an incident . . . which is likely to throw some light on the vexed question of the genesis of the Students' Representative Council. Mr Bell, who had been my fellow-student at Jena for two seasons, in June 1883 paid me a visit at Strassburg. It was a broiling day. We inspected the new University buildings, and outside the door of one of them he noticed a placard relating to the '*Studenten Ausschuss*'. 'What is that' he asked; 'there was nothing of that sort at Jena.' I explained, and forthwith procured a copy of the regulations of that mysterious body. 'We must have something of the kind at home,' was his comment, after he had studied the document for some time in the shadow of the great Cathedral. I was not surprised, therefore, to hear soon after that Mr Bell had summoned the presidents and secretaries of all University societies to meet in his rooms at 30 Walker Street and frame a constitution. . . . Personally I can hardly claim any credit for my share in the matter, but I am

22

proud to think that, like so many choice and noble things, the Students' Representative Council was made in Germany'.[3]

The principal, Sir Alexander Grant, was sympathetic to Bell's idea but advised him to delay any action until after the rectorial election. On 17 January 1884 the project was launched at a meeting in the humanity classroom, followed by an inaugural meeting, attended by ninety-seven representatives of faculties and societies, nine days later. The S.R.C. had three functions which were later defined as: '(a) To represent the Students in matters affecting their interests; (b) To afford a recognised means of communication between the Students and the University authorities; (c) To promote social life and academic unity among Students'. The representatives were returned by constituencies according to classes in the faculties of law, arts, and science, and according to faculties in divinity and medicine. The officers included three presidents, who took the chair in rotation at council meetings, and two joint secretaries and treasurers.[4]

The S.R.C. in Edinburgh began with mixed motives (a very small minority, it was said, wanted to use the council to fight the senatus, but this attitude was not tolerated)[5] and with a condition which has dogged S.R.C.s ever since and has been the commonest complaint in student newspapers: the apathy of the bulk of the students. The only opposition came from the medical students, apparently for the fear – a surprising one to come from medical students – that this would only add to the number of meetings at which disorder might occur. Their fears were groundless, for one of the first tasks undertaken by the S.R.C. was to provide stewards and to keep order at the rectorial address given by Lord Iddesleigh. It succeeded. The proceedings were harmonious and dignified and the infant S.R.C. earned a commendation from the principal: 'Gentlemen, you have saved the Republic!'[6] A few weeks later the university celebrated its tercentenary; once again the S.R.C. earned golden opinions for its contribution to the sobriety of the occasion.

This early co-operation on two important public occasions, coupled with a non-belligerent attitude toward the authorities, ensured good relations from the start between the S.R.C. and the professors. When the council took stock of its progress after twenty-one years it could look back upon several substantial achievements. Through its influence an athletic ground and a union had been acquired; by 'firm but friendly pressure' on the senatus it had secured improvements in the university library; from 1889 it sponsored an influential magazine founded two years before, *The Student*, which would put to shame the brash student newspapers of the 1960s. The S.R.C. organised what may have been the first staff–student consultative committee: a commission on clinical instruction, with senior and junior members on it, which substantially influenced clinical instruction in Edinburgh.[7] Of course all was not sweetness and light. There were grievances about the high failure rate for the M.A. degree. The professors, we are told, did not receive the medical commission's recommendations with enthusiasm. The students did not approve of all the professors. There was, for example, in 1887 an outspoken publication on the need for reform in the faculty of arts.[8] Students, the article says, 'are beginning to grumble at having to go to Professors whom they cannot follow, and to study subjects in which they have no interest, and they wish for either a wider range of subjects or a choice of teachers'. Their remedy was an interesting one: to allow anyone whom the court considered qualified to 'set up his plate' as it were, in the university, and to offer lectures, as the *Privat Dozent* at that time could in Germany. Since the teacher collected the fees and they were part of his emolument, this would produce a refreshing open market in higher education. So there were students who made a case, doubtless an unpopular one with the senatus, for what they called extra-muralists, attached to the university, but offering courses in competition with the regular professors. In philosophy, for instance, why should they have to be exposed to 'the sterilising influence of a systematic dosing of one school' when a variety of extra-muralists might offer them an eclectic choice? (The present-day student who believes that there should be a choice in the curriculum between capitalist economics and Marxist economics would be surprised and shocked to know that some members of his great-grandfather's generation had similar views about philosophy.) 'Let us have no monopolists', wrote a columnist in *The Student* in 1889; 'let us give a chance to every duly qualified teacher who chooses to come among us; and then, on the principle of the survival of the fittest, the best men will soon come to the front.'[9] His great-grandchild, organising a Free University in Bristol or Cambridge in 1969, could not have put it better.

On its twenty-first birthday, in 1905, the Edinburgh S.R.C. was able to look back too on three more notable achievements. The idea of an S.R.C. had colonised the other Scottish universities and some of those in England. The S.R.C. had put the views of the students to the government over the Universities (Scotland) bill of 1888 and to the commissioners appointed to put the act of 1889 into operation. And, most important of all, the Scottish S.R.C.s, by virtue of their record of responsible participation and not through the modern strategy of confrontation, had become incorporated by parliament in the constitutions of their universities and received statutory privileges. We now go into some detail about these achievements.

Within two years of the birth of the Edinburgh S.R.C. there were S.R.C.s of similar pattern in the other Scottish universities. Aberdeen followed in December 1884, St Andrews a month later, and Glasgow in 1886. Two years later, in 1888, a further step toward cohesion was taken. The president of the St Andrews S.R.C. wrote to each of the other councils suggesting that a joint committee should be set up to consider the legislation proposed for the Scottish universities.[10] Out of this co-operation there came a decision to hold an annual conference of representatives of the S.R.C.s of all Scottish universities, the beginning of an *entente universitaire*. A consortium called S.R.C.S. (Students' Representative Councils of Scotland) was set up which met every year, except for a break from 1915 to 1918, from 1888 to 1935. In 1935 it was metamorphosed into the Scottish National Union of Students. These developments of the student estate were observed from across the border and across the Irish Channel; and by the time the Edinburgh S.R.C. celebrated its majority it was able to invite to its dinner delegates from 'sister councils' in England and Ireland, although it was not until 1922 that a National Union of Students was established in England.

In 1887, barely four years after its foundation, the S.R.C. in Edinburgh took an interesting initiative. In November of that year (some months before the approach to S.R.C.s from St Andrews) it presented a memorial to the Scottish members of the government with the intention of influencing the forthcoming bill for the reform of the Scottish universities.[11] We deal with the tortuous and languid progress of the nineteenth-century bills and commissions on Scottish universities in the next section (p. 27). What is relevant here is the sense of responsibility which the memorial displays. First the S.R.C. asked that students and graduates should be included among the persons who might be called upon to testify before a statutory commission. Then the S.R.C. went on to mention some of the reforms it would like to see. The catalogue reads like an S.R.C. submission to the University Grants Committee in the 1960s: an improvement in the staff–student ratio; the setting up of boards of studies, e.g. for classics; a modification in the heavy reliance on systematic lecturing; rearranging the grouping of examinations to allow greater freedom of choice; introducing tests other than the existing examinations as qualifications for graduation; vesting the election of professors in a board 'qualified to estimate the merits of candidates as teachers and as specialists'.

Six months later, in May 1888, the Edinburgh S.R.C. submitted a further memorial to the government: an elegantly printed document (which we reproduce in an appendix)[12] signed by the presidents of all four representative councils, and the outcome of the joint consultations proposed by St Andrews. By then the government's legislative proposals were no longer a matter for conjecture. The Universities (Scotland) bill of 1888 had been introduced in the house of lords on 19 March, and this further memorial, carefully timed to precede the committee stage of the bill, set out the amendments which the students considered necessary to safeguard their interests. Since much of the detailed regulation of the Scottish universities was to be referred to a statutory commission, the students were mainly concerned here with their constitutional position. They asked for increased representation on the university courts (four instead of two members), student representation on committees of the senatus, and clarification of the relations between the statutory commission, the courts and senates on the one hand, and students and S.R.C.s on the other. These requests (they were too courteously worded to be called 'demands') were pressed on the lord advocate when a deputation from all four S.R.C.s waited on him on 31 May 1888.[13] He dealt with them gently but firmly. Voting power, he told the deputation, was of less importance than the power of making their views known. This they could do already if they elected the right kind of rectors. 'Use what you have' was his advice.

In February 1890, the Edinburgh S.R.C. followed up these earlier memorials to the government with one to the commissioners appointed under the Universities (Scotland) Act of 1889. This, too, was a formal printed document (which we also reproduce in an appendix)[14] and again the whole tone and content testify to the intellectual maturity and serious intent of these Scottish students. It is difficult to conceive that any comparable document could at that time have come from the undergraduates of Oxford or Cambridge. It contains one bread-and-butter request: that the S.R.C. should receive an assured revenue (they suggested one shilling per matriculated student, by increasing the matriculation fee from a pound to a guinea). After this modest claim the petition gets down to academic matters: that draft ordinances of the court should be submitted for comment to the S.R.C.; that the S.R.C. should submit to the lord rector names for his assessor, 'one of which he shall select'; that all students entering the university with a view to

26

graduation should have to sit a matriculation examination, 'and that at least four compulsory subjects be passed at once'. For the rest, there are several requests which demonstrate the heavy influence of medical students in S.R.C. affairs (reform of medical examinations, remedies for overcrowding of classes, and a suggestion that the professors' obligation to deliver 150 lectures a year should be taken to include other types of instruction as well so that 'Practical, *viva voce*, and Clinical Instruction' might be given much greater prominence). On behalf of arts students there are requests for a degree in music, chairs in modern languages and history, and a choice among optional subjects for the M.A. degree. Altogether an impressive document.

Participation and recognition

The *Act for the better Administration and Endowment of the Universities of Scotland* was passed in August 1889. It appointed commissioners to carry out the intentions of the act and they laboured at this until the turn of the century. The commissioners were specifically empowered to call students into consultation. Among the commissioners' powers was one (section 14 (12)):

> To lay down regulations for the constitution and functions of a students representative council in each University, and to frame regulations under which that council shall be entitled to make representations to the University Court.

The act provided also that the rector (who since 1858 had been elected solely by the undergraduates) 'may, before he appoints his assessor, confer with the students representative council'. The courts were to be larger than they were under the earlier constitutions – eighteen instead of six to eight – and this reduced the relative voting strength of the students' representatives; but this was more than remedied by the recognition of S.R.C.s and provision for their statutory right of access to the university court. It was another step forward in the establishment of a student estate.

To explain how this state of affairs was reached we must invite the reader to accompany us through some sixty years of dilatory parliamentary attention to the universities of Scotland. We begin with the royal commission of 1826–30. This commission swept under the carpet the matter of rectorial elections. In their evidence the commissioners heard all sorts of objections to student suffrage and little in its favour.

27

But they evidently decided that it would be impolitic to tamper with existing practice and they left arrangements practically as they were: student elections by nations in Glasgow and Aberdeen; in St Andrews the undergraduate constituency to be senior students only; in Edinburgh students to take no part in rectorial elections at all. They added graduates to the constituency in all Scottish universities. It was this evasion of the issue which drew the criticism from Cockburn which we quote at the end of Chapter 1.

No legislation followed the publication in 1830 of the commission's report, and parliament dropped the question of major reform in the Scottish universities for a quarter of a century. They continued to be autonomous, and selfish, oligarchies of professors. Meanwhile much had happened to universities in the south. The pace of reform in England's ancient universities had been hastened by royal commissions. The University of London was beginning to earn a grudging respect from intellectuals. Another English university had been set up in Durham, in Manchester Owens College opened its doors, and the Irish Universities Act of 1845 had led to a young and vigorous Queen's University of Ireland. The time had come to blow the dust off the commission's report of 1830 and to reconsider its recommendations.

In February 1857 the lord advocate (Moncreiff) invited James Lorimer to draft a bill to give effect to some of the reforms advocated in 1830. Lorimer was the right man to be charged with this assignment, for he was a leading light in a body called the Association for the Improvement and Extension of the Scottish Universities. He began with an outline of reform for faculties of arts, which included one singularly democratic provision, namely that the faculty of arts should be presided over by a court, comprising the principal and the professors; but not these only: there should also be government-appointed examiners and graduates equal to half the number of professors. Half these graduates were to be elected by their fellow graduates, and half by matriculated undergraduates in their third and fourth years. This would have been student participation with a vengeance.[15]

The proposal was dropped and the first version of the bill, when it did appear in April 1858, would, had it been passed in that form, have deprived the students of their residue of privileges, for it provided for rectors to be elected not by the students but by a new body (which did in fact come into existence) called the general council, consisting of the chancellor, the court, the professors, and the graduates, but deliberately excluding all students. The court was to have considerable powers, even over the senatus, although it was not until later that it was given

28

financial control of the university. At the second reading of the bill (on 10 June 1858) two Scottish M.P.s (both members of the Improvement Association to which Lorimer belonged) sought to secure an exclusively student franchise for rectorial elections in all Scottish universities. One of these M.P.s was Alexander Dunlop (an unlikely champion of student rights, for his life was spent largely on ecclesiastical reform); the other was E. Ellice jnr. The proposal was at variance with the traditional concept of the rectorship, which was that the rector represented the whole of the university, not the students alone; but the debate proceeded in complete disregard (and possibly ignorance) of this academic consideration. The lord advocate was sympathetic to the proposal; he confessed to having a great bias in favour of election by the students. The next day an amended bill was printed which put rectorial elections in the hands of the general council *and* the matriculated students. This did not satisfy Messrs Dunlop and Ellice jnr. They pressed for students to have the sole franchise.[16] The effect of the amendment, Mr Dunlop said, would be to swamp the voices of the students; and Mr Ellice jnr added that he saw no grounds whatever for interfering with a right which the students had exercised most satisfactorily. The lord advocate beat a retreat and on 1 July the bill was reprinted to provide for the rector to be elected solely by matriculated students of each university. Some M.P.s still demurred. Would it not be desirable to have the professors associated with the students in these elections in the interests of 'good order'? To which Mr Dunlop replied that the professors might make any regulation they liked for preserving order, 'but the students ought to be left in full, free, and unfettered exercise of their electoral rights'.[17] The house of lords put in an amendment reintroducing voting rights for professors. But the commons rejected it and justified their rejection by reporting to their lordships that they disagreed with it 'Because by making Professors Co-electors of the Rector with their Students they would be placed in a Position hurtful to their Dignity and Influence'.[18]

The bill was given the royal assent on 2 August 1858. Thereafter the rector no longer embodied the corporate identity of the whole university; he became the representative of the students. The bill provided a new and substantial foundation for the student estate, for the rector, now to be indisputably the students' elected man in all four universities, was president of the court, had a casting as well as a deliberative vote, appointed an assessor, who also had a vote, and remained in office, as also did his assessor, for three years.

It was now up to the students to elect rectors who would represent

29

them. In Edinburgh their first choice was an absentee, W. E. Gladstone. But he served them well, for in his rectorial address for 1860 he put the weight of his great prestige behind the student estate: '. . . the Legislature of our own day', he said, 'has, by a new deliberative Act, invested you, the youngest members of the University, with a definite and not inconsiderable influence on the formation of that Court, which is to exercise, upon appeal, the highest control over its proceedings . . . we think it eminently British to admit the voice of the governed in the choice of governors. . . .'[19]

For eighteen years the Scottish universities ran under the new legislation, with a two-tier system of government: the old senatus of professors, presided over by the principal; the new court of no more than six to eight persons of whom four were assessors (five in Edinburgh) and only one of the four represented the professors; and a general council whose main function was to act as an electoral college for one of the assessors. Conditions were improved, but not improved enough. There were still many things which needed to be put right: over examinations and academic standards; over finance; and, still, over the rectorship. For (as is evident from our description of the inauguration of Maitland at Aberdeen in 1861) not all rectorial elections were as felicitous as that for Mr Gladstone.

So in 1876 another commission was appointed to inquire into the universities of Scotland, with very wide terms of reference which included mode of government, examination, the creation of new professorships, the recognition of extra-mural teaching, emoluments and finance.[20] Its members were very different from the patrician commissioners of 1826; they included three men who were very knowledgeable about universities: T. H. Huxley, Lyon Playfair and J. A. Froude. Huxley's incisive questions must have disturbed the complacency of some of the witnesses. He wrote, after one of the meetings, '. . . the chief witness we were to have examined today, and whose due evisceration was one of the objects of my coming, has telegraphed to say he can't be here'.

Naturally the question of suffrage for the rectorship was raised. There was general agreement that voting by 'nations' and not by simple majority was objectionable; but most witnesses, especially from Edinburgh and Glasgow, did not wish the students to be disfranchised. Men as distinguished as Grant and Caird supported the students' rights. From other quarters there was strong opposition. The professor of church history in Aberdeen was uneasy because in his university the students had on one occasion had the idea of electing a rector from their own number. If this were to happen 'it might prove a very serious and awkward matter'.[21] His colleague, the professor of humanity, who also spoke for the general council, was more emphatic. The present system, he said, is 'an indefensible blot' on our arrangements. He would have the rector elected by the general council.[22] The professor of anatomy was more sympathetic to the student cause. He – like other witnesses – wanted voting by a simple majority, but 'I have no sympathy at all with the wish of some, that the election of the Rector should be taken from the students'. Any disadvantage, he went on to say, is 'more than compensated by the training it gives the student in the exercise of his judgement in the affairs of the University'. And he ended, possibly with a deliberate innuendo against someone he disliked: '. . . viewed in its results in Aberdeen, the members who have been sent into our Court by the students will compare very favourably indeed with those who have been sent in from the other electing sources.'[23]

The commissioners were obviously less interested in the rectorship and student participation than in other issues; for they did not call for any evidence from students nor did they receive any. The only witness who claimed to speak on behalf of undergraduates and recent graduates was Benjamin Costelloe, a Glasgow M.A., and his evidence was largely on fellowships, scholarships, bursaries and grievances about the curriculum. He was, of course, strongly in favour of the student franchise, but he put up a disappointing performance when examined on the value of rectors to the student body.[24]

In their recommendations the commissioners carefully deployed all the arguments against the student franchise, and concluded that they were not convinced by any of them. They did, however, recommend that in Glasgow and in Aberdeen there should be no more voting by nations, and that rectors should be elected, as in St Andrews and Edinburgh, by a simple majority vote among the undergraduates. And they recommended that there should be an increase in the representation of the general council (the graduates) on the court, without any corresponding increase in representation from students. But there is no reason to suppose that this was a deliberate move to diminish student influence; more probably it was a move to strengthen the influence of educated citizens in the affairs of their universities.[25]

The commission published its report in 1878. Its publication was followed by a spell of parliamentary inactivity toward the Scottish universities, though they did not have to wait (as they had waited after 1830) for a generation before Westminster turned its attention to their affairs. A bare five years afterwards, in 1883, a bill was introduced into the house of commons to give effect to many of the commission's recommendations. This was followed by bills in 1884 and 1885. None of them was given a second reading. A bill was introduced for the fourth time in 1887. It proposed, *inter alia*, that the rector's assessor should have no vote at the court if the rector was present and that the general councils and the senates of the universities should each elect four assessors to the courts. This bill, too, was withdrawn. By this time both the graduates, through their general councils, and the undergraduates, through their S.R.C.s, were able to organise and put forward collective opinions which were intended to influence the fate and content of the next version of the bill.

In March 1888 the general councils of Edinburgh and Glasgow sent a deputation, led by Lord Wemyss (and including Haldane, who was to play a leading role in university reform), to Whitehall to meet the secretary for Scotland (Lord Lothian) and the lord advocate (J. H. A. Macdonald). The deputation made it clear that they wished students to have a voice in the government of the Scottish universities and Haldane, though he referred to the new S.R.C.s as 'a sort of Vigilance Committee', expressed his admiration for the way they were working and his confidence that they would be reliable representative organisations.[26] Lord Lothian (whose subsequent actions confirmed his view) replied: 'I am most anxious that the students should be represented, and with reference to the Rector's Assessor, I am of opinion that the students should have a voice in the nomination.'[27] Two months later a deputation of S.R.C.s from all four universities put their views about legislation before the lord advocate; they wanted two direct, and two indirect representatives on the university courts and student representation on standing committees; and we have already recorded the lord advocate's reply: 'Use what you have.'

The bill of 1888 was based on that of 1887, with (for the theme of this book) four important changes: the membership of courts was increased by the provision for two assessors appointed by the Crown, and representatives from any affiliated colleges; the rector's assessor was no longer to be deprived of his vote if the rector himself were present; the courts were to assume powers over finance and therefore to become much more powerful bodies than heretofore; and, most important of all: 'The rector may, in making the choice of his assessor, take the assistance of the students' representative council in such manner and subject to such regulations as the Commissioners after consideration of any representations from the students' representative council may determine.' For the first time in history, the organ of student government was included in a proposal for legislation by parliament.

The Edinburgh correspondent of *The Times*, in its issue of 30 March 1888, welcomed the terms of the bill but singled out for criticism one point which, if it had appeared in *The Times* eighty years later, would have filled the correspondence columns for days afterwards with indignant letters from dons. The criticism was that the students, who contributed more largely than any other body to the income of the university, were inadequately represented in its government. For the rector and his assessor would now constitute only about one-eighth of the votes on the court, so '... the voice of the students', wrote the correspondent, 'is kept in the background and their desires are rendered ineffectual'. The courts of the Scottish universities, now that they had the management of finance, should give appropriate representation to all the bodies that contribute to the universities' revenues: students, graduates, and the public.[28]

When the bill came up for a second reading in the house of lords, not all their lordships were as well disposed toward the claims of students as the correspondent of *The Times* had been. A passage from *Hansard* is worth preserving:

> He [the earl of Rosebery] should like to say a word on a clause which was new to him. It was the clause where the Rector in making a choice of assessor had to take the assistance of the Students' Representative Council. But that Council was not, he thought, an expression which was defined in the Act. The clause itself was of an absolutely novel character, and he thought his noble Friend in making further observations with reference to the Bill would do well to give some explanation of that clause. He must honestly say that he thought in so large a proposition as this no clause so vague and so absolutely destitute of guidance had ever been submitted to Parliament.[29]

Lord Lothian met his objection by a simple amendment to the bill: ' "Students representative council" means a students representative council in any University, constituted in such manner as shall be fixed by the Commissioners under this Act.' This gem of tautology appeared ni the final act which was eventually passed and it is not on record that the earl of Rosebery was dissatisfied with it; indeed, later in the debate he spoke in favour of recognition being given to S.R.C.s. His noble friend the duke of Argyll, during the committee stage of the bill, had other grounds for objection, namely the implied obligation that the rector should consult the S.R.C. before appointing an assessor. This, said the noble lord, would place the rector 'in an exceedingly inconvenient and invidious position. The students were eminently capable of deciding upon a man of eminence as Rector, but he did not think they were so well able to choose a good man of business for the working purposes of the University. He would, therefore, suggest that the words he had quoted should be struck out, so that the Rectors should be left free, as they were now, to choose their assessors.'[30] Lord Lothian said he was not prepared to accept the amendment. Then the earl of Camperdown raised an objection. Why should the commissioners be obliged, as they were by sub-section 13 of clause 14 of the bill, 'to lay down regulations for the constitution and functions of a Students' Representative Council in each University'? He doubted whether parliament should compel the commissioners to do this, for the noble lords 'knew nothing about these Students' Councils, and he did not think it was wise to mention them in this Bill'.[31] He later moved the deletion of the tautological definition of an S.R.C., not because it was otiose, but for all the reasons which reactionary adults have been in the custom of using, and still to this day use, to keep responsibility out of the hands of the young. Undergraduates are a fluctuating body and it would be difficult to lay down rules for organising them. Anyway the duty to be put upon them: 'to select an assessor' (he overlooked the fact that the bill provided only that the rector might *consult* S.R.C.s over the selection), was perhaps the one 'which, of all others, they were not competent to discharge'. Furthermore 'a proposal of this sort was objectionable in principle . . . here they were proposing to recognize the students as a part of the University, just as much as they recognized the Senatus or the General Council. Such a proposal had never been made with reference to any University in any other part of the world. . . . Their Lordships would see that hereafter, the body of students having been once recognized, their Representative Council would, no doubt, make claim to be recognized in other matters connected with the discipline of the University. . . . When he was an undergraduate he should have thought this a very improper proposal, and he held the same view of it now.'[32]

Lord Napier and Ettrick took a more realistic line: 'There was no doubt', he said, 'that students in the Scottish Universities were an active and rather aggressive body at the present moment. He thought they would take an active part in the management of the Universities and he therefore thought it would be a wise thing to recognize them as a factor in University affairs, and to give them a recognized constitution and status.'[33]

The marquis of Lothian said he hoped their lordships would now be satisfied with the discussion which had taken place on the matter; he admitted that there was a great deal of force in what the noble earl (Camperdown) had said; but he conceded nothing. On 25 June the bill had its third reading in the house of lords. Lord Rosebery, now willing to champion S.R.C.s, had an additional provision added to the bill, to enable S.R.C.s to be entitled to make representations to courts. The bill was passed and sent to the commons. Twice a second reading of the bill was deferred and on 15 December 1888 it went the way of its four predecessors: it was withdrawn because the government was unwilling to find sufficient parliamentary time for it.

But this time the period of dormancy was a short one. Eleven weeks later the bill reappeared, in terms almost identical with those of the bill passed in the house of lords in 1888, as the Universities (Scotland) bill, 1889. At the second reading in the commons it was warmly commended by Haldane. '. . . I consider', he said, 'that a University should be regarded as a kind of democracy where there is citizenship and where all internal affairs should be under the control of the various classes interested. The Students' Council is a thing that the students have to thank the Lord Advocate for.'[34]

In the committee stage another champion of the students protested at the proposed increase in the size of courts (from six to eight, to eighteen) without a corresponding increase in student representation. That this should happen 'while the vested interest of the professors . . . is multiplied by four' (there were to be four assessors from the senatus in place of one), he described as 'perfectly monstrous'.[35] But the bill was passed unaltered in this respect, and it received the royal assent on 30 August 1889. In Scotland the student estate, in its embodiment as an S.R.C., was now on the statute book of the British parliament.

The commission appointed by the act made a happy choice of secretary: it was Fitzroy Bell, who had founded the first S.R.C. in Edinburgh. Over the ensuing decade ordinances trickled out from the commission. We reproduce at the end of this chapter the enactments of particular relevance to our theme. But before doing this we must try to assess the significance of the part the students played in this historic legislation.

Assessment is not easy. We cannot with certainty separate the direct influence of the students' memorials to the government and their evidence to the commissioners from the influence of ideas which were in any case 'in the air' among legislators at the time. For example (to jump seventy-five years ahead in our story) we describe in Chapter 5 the pressure brought by students upon the Privy Council at the time of the granting of charters to the new technological universities in Britain. The students, quite properly, claimed that their pressure was effective; but over some measures (such as disciplinary arrangements) they were pressing at an open door, for the University Grants Committee, which advises the Privy Council about charters, shared the students' views over these measures; so did the secretary of state himself. Similarly (we now take the reader back to the nineteenth century) it is known that Lord Lothian gave notice of an amendment to the bill of 1888 on 17 May,[36] which was the day he acknowledged the memorial from the four S.R.C.s of the Scottish universities, dispatched from Edinburgh only two days earlier.[37] This was to empower commissioners to lay down regulations for the constitution and functions of a students' representative council in each university: one of the amendments which the students asked for in their memorial. Did Lord Lothian have prior knowledge of this request from the students he represented as rector? (The Edinburgh *Student* lists among his graceful acts the way he 'listens attentively to the Secretary of your Council on the subject of the Universities Bill'.)[38] Or was he simply responding to the objection which Lord Rosebery had raised on the second reading of the bill?[39] (Lord Rosebery was known to have taken a deep interest in the Scottish universities, and to have drawn up the first of the draft bills for their reform with his own hand.)[40]

We cannot answer these questions, but we can point to other evidence that the efforts of the students were fruitful. First, there was the effect upon themselves. It is not an exaggeration to say that from 1887 to 1900 Scottish students who cared to interest themselves in university reform had opportunities to discuss it and to present their views; indeed were encouraged to do so. 'Probably next session', said Sir J. Donaldson in an address to students as principal of the University of St Andrews in October 1890, 'there will be great alterations . . . you as students may help in moulding these alterations so as to make them beneficial.' He then went on to enumerate topics on which student opinion would be valuable: courses for the M.A. degree, the length of the academical year, the training of teachers. '. . . a great gain would be secured for our country if, by the discussion of [these and other similar subjects] you helped to create a public opinion which could stimulate and direct the Legislature.'[41] And the commissioners, in addition to receiving written and oral evidence from students, paid them the compliment of conceding what parliament had withheld: the privilege of receiving draft ordinances for comment.[42] There is no doubt that the student estate grew in stature as a result of the deserved response it obtained from university and government authorities. This was one fruitful consequence of the memorials.

There were other, more specific, fruitful consequences. It may well be that students influenced the government to provide that the commissioners should be empowered to frame regulations under which S.R.C.s should have direct access to university courts, and also that students should be specifically mentioned among those from whom the commissioners might take evidence. And there can be no doubt that the commissioners were influenced by the students' evidence when they came to draft ordinances. For example, ordinances authorised the provision of a revenue for S.R.C.s. They enabled S.R.C.s to petition the senatus as well as the court – this was not provided for in the act, but it was one of the amendments which the students had asked for in 1888. Over academic matters many of the students' requests were granted: e.g. a qualifying preliminary examination, improved staff–student ratios, establishment of faculties of science, boards of studies. In these academic matters, it can be said of course that student opinion was merely flowing with the tide. We agree, but we add that our impression of the work of S.R.C.s in Scotland over these years is that student opinion helped to create the tidal flow. In 1890, as in 1970, it is easy to tell students that their proposals have been familiar to the authorities for years; nevertheless a little pressure from students, especially when it is applied with the dignity and urbanity to be found in the Scottish memorials, is a healthy encouragement to the authorities to do something about the proposals.

So the commissioners in the 1890s were aware of the views of the student estate in Scotland and responsive to them. As examples of their response we quote two of their enactments:

Ordinance No 27[43]

[Edinburgh, No. 6. Regulations as to Application of parliamentary grants as to salaries and for the Institution of a fee fund, and for other purposes.]

At Edinburgh, the Fifth day of June, Eighteen hundred and ninety three years

. . .

Therefore the Commissioners . . . statute and ordain, with reference to the University of Edinburgh as follows:

. . .

XI. The whole revenues of the said University, other than those paid into the Salaries Account and the Fee Fund Account, but including any surplus income arising upon the Fee Fund, shall be paid to the account of the General University Fund, and shall in so far as not specifically appropriated by any Act of Parliament, Ordinance, Deed of Endowment, or other instrument in force at the time, be applied by the University Court for the following purposes, which shall rank according to the order in which they are named, subject to the provisions hereinafter contained:

1. Paying expenses of administration, including such provision as the University Court may think necessary to enable the Senatus Academicus and the General Council to discharge their duties, and including also such sum, if any, as the Court may think fit to grant towards the expenses of the Students' Representative Council.

. . .

A. S. Kinnear, *Chairman*
Approved by Order in Council, dated 23rd November 1893

Ordinance No 60[44]

[General, No. 22. Regulations for the Students' Representative Council.]

At Edinburgh, the Fourth day of February, Eighteen hundred and ninety-five years

Whereas by the Universities (Scotland) Act, 1889, a 'Students' Representative Council' is defined to mean a Students' Representative Council in any University, constituted in such manner as shall be fixed by the Commissioners under the said Act; and whereas by section 14, sub-section 12, the Commissioners under the said Act are empowered to lay down regulations for the constitution and functions of a Students' Representative Council in each University, and to frame regulations under which that Council shall be entitled to make representations to the University Court, and whereas such Students' Representative Councils already exist in each University:

38

Therefore the Commissioners under the said Act statute and ordain as follows:

I. The Students' Representative Council in each University shall submit to the University Court for approval the regulations under which it has been formed or now exists, and these regulations as approved, or with such alterations as may from time to time be approved by the University Court, shall form the constitution of the Students' Representative Council, and shall, subject to the provisions of this Ordinance, determine the functions thereof, and the mode of election thereto.

II. After the University Court has approved of the constitution of the Students' Representative Council in any University, alterations in the said constitution shall be of no effect unless and until they shall receive the approval of the University Court.

III. (1) The Students' Representative Council shall be entitled to petition the Senatus Academicus with regard to any matter affecting the teaching and discipline of the University, and the Senatus Academicus shall dispose of the matter of the petition, or shall, if so prayed, forward any such petition to the University Court, with such observations as it may think fit to make thereon.

(2) The Students' Representative Council shall be entitled to petition the University Court with regard to any matter affecting the students other than those falling under the immediately preceding sub-section.

(3) Nothing contained in this section shall be held to prejudice any right of appeal which may be competent under section 6, sub-section 2, of the said Act,* nor the powers and jurisdiction of the Senatus Academicus with regard to the teaching and discipline of the University.

IV. This Ordinance shall come into force from and after the date of its approval by Her Majesty in Council.

. . .

A. S. Kinnear, *Chairman*

Approved by Order in Council, dated 29th June 1895

---

* This gave power to the university court to review any decision of the senatus academicus which might be appealed against by a member of the university having an interest in the decision.

3 Student Awakening in the South

Student organisation and statutory recognition

We have already introduced the reader to the twenty-first birthday party of the Edinburgh University S.R.C., held on 28 January 1905. As is permissible at such parties, the speeches were somewhat self-congratulatory, though the spectre of student apathy hovered even over that occasion, in the speech in reply to the toast of the S.R.C. The interesting point is that the effectiveness of the Edinburgh S.R.C. since 1884 – and it had been effective – had not been in its influence on the court through rectors and assessors: it had been mainly in the direct influence of the S.R.C. on the senatus. For notwithstanding the privileges of electing a rector and advising on the nomination of an assessor accorded to the students in the act of 1889, the students continued to elect ornamental rectors and they did not use the rectorship as the main channel for pressing their views. The likely reason for this is that the S.R.C. soon found that its power under the ordinance, to 'be entitled to petition the Senatus Academicus with regard to any matter affecting the teaching and discipline of the University', was an easier way to get things done. On one occasion five years after the S.R.C. was founded, the student magazine made this quite explicit: 'It has been exceedingly fortunate that instead of estranging the Senatus and the students, the Council [the S.R.C.] in its work has brought them closer together, and has produced a feeling of mutual trust which we of the old times hardly expected.'[1] And the writer went on to say that Edinburgh University 'no longer presents the anomaly that the undergraduates for whom the University exists, and who form numerically by far the largest part of its working members should have no other means of expressing their views on questions of University polity than by electing an absentee Rector once in three years'. The success of the Scottish S.R.C.s lay in the fact that they had brought 'an unbroken current of suggestion to play upon the legislative centres, day in and day out, for one-and-twenty years'.[2] And the most effective legislative centre in academic matters was the senatus.

40

It was this concept of student government as an organ of junior partnership with the professors, not as a trade union pledged to oppose them, which was adopted in other Scottish universities and which, by the time the Edinburgh S.R.C. celebrated its twenty-first birthday, had spread to the south. The S.R.C.s of other universities were described as 'sister councils' on the toast list at the Edinburgh dinner; in fact it would have been more accurate to describe some of them as 'daughter councils' for the first of them, at any rate, was directly descended from the Scottish model. In proposing the health of the sister councils, the speaker described them as displaying 'the potential force which representation gives to everything'.[3] We turn now to consider the origin and growth of some of them.

It would be incorrect to assume that all organised student activity in the south took its lead from Scotland. We have already given a picturesque example of cohesion among the medical students in the college in Gower Street It was a spasmodic cohesion, but students in the London colleges did form various flourishing societies and launched a number of short-lived but enthusiastic magazines. The societies fragmented rather than united the students, and when they did coalesce to form a union, as they did at King's College in the 1870s, no corporate strength came out of the coalition. The King's College union survived only from 1878 to 1882, and then dissolved through lack of premises and finance. A similar union was formed at University College by H. Morley in 1884, but this, too, expired with the departure of Morley in 1889.

The weakness of corporate life in the London colleges had several causes. Most of the students lived at home, dispersed in the suburbs around London, unable (unlike many of the Scottish students) to walk to the university from their homes. They inherited no tradition of citizenship of the university or of the college: there was no question of the matriculation oath making them *civis universitatis*. And – a very important factor – their professors, too, inherited no tradition of academic citizenship; until quite late in the nineteenth century they had no share in college government; though some of them were very distinguished scholars, they taught a curriculum they had not designed, for examinations they did not set; they did not even have security of tenure. Not only among students, but among professors, there was a total absence of the 'largeness and variety of intercourse, the abundance of congenial society' (this is the way Seeley put it in 1868) 'which makes the special charm and exhilaration of university life. . . . To be a London student has not hitherto meant to be a member of a vast student world. Membership at one college has not been a passport to the society of other colleges. The London students never assemble except for examination.'[4]

From written recollections of that time one gets the impression that it was the professors more than the students who felt the need for a corporate student life, and it was professors, not students, who were the moving spirits in trying to create some corporate spirit at University and King's Colleges; perhaps it is on this account that the ventures failed: they were not founded on the initiative of the students themselves. In University College two devoted and distinguished teachers took the initiative: Seeley and Morley. It was Seeley who founded in 1868 *The London Student*, which perished after five issues. He believed that student life should be organised at university rather than college level (the colleges, he thought, were 'too small to form the basis of prosperous common undertakings'). Eighteen years later Morley launched another journal, *The University College, London, Gazette*, which survived for twelve issues. It was Morley who organised 'at homes' for the students; and it was Morley, not a pressure group of students, who wrote in 1879: 'I am not at all sure that I shall not propose the setting up of something of the nature of a students' committee empowered to send facts and suggestions to the Senate.'[5] In 1884 Morley did set up a University College Society open to governors, teachers, and students. The society acquired a reading room and tennis courts and, under Morley's guidance, issued the *Gazette*. When Morley retired the life went out of the movement and it was not until the initiative came from students themselves (though still with the help of a professor, Schafer) that a viable student organisation was founded at University College. This was in 1892 and it belongs to a later episode in our story.

There was, of course, a degree of liberty not to be found at Oxford or Cambridge, at any rate for those students who could escape the sanctions of a Victorian home in Streatham or Leytonstone. C. H. Pearson speaks of the feeling of freedom after the regime of a boarding school, even to the extent of signing the Chartist petition.[6] Not that the colleges did not apply strict rules to the students while they were on the premises. The medical school of King's College, for instance, issued prohibitions respecting the admission of dogs and ladies into the college and it forbade not only the use of firearms, but the placing of flower pots on window ledges.[7] And when the debating society of University College in the 1880s was infested with a number of radicals who wanted to propose the motion 'That the Social Reform of University College is hopeless' the authorities vetoed the debate.[8] But by and large the non-academic preoccupations within the college of London students in the nineteenth century were parochial and domestic, such as playing fields for athletics (very necessary and in London very difficult to secure); or frankly trivial, such as the dispute in 1902 over the playing of ping-pong in the games room at University College, because the noise disturbed chess players in an adjoining room.

In the provincial colleges in the 1880s corporate life was not much better than in London. In Owens College, Manchester, a union was formed in the foundation year of the college (1851); but it was essentially a debating society. When the college received its charter as Victoria University in 1880 there was a coalescence of societies, with delegates from each, into a union, but its activities were to promote social life among undergraduates and not to constitute the body of a student estate in the university; though later on, owing to the peculiarly powerful spirit of independence infused into the university by men like Tout and Alexander, student life became very healthy there. Anyone surveying the influence of students upon universities in Britain in, say, 1890 could not fail to conclude that there was no activity south of the Tweed to compare with that to be found in the Scottish universities. In Oxford and Cambridge the undergraduates were legally part of the corporation of chancellor, masters, and scholars; but they took no part in university government. In London, Manchester, Leeds and elsewhere there were many active student societies, sometimes consolidated into unions; but, except sporadically over some particular crisis, there was no expression of solidarity of opinion, and no effective machinery for representation of the student view, such as existed in Scotland. Nor was there any co-ordination of student opinion between universities, such as the Scottish S.R.C.s had organised in order to put their collective views before the government.

The seeds of Scottish influence were bound to spread to England. The first institution where they germinated and took root was University College, Liverpool. It is often difficult to explain how some student movement begins in one university rather than another; but there is no difficulty in explaining why Liverpool was the pacemaker for student representative government in England; it was due to the influence of one man: Ramsay Muir, the son of a Scottish presbyterian minister in Birkenhead.

Ramsay Muir was born in 1872 at Otterburn. His father moved to Lancashire when the boy was only eight months old, and Ramsay had all his schooling in Birkenhead; so he had no direct experience of a Scottish education. In 1889 he went to the University College at

Liverpool (one of the constituent colleges of Victoria University). His memories of it, at that time, written about fifty years later, are the clue to his great interest in student affairs:

> ... as yet the college was no more than a mere knowledge-shop. It had not begun to be a focus of intellectual life. There were almost no opportunities for the students to meet one another or to carry on the vital, if often shallow, talk which is the most valuable element in University life. They all lived at home, and scattered to every part of a wide area when lectures were over. .... The college had not begun to become a living society.[9]

But even a 'mere knowledge-shop' is fertile ground for a man of high quality, and Liverpool gave Muir the three great influences of his life: the very poverty of student life which, in Muir's mind, demanded reform; a library, from which he read, among other things, Newman's *Idea of a university*; and J. M. Mackay, the professor of history, 'the most dominating personality I had ever met', a highlander, educated in St Andrews and Edinburgh, steeped in the Scots tradition, with a passionate, almost mystical concept of what a university should stand for; a man of vision and fire. He was an example of a phenomenon which one finds occasionally in the academic world: not, by all accounts, a good scholar; evidently, on Muir's testimony, a poor lecturer; not even a coiner of memorable phrases. But he had that personality which is now called charismatic. For those prepared to wait there were moments of greatness. And, as one of his colleagues, Walter Raleigh, said of him: for years he thought of nothing else beside what a university is – or ought to be – *for*. So although, as the pedants would say, he was not quite *sound*, his influence on the idea of a university at the turn of the century was immense; we shall describe some of it when we come to consider the foundation of the University of Birmingham. His ideas about the status of students were clear. This is what he said in an address to the Arts Students' Association at Liverpool University College in 1900:

> The self government which under Crown Charter, the Court and Council, the Senate, the faculties and the schools enjoy, students should exercise. In their own societies they shall manage their own affairs, with an infusion of resident graduates to give guidance, tradition and experience. Their discipline they should maintain themselves, when out of class. Like the staff they fall naturally into faculties with representative councils and a general representative

44

council, a Students' Senate. Self government is part of their education, whether for their profession or for national or civic life.[10]

This address was given eleven years after Muir went to the college. It illustrates the sort of man under whose influence Muir willingly came. But it was the pupil, not the master, who had already taken the first steps to turn this rhetoric into fact. In his third year ('when I was living on the chopped straw of a pass course') and in his fourth year, when he read for honours in history, Muir founded the first organ of representative government in an English university. He tells the story himself: 'The student-body must somehow become a real corporate body, not a fortuitous collection of atoms. So I wrought out the idea of establishing a Students' Representative Council such as existed in the Scottish Universities, but not, as yet, in any of the English Colleges.'[11]

His strategy was admirable. He became one of the editors of the *University College Magazine*, changed its character and doubled its circulation and 'preached in every number the necessity of organising student-activities by establishing an elected S.R.C. to look after student affairs'.[12] The Victoria Building was to be opened in 1892 and Muir resolved that this was the time to act. He invited five students to form, with himself, a provisional committee. They secured the approval of the principal (Rendall) at an interview 'during which we all sat on the edges of our chairs'. They then summoned a mass meeting in the new arts theatre on 18 October 1892. The mass meeting decided to establish an S.R.C. and elected a committee to draw up its constitution.

The infant council's first encounter with the Establishment was not altogether a happy one. The authorities decided that students should not be present at the formal opening of the Victoria Building in the arts theatre through lack of space. A strongly worded petition of protest was organised, signed by practically every student. The authorities relented and reserved the gallery for students. This was a satisfactory victory, but unfortunately it did not satisfy some of those who resented the original decision to exclude them. Accordingly they disrupted the proceedings, which had doubtless been planned with heavy Victorian pomposity, by a combination of noise and high jinks. The high jinks took a form which senior academics (such as one of the authors of this book) regard with nostalgia compared with the witless obstruction adopted by some modern demonstrators. The gallery in the arts theatre was semi-circular. As the chancellor of the Victoria University, resplendent in his robes, rose to speak, a monstrous biscuit, three feet in diameter and specially baked for the occasion, descended slowly from a wire strung across the gallery, until it hung in front of the chancellor and obscured him from the audience. An inscription on the biscuit explained that it was presented to the senate, 'which took the biscuit for its impertinence in trying to exclude the students'.

There is no need to describe the indignation, the censure, the murmurs of 'I told you so' which followed this episode. The inevitable public condemnation – not for the last time – had a beneficial effect, for it united the students in a common cause of self-defence, and it provided a challenge to the S.R.C. to discipline its irresponsible members. The S.R.C. accepted the challenge and determined that on future occasions of this kind all noise should stop at a signal from the S.R.C.'s president.[12]

Muir did not enter the promised land of the S.R.C. for in 1894 he left to go to Balliol. But he kept closely in touch with his old college, and wrote for the college magazine (now taken over by the S.R.C. and christened *The Sphinx*). Although captivated by the graciousness of Oxford after the 'sordid slum' in Liverpool, he eagerly left, after having won first-class honours in Greats and modern history, 'to translate into reality my boyish dreams of the city University'. His boyish dreams came true. His academic career was spent in city universities. He returned, after a brief sojourn in Manchester, to Liverpool, and took part in drafting the charter which made it an autonomous university, and which (as we describe later) gave statutory recognition to the S.R.C. he had founded eleven years earlier.

Close on the heels of the S.R.C. in Liverpool there was a similar (though, so far as our evidence goes, coincidental) development at University College, London. This, too, began with propaganda in a college magazine. We have already (p. 42) described how the college authorities vetoed a debate because it seemed likely to ventilate radical sentiments. There were in the 1880s other clashes with authority: an arbitrary closing of the college at five o'clock; insufficient support for athletic activities, and so on: enough to create a current of discontent. The current in turn created a channel of communication (a phenomenon familiar to dons in the 1960s!) which took the form of a new journal with a provocative title – *The Privateer*. Like its predecessors it was short-lived; it ran only for eleven numbers in 1892–3. Unlike its predecessors, it was not a paternalistic gesture imposed upon the students by a professor. The college office viewed it with distaste and at first forbade the beadles (the name for porters in University College) to keep copies on sale. The editorial response was refreshingly independent: '*The Privateer* intends to protest and fight only when the

46

Office gives way to excess of zeal and oversteps its boundary line, or when it neglects to do that to which the students seem to have a distinct right.'[13]

The main grievance among the students was the inadequacy of arrangements for athletics, and it was this issue which brought the students together in a general meeting under the chairmanship of the distinguished professor of physiology, Edward Schafer. It was decided to form a combined athletic and social union, and a proposal to this end was sent to the college council in November 1892. Five months passed with no response from the council. The students, evidently encouraged by Schafer, kept up the pressure; a further meeting under his chairmanship was held in June 1893; and the council approved the proposal. The union began, with modest accommodation handed over by the college, on 1 October 1893 under Schafer's reluctant presidency; he, very properly, wanted them to choose a student president. The union's main interest was to promote social life among students. It did not at first generate much enthusiasm. It depended at first upon voluntary membership and it collected only 133 subscriptions from a student population of over 1200. But it was the beginning of an articulate student organisation in London and with the encouragement of Gregory Foster, who became principal in 1904, it performed for the college what S.R.C.s were performing for universities elsewhere.

We shall not disturb the flow of this narrative to describe the foundation of other S.R.C.s in England; in Leeds, shortly after a merger of three student societies in 1891;[14] in 1897–9 in Durham;[15] in 1900 in Belfast, following a campaign in a college magazine.[16] We now turn to the next step taken in England to recognise the student estate: the statutory provision for student representative government in the charters of universities.

The turn of the century was a time of great change in the new universities and university colleges in England. The Victoria University was soon to dissolve its federation into three autonomous universities, in Manchester, Liverpool and Leeds. University College, Sheffield, was soon to become a university. A University of Wales had recently been founded. The University of London was undergoing one of its periodic spasms of reform. And Joseph Chamberlain had determined that there should be a university in Birmingham.

Chamberlain had not attended a university. He left school at eighteen to go into his father's office and his life had been spent in business and in civic activities in Birmingham, followed by his career in parliament. The establishment of a federal university with colleges in Manchester,

Liverpool and Leeds was a natural challenge to the midlands and as early as 1888, influenced by Seeley, Chamberlain was urging the case for 'a true Midland University' in Birmingham. There was already one institution of higher education, Mason's College, but its scope was insufficient and its resources poor. In 1897 Chamberlain was elected lord rector of Glasgow University. He travelled north to deliver his rectorial address. 'The proceedings', wrote his biographer, 'made a deep impression on him, and just before leaving Glasgow he remarked: "When I go back to Birmingham I mean to have a University of my own." '[17]

Chamberlain was not a man to leave the design of the new university to experts; he himself exerted a considerable influence over the constitution, and there is no doubt that his views were influenced by his office, as the elected representative of the students, in Glasgow. There was, moreover, a second influence from Scotland, even more powerful: J. M. Mackay, of Liverpool, comes on the stage again, this time as a sort of consultant to the professors who were involved in designing the constitution.

We have elsewhere described the exciting dispute between a group of professors and the sub-committee charged with drawing up the charter for the University of Birmingham.[18] The outcome was a victory for the professors, led by E. A. Sonnenschein, which established Birmingham as a 'faculty-run' university. The inspiration behind Sonnenschein's campaign was Mackay. In 1897 Mackay made his first report as dean of the newly constituted faculty of arts in Liverpool. It was in his most impressive prophetic style; some rhetoric ('we are at the making of a University'); some heresy ('the examination mill is condemned already'); some exhortation ('Let us turn to Edinburgh'), and an important statement of principle: 'The Faculty at its full extension includes the teaching staff, the graduates, and the students. . . . Nor can our students breathe the atmosphere of a University except where circulates the breath of liberty and the exercise of rights that are duties. In their own societies, organised by them on the lines of the Faculties, and in their Representative Councils, . . . they have recovered an inalienable claim of their predecessors.'[19]

The report was published. Sonnenschein in Birmingham, thinking about the possibility of a university in the midlands, read it eagerly and when the time came to lay detailed plans, he secured the willing co-operation of Mackay. 'Many a night', wrote Sonnenschein, 'have I burned the midnight oil in his company, both in Birmingham and in Liverpool. . . . What we felt was that we were assisting at the birth of a new type of University in England. . . .'[20] Mackay's ideas fell on fertile soil. Joseph Chamberlain at a lunch preceding a governors' meeting on 13 January 1898 laid down the general policy he desired to see in the constitution of the university: it should be an institution, he said, where professors and students should be associated together as students.[21]

The charter was granted in March 1900. It required the university to establish a guild of graduates and a guild of undergraduates. The undergraduate guild was to have functions similar to those of a Scottish S.R.C. At the same time the charter provided for representatives of these guilds to be elected to the court of governors; this was in place of the Scottish tradition of representation through a rector and his assessor. It was a provision which obviously pleased Sonnenschein, for he singled it out for mention in an article he wrote for *The Times* about the new charter: 'A feature of truly medieval character in the best sense of the term is the provision by which the "Guild of Undergraduates" will elect three members to the supreme governing body.'[22] Sonnenschein had been reading Rashdall's book on the medieval universities (it had been published only four years earlier). Perhaps he saw in the new provision a sign of revival of the ancient *universitas*. The text runs:

15. There shall be a Guild of Graduates of the University and a Guild of its Students each of whom shall have such and so many Representatives on the Court of Governors as may be provided by the Statutes of the University. The constitutions functions privileges and all other matters connected with the said Guilds requiring to be prescribed shall be prescribed as may be provided by the Statutes.[23]

It has to be made clear straightaway that student representation on the court in Birmingham is a very different thing from representation on the court of a Scottish university. A Scottish court – even after its enlargement from its original six to eight members, to sixteen members – is an executive body with heavy responsibilities. The court at Birmingham (and the same is true of the courts in those other English universities which have them, and in the University of Wales) is an assembly running to over one hundred and sometimes two or three times that number, meeting infrequently to hear the vice-chancellor's report and serving mainly as an electoral college for certain offices. The presence of three representatives of students on this sort of court is a somewhat dilute form of participation. Still, the charter did provide specifically for undergraduates themselves to elect these representatives; and in 1903 there were two undergraduates, James Hector Barnes and

49

L. G. J. Mackey among the three delegates sent by the guild of undergraduates to sit on the university's governing body.[24] The third delegate was the Rt Hon. Lord Avebury, a distinguished naturalist but chiefly remembered to laymen as the author of a best-seller entitled *The pleasures of life*. The guild was given by ordinance powers similar to those enjoyed by Scottish S.R.C.s: it was to be 'the recognised means of communication between the Undergraduates on the one hand and the Court of Governors, Council, Senate, and other authorities of the University on the other hand'.[25] The guild was allowed to petition or make representation to the council or senate on any matter affecting the interests of the undergraduates.

Three years later Liverpool and Manchester embodied in their charters provision for student representative government. The Manchester S.R.C. was 'to promote the general interests of the students and to represent them in matters affecting their interests', and 'to afford a recognised means of communication between the students and the University authority';[26] and the prescribed channel of communication was through the vice-chancellor.[27] The Liverpool organisation was to be called a guild (Muir's S.R.C. was duly transformed into the guild, Muir himself assisting in the transformation) with a representative committee of undergraduates.[28] The guild at Liverpool, but not the S.R.C. in Manchester, had the right of electing representatives to the court. The charters for Leeds (1904) and Sheffield (1905) offered no statutory recognition to S.R.C.s, although in Leeds there was already student representative government. The one university where student representation languished to the point of death at this period (the early years of the century) was Durham; due, perhaps, to its collegiate organisation. (In Oxford and Cambridge S.R.C.s did not even start until the 1960s.) Durham had had a union, which was a students' debating society, since 1842. In 1897 the college of medicine formed an S.R.C. on the Scottish pattern and in 1899 the Durham colleges formed a separate S.R.C. (a few months later the student magazine has such comments as 'There was a miserable attendance').[29] A university S.R.C. struggled into existence in the following years, and in 1907 the magazine wrote hopefully that 'the 'Varsity S.R.C. has met once this term. . . . In due time it should make itself felt as the conscience and voice of the undergraduates.'[30] But there was no very encouraging response. The Durham University bill of 1908 made no provision for student representation, and when the Durham students, backed by a resolution from a students' congress, pressed for representation and were ignored, nothing more happened.[31]

50

By 1909 three English universities – Birmingham, Liverpool and Bristol – had statutory provision for undergraduates to participate in university government by membership of their courts. Three others, which had acquired university status since the beginning of the century (Manchester, Leeds and Sheffield), had no such provision. It was clear from the beginning that the privilege of undergraduate representation on the court was an honorific token; it conferred status and the opportunity for influence upon the student body, but it was not an instrument for what would nowadays be called student power; at any rate it was not used that way. *De facto* influence lay through direct communication between student representatives and the university officials, which charters also provided for: sometimes, as in Manchester, through the vice-chancellor, and sometimes, as in Birmingham, through council or senate. Even in Scotland, as we have seen, it was the 'un-broken current of suggestion' playing upon principal and senates, rather than the advocacy of rectors and assessors, which was the common machinery for bringing about change.

But the impression one gets is that students in the early years of the twentieth century were a contented lot, and did not press for much change. Much of their contentment was due to apathy. They accepted without question a social system which excluded, on grounds of finance and not of intelligence, many of their contemporaries from the benefits of higher education. They surely grumbled, but their grumbling did not rise to the temperature of protest, about the poor libraries, insufficient lodging or hostel accommodation, and lack of amenities in the civic universities and colleges. They were resigned to a providential superiority of Oxford and Cambridge; and the students of Oxford and Cambridge, now better taught and better looked after than their predecessors had been, enjoyed, without much twinge of conscience, the most luxurious higher education in Europe. When students met for annual congresses (which we discuss below) the items on their agenda had none of the hot political overtones of a modern conference of the National Union of Students; every year from 1904 to 1909, for instance, one item (though not the only one) on the agenda which provoked animated discussion, especially between Scottish and English delegates, was the Students' Songbook!

It was in three of the older university institutions – Queen's, Belfast, London and Wales – that there occurred significant discussions about participation. The creation of a crop of new universities at the turn of he century had precipitated the need to reassess progress in some of their elder sisters; so between 1901 and 1916 there were commissions on all three of these institutions; and in all three the commissioners took evidence from students.

From the point of view of student participation the most interesting of these was the commission on university education in Ireland (1901). The commission, under the chairmanship of Lord Robertson (who as lord advocate had piloted the Scottish bill of 1889 through the house of commons), had to tackle intricate and delicate political problems. Student affairs were not high in its list of priorities. However the student body at Queen's, Belfast, was a very lively and active one, owing partly (as in London) to the predominance of medical students, and partly to the fact that most students, whether living at home or in lodgings, were within easy walking distance of the college, so that student life was not – as it was in London – cut off by the evening commuter trains from Charing Cross and Euston. On 5 April 1902 the commission heard evidence from the president of the S.R.C., Samuel Irwin (who subsequently served for a generation on the governing body of Queen's University and never lost his interest in student affairs).[32] Irwin was a medical student who had, as was common in those days, first completed an arts degree. He put fourteen points before the commission. He made it clear that he was mandated by the S.R.C., for at the outset of his evidence he said: 'Into the broader question at issue' (the future of the Royal University of Ireland) 'I am not instructed to enter'; so his views can be taken as representative of the opinion of reflective students in Ulster at that time.

The first of his fourteen points was admirably blunt:

> In any reorganisation of this College, none would, from the students' point of view, be satisfactory, which did not give them a voice in the management of those affairs which are to them of vital importance. To effect this, we venture to propose that a students' representative should have a seat on the governing body.

Substitute 'demand' for 'venture to propose' and the sentence could be lifted into the 1960s. But it was not as revolutionary as it sounds, for Irwin went on to say that what the students had in mind was the Scottish arrangement of a rector and rector's assessor, the one elected and the other nominated by the students. Some of the other fourteen points illustrate well how students – even the unsophisticated sons of farmers and businessmen from County Antrim and County Londonderry (Irwin's own home) – do produce mature and responsible

52

opinions when given the opportunity to do so. 'We protest', said Irwin, 'in the strongest terms against the present practice of making the students of Queen's College, Belfast, travel to Dublin for practically all examinations. . . . We also complain of the present method of holding the oral examinations in the Royal University. A candidate is often asked to undergo the severe strain of an oral examination after having spent four hours in a waiting room; or he may be told, after the same time, that he will not be examined orally until the next day. . . . The present method of appointing Examiners is most unsatisfactory. . . . We would suggest that, in each subject, there should be an Examining Board, composed partly of those engaged in the actual teaching of the subject and partly of extern Examiners. An arrangement of this kind is found to work satisfactorily in Edinburgh University.' And a very perceptive observation on the arts curriculum: 'In all examinations in classical subjects there should be prescribed *authors* rather than pre-scribed *books*. This would prevent "cramming" to such an extent as exists at present. . . . If this were done students would be compelled to read much more widely and with a far truer appreciation of the merits of the Classics.' (There was a motive behind this, namely to enable Irish students more easily to qualify for English civil service examina-tions.) Among other views on academic work put forward by Irwin on behalf of the S.R.C. were Greek as an option in place of Latin or mathematics; a pass course for the B.A. in history, political economy, and jurisprudence or English; an improvement in the staff-student ratio (to give professors more time to devote to honours candidates); the need to have strong schools of biology, geology, and mineralogy in a college where medicine and engineering were taught; and the need for post-graduate scholarships in medicine 'for graduates in Medicine to remain in connection with the College and to take up research work'.

Only after this catalogue of academic needs and grievances did Irwin turn to the social needs of students at Queen's: halls of residence and athletic grounds. As in London, students who wanted to play games had to play for clubs in the town 'and there is lost to the students all that good fellowship and comradeship which men associated with each other in sport enjoy; and there is lost to the College the loyalty to it which such feelings beget'.

There was no dialogue between Irwin and the commission after he had given his evidence; nor did the commission recommend any form of student representation. But the S.R.C.'s ideas fell on fertile ground, for when, under the Irish Universities Act, 1908, Queen's College became Queen's University, the act provided for a more intimate student participation than existed in any other university in the kingdom. The president of the S.R.C., if a graduate (and he frequently was a B.A. proceeding to a degree in medicine or law), had *ex officio* a place on the senate. The senate, in Belfast, is the supreme governing body, both *de jure* and *de facto*. It corresponds to the Scottish court and the English council. This was a far more realistic recognition of student status than membership of the elephantine English court, or even than vicarious membership of the Scottish court.

Nine years later the Haldane commission was wrestling with the affairs of the University of London. It – like the commission on Irish universities – was preoccupied with what, at that time, were much more important issues than student representation; but it, too, received a statement from the University of London S.R.C. and examined two representatives, W. H. Lister and L. F. Thompson. The S.R.C. statement began with a declaration, not entirely accurate, but almost identical with that made by the Belfast S.R.C.:

> No reorganisation of the University would be satisfactory from the students' point of view unless it allowed student representation on the Senate. In support of this we would respectfully point to the example set by the Scottish universities, where students have a direct voice in the management of university affairs, through their Lord Rectors; and we would further point out that the principle has been admitted in the constitutions of the Universities of Birmingham, Liverpool, Leeds, and Belfast.[33]

The statement goes on to explain that what the S.R.C. has in mind is not direct representation by a student, but 'some prominent man, preferably a graduate'; though the request ends with the firm condition 'it is to be understood that nominations to such an office could only be accepted if confirmed by the Students' Representative Council'. The other points were an objection, felt strongly in London, that there was no distinction made to enable people to know whether a degree had been taken internally or externally, 'by methods the very reverse of those which it is the object of a university to enforce'; too much lecturing and too little personal teaching; and criticisms of the conduct of examinations.

It is noteworthy that both in London and in Wales the commissioners invited students to present oral evidence. This, we think, may well be due to the fact that Haldane was chairman of the commissions inquiring into both these universities. His sympathy with the student view, and

54

his advocacy of the student interest, are a recurrent pattern in our story. The discussion between the students and the commissioners which followed disclosed that the S.R.C. – or at any rate its delegates before the commission – had a curious concept of the value of representation on the senate. 'What was at the back of our minds', said Mr Lister, 'was not so much the fact that representation would be of value, but that the actual election would be the great point if you granted us this. That the election taking place once in two years or something of that sort would be a most tremendous help in bringing to the students of London the realisation that they are units of one whole University, especially if carried out on party grounds. . . .' 'Political party grounds?' asked one of the commissioners. Yes, was the reply.

Perhaps it is fortunate that the commission did not recommend this pattern of student representation for an institution so diffuse as the University of London. Haldane, notwithstanding – or perhaps because of – his Scottish experience, preferred the new pattern of the English civic universities: the commission recommended that two representatives of the S.R.C. should serve on the court, which it had in mind should be a body comprising some 200 persons.[34]

Our last example comes from Wales. There a royal commission, again under Haldane's chairmanship, was appointed in 1916 to inquire into the organisation and work of the federal University of Wales and its constituent colleges. The commissioners' main task was not unlike the task of the Irish university commissioners: the problems of a federal university inextricably tangled up with celtic tribal politics. But they, too, found time to examine representatives of the S.R.C. of the University of Wales, which had been set up in 1914. The S.R.C. produced a terse and lucid memorandum with three recommendations:

I. That the University should retain its constitution as the federation of the three Colleges situate at Aberystwyth, Bangor and Cardiff respectively.

II. That the said University be represented in Parliament.

III. That the students be granted the right of appointing a representative to such governing bodies of the University and of the constituent colleges as may deal with matters affecting the interests of the students.[35]

The first two recommendations were supported with the argument (which still unites the colleges of Wales into one university despite the majority recommendation of a more recent commission) that 'the distinctive feature of the University of Wales is its national character'. The annual meetings of the S.R.C. had brought students together from all the constituent colleges and this had become 'an essential factor in the conduct of Welsh students' activities'. For the third recommendation the Welsh S.R.C. was prepared to adopt the Scottish model: 'a graduate of some standing' to represent it on the senates of the colleges and the university.

On 15 December 1916, three students met the commission: Marion Soar, Illtyd David and Cyril Rosebourne. Haldane asked them whether, in asking for representation, they did not mean the court of the university (a body over 100 strong) and not the senate (which is an academic body). By 1916 student politicians had evidently realised that token membership of courts was not an effective device for representation and that the effective influence in the civic universities came from the assembly of professors – the senate. 'What we had in mind', said Mr Rosebourne, 'were the University Senate and the College Senates rather than the Court.' Haldane demurred, and asked what about the council (the effective supreme governing body composed of a mixture of academics and laymen). 'What we had in mind when this resolution was passed', insisted Mr Rosebourne, 'was the Senate.' Haldane replied: 'I see you have fixed your mind upon the Senate. But, no doubt, you are not averse to our considering the other bodies in addition or alternatively, as the case may be.' Mr David then illustrated how the senate would be the appropriate body, for topics upon which 'the views of the students might very profitably be heard' included the structure of degrees, the excessive number of lectures and the pattern of examinations. At this point Haldane, scenting danger, made a comment which has great relevance to the students of 1970 (though it is perhaps inconsistent with one he made in a different context, as a young M.P. supporting the Scottish Universities bill twenty-seven years earlier, and which we quoted on p. 35):

> Of course, a university is not a democracy; you cannot govern it through the students. That was done in the case of the mediaeval universities in Italy, I believe, with the possibly beneficial result that only those professors survived who were the fittest, and that those who were not agreeable to the students were hunted out. You are not suggesting that we return to that state of things . . . where the government was a sort of democracy?[36]

– to which Haldane got the retort he deserved. Miss Soar (clearly a young lady flourishing forty years before her time) replied: 'If it led to the survival of the fittest it was surely a good thing.'

The lively students of Wales did not get all they asked for. But they did have the satisfaction of knowing that they had made an impression on the commission, for the commissioners in commenting on the arguments which they had heard in favour of preserving one single federal university – and which they accepted – wrote: 'It is interesting also to note that this view has the strong support of the Central Students' Representative Council.'[37] The students had the satisfaction, too, of getting statutory provision for two members of the central S.R.C. of the university to serve on the court. And the commissioners, realising perhaps by then that the courts of civic universities were not very useful bodies, included in their recommendations suggestions for infusing life and some influence into the court of the University of Wales. They supported the proposal from one of their witnesses that the court at its half-yearly meeting should not hurry through its agenda in one day 'with its attention divided between the business and the clock or railway guide', but should settle down for four or five days to discuss higher education. 'Great projects of reform and development might be discussed and even if there were no immediate result these discussions would be at once the outcome of public opinion and the means of bringing it to ripeness.'

Neither in Wales nor elsewhere have university courts risen to this challenge. Those who dismiss with a shrug the cumbersome proceedings of student conferences do well to remind themselves that courts, which might have become the popular parliaments of the civic universities, have put up an even poorer showing; the students do at least talk earnestly and at inordinate length about things that matter.

A false start in cohesion

If the expression 'student estate' is taken to cover recognition by parliament that students have collective rights and responsibilities in universities, then by the end of the epoch marked by November 1918, there was a student estate in Britain, not everywhere (Oxford and Cambridge were still immune from these currents of thought – Miss Soar would have had no sympathetic hearing there); not influential outside universities, and only spasmodically inside them; and, except in Scotland, where the S.R.C.s of all four universities had combined to put their views to the government as long ago as 1888, not co-ordinated for any common cause. By 1970 the 'student estate' has come to mean much more than this, and we now turn to the first attempts at inter-university co-operation south of the border.

Affiliation, followed by schism, is a common feature of human communities, whether they are the christian church, the trade union movement or students' representative councils. It was not surprising, therefore, that S.R.C.s, having received statutory recognition in university charters, should want to assemble together in an annual congress. The idea was discussed by English student delegates at the celebrations of the ninth jubilee of the University of Glasgow in 1901. It was planned to hold a congress in Belfast in 1902 but the project was abandoned, chiefly owing to the difficulty of finding accommodation.[38] But in 1904 the plans were fulfilled: the first Inter-Universities Students' Congress, with representatives from all universities in England and Wales, was held in Manchester.[39]

This first congress was blessed from on high; there were congratulatory telegrams from the prince of Wales, the duke of Devonshire, and Mr Joseph Chamberlain. And a splendid initial motion was proposed by the distinguished physicist Professor Schuster, condemning the existing state of examinations. The motion was passed unanimously. But this promising start was not sustained. The congress then passed resolutions deciding to establish an inter-university magazine and a British Students' Song Book, and it set up committees to work on the magazine, on residential halls, and (inevitably) to consider a constitution for the congress. It was decided, too, to extend a fraternal invitation to representatives of the universities of Scotland and Ireland to attend the next congress. This took place in University College, London, and was the first British Inter-Universities Students' Congress.[40] There were sixty-three delegates. All universities in the kingdom were represented, except Oxford and Cambridge. It lasted from 28 June to 1 July. Serious matters were discussed such as employment registers, mutual recognition between universities of work for degrees (a topic which, if it had been successfully pursued, would have changed the history of higher education in Britain) and, again, halls of residence (the committee had duly delivered its report). In 1906 the congress was held in Edinburgh.[41] There was a discussion of a further report on halls of residence and a resolution in favour of partial control of halls by the students living in them.

It is worth while to digress for three paragraphs to discuss the topic of residence. Outside Oxford and Cambridge provision for student residence was very poor. At a time when Columbia University alone had dormitories for 1000 students there were, except in the two ancient universities, only eleven halls for men, with 470 places, and fourteen halls for women, with 729 places. The difficulties about providing more places were primarily, of course, that the new universities could not afford to build them, but also that they were more expensive than lodgings (the cost at Dalton Hall, Manchester, was £90 a year), and, according to one critic, 'the fear of curtailment of liberty'. Following the first report of the inter-universities halls of residence committee in June 1905 there was an interesting series of articles in *The University Review*, which illuminate again the great differences between Scottish and English universities and the powerful influence which Oxford and Cambridge had upon notions of student residence in England.[42]

In 1887 Patrick Geddes, who brought to the vague and misty subject of sociology the austere discipline of a man trained in biology under T. H. Huxley, put one of his sociological ideas into practice by founding University Hall, Edinburgh, a student residence which had no warden and was run by students themselves. By 1905 it was the largest hall of residence in the country and it contained nearly one-third of the total number of men in residence in such halls in all Great Britain. One of its virtues was its cheapness (it cost students less than half the cost at Dalton Hall); but a far more important virtue was the educational value of living in a self-governing hall of residence. Students, it was claimed, did not act defiantly, because there was no one to defy. It could be inferred from this claim that a warden might be what is now called 'counter-productive' educationally.

This good example from Scotland was not looked on with favour by some English wardens who responded in the pages of *The University Review*. The principal of Dalton Hall asserted (with justice) that wardens have a positive educational mission; they are not just policemen. 'Discipline', it was blandly said, 'is hardly felt by men of good manners.' Self-governing halls without wardens might be suitable for Scotsmen; the Scottish student 'is more self reliant from his early boyhood, and generally more in earnest'. In 1906 Geddes himself addressed the University Extension Students' Guild of the University of London on the sociology of student residence, and again advocated student communes. Unfortunately the discussion seemed to die out after 1906. In the long run the English idea prevailed. 'The men', wrote the principal of Dalton Hall, 'are at an age when, if they lived at home, they would be helped by the guidance, and be much under the reasonable control of their fathers. I see no reason why the same men, when massed together, should do better without such equivalent for fatherhood as a warden can offer.' It is interesting to speculate how differently the English universities might have developed if the University of

Edinburgh had, in 1905, a second time set a pattern for the evolution of the student estate.

We must now take the reader back to the attempt at cohesion which was being made through the inter-university congresses. There were only two instances of the congress combining to help one of its constituent S.R.C.s. The students of Durham had a grievance that their revised constitution would not grant them representation on the governing bodies of the university or its constituent colleges. A motion was passed urging on the authorities 'the extreme desirability of undergraduates being represented' on these bodies.[43] The act of 1908 contained no such provision, but there is no record that students in Durham or elsewhere protested about this. At a later congress, in Birmingham in 1910, it was agreed to impress on the royal commission on the University of London 'the necessity for the representation of the S.R.C. of that University on the Senate by means of a Lord Rector';[44] but the commissioners were not likely to have been swayed by this pressure in their recommendation for student representation on the court.

The annual congresses were agreeable social occasions, and a useful means of diffusing through British universities a certain corporate consciousness. Their weakness was that there were, in those years, no issues on which students, as students, felt passionately. To be a student, as Seeley had said long ago, did not mean for them membership of 'a vast student world'. It is not surprising, therefore, to find a maggot of self-doubt lodged in the minds of the organisers of the congress. The public notice of the 1909 congress, held in Durham, referred to scepticism about the congress arising perhaps out of the 'not unnatural hesitancy' of the authorities 'to immediately approve of any organized movements of "irresponsible" undergraduates'.[45] In 1910, when the congress met in Birmingham, the suggestion was made that congresses should be held biennially instead of annually. By 1911 there was an unconcealable disenchantment with the congresses. On 13 November 1911, the Durham S.R.C. resolved to discuss a motion to withdraw from the congress; and early in 1912 the cracks of schism appeared. The Scottish Inter-Universities Conference, by three votes to one (Aberdeen dissenting), resolved 'that the four Scottish Universities sever their connection with the British Universities Congress'.[46]

4 National Co-ordination

The National Union of Students

Between 1914 and 1918 three-quarters of a million men from the United Kingdom were killed and another million and a half permanently injured.[1] The students who assembled in Britain's universities in October 1919, both those from the trenches and those fresh from school, were the survivors of a holocaust, a major discontinuity in history. The glamour of war – still present in 1914 – had been dispelled. Those who had learnt what war was like were eager to secure peace in their time; among thoughtful ex-service students there was an enthusiasm for international friendship.

An opportunity to develop this friendship came in 1919. French students organised a student congress at Strasbourg to celebrate the reopening of the university there under French rule. Delegations were invited from allied and neutral countries. Scotland, having an official federation of Scottish students, was able to send a delegation; but there was nobody to appoint a delegation from elsewhere in Britain, and England was represented only by some students who went in their personal capacity. The congress set up a *Confédération internationale des étudiants* (C.I.E.) with seven member countries. Ten other countries, including England, whose students were present unofficially, were offered associate membership without voting rights. The C.I.E. determined to hold an international congress every three years and to elect a council and an executive to provide continuity between congresses. The constitution specifically excluded discussion of religious or political issues. Ex-enemy countries were barred from membership until they had been admitted to the League of Nations.

The first congress was held in Prague in 1921. Six hundred students attended, including about a hundred 'unofficial' delegates from England, organised by Malcolm Thomson of the International Students' Bureau. The congress was dominated by French and francophil students and it was not long before the post-war idealism of nordic youth came under strain. Cracks appeared in the C.I.E.: some wanted overtures to be made to students of ex-enemy countries; others did not. There was a move, which the English group opposed, to set up an independent international organisation. Failing this, the Dutch and Scandinavian students urged the English to qualify for full membership of the C.I.E. by establishing in England a national union of students which could appoint official delegates to the C.I.E. to counteract the excessive influence of the French.

The delegates on their return to England set up an Inter-Varsity Association under the chairmanship of F. S. Milligan of Birmingham. It was not widely representative of English universities and it lasted only a few months. But it served an essential purpose, for it called a conference in London in September 1921, attended by students from universities and university colleges in England and Wales. The conference dissolved the Inter-Varsity Association, decided to establish a National Union of Students, and drew up a first draft of a constitution. Five months later, at a further meeting of student representatives in London, fourteen student organisations (from Durham, London, Manchester, Birmingham, Liverpool, Leeds, Sheffield, Bristol, Nottingham, Aberystwyth, Cardiff, Bangor, Swansea, and the women students of Oxford) formally supported a declaration establishing a 'National Union of Students of the Universities and University Colleges of England and Wales', and approved a revision of the draft constitution. Three colleges—Exeter, Reading and Southampton – did not subscribe to the statement, and delegates from the Oxford and Cambridge Union societies had to explain that they had no authority to associate their universities with the declaration because neither Oxford nor Cambridge had a representative student organisation: an obstacle which continued for years to exclude these two universities from playing a full part in national student affairs. Students from these two universities did, however, play some part in the building up of the N.U.S.; indeed, the second president was an Oxonian. The original constitution embodied one object for the N.U.S., namely:

> To represent past and present students from a National and Inter-national point of view, and to render possible the co-operation of the body of students in England, Wales, Scotland, and Ireland with the students of other lands.

To this one object the executive of the council added, at its meeting later in 1922, another object:

> To promote the educational and social interests of students in entire independence of all political or religious propaganda.

Membership was open to the student organisations of universities and university colleges (it was not opened to student organisations in institutions of further education until 1937). The union was administered by a council composed of representatives of each affiliated organisation (two from each, with additional delegates – one per thousand members – from larger institutions, up to a maximum of seven); and a small executive elected from the council. Normally the council met once a year and the executive once a term.[2]

Its first president was Ivison Macadam, who had served in the Royal Engineers, and had returned to King's College, London, where he had become president of the college union. He was inspired by the ideals of internationalism implicit in the C.I.E., and he brought to the new movement a typically Scots combination of shrewdness and vision. Ideals had to be translated into organisation. Continuity had to be assured. This required accommodation and an executive staff; and this required money. There were two ways to raise money. One was to foster the international activities of the N.U.S. by promoting student travel abroad. Accordingly Macadam organised a tours department which has not only contributed, in ways that cannot be measured, to international understanding, but has also proved to be a valuable source of income. The other way to raise money was to enlist public interest. This was a romantic episode in Macadam's pioneering work. Inspired by Barrie's famous rectorial address at St Andrews on *Courage*, calling for a league of youth, Macadam wrote a letter to *The Times*, declaring that there was a 'league of youth' in Britain, the infant N.U.S. Letters from undergraduates to *The Times* do not normally attract attention. This letter attracted much more than attention: it attracted a fairy godfather. Macadam was called out of a lecture at King's to answer a telephone call. The call was from Bertram Hawker (who was a virtuoso in modesty and managed to keep his name out of the archives of the movement). Hawker was impressed by this undergraduate's letter and offered to help him launch an appeal. The appeal (signed by Balfour and other distinguished figures) gave the N.U.S. a start. It was promoted not only in London but, with C. P. Scott's help, in Manchester. With Hawker's help a house was purchased in Endsleigh Street as a headquarters. It was opened by Lord Haldane, who had championed student affairs for a generation. Fortunately Macadam did not fade out from the N.U.S. at the end of his presidency. He stayed on until 1930 as honorary organising secretary, and this enabled him to lay firm financial and administrative foundations for a movement which might otherwise have evaporated through the constant flux of student-officers. His ambition to give what would now be called a 'good image' to the N.U.S. was helped by another exciting episode. A meeting of C.I.E. representatives was to be held in England. What could be provided for the delegates which would be typically English? Macadam had the answer: an English country house. To provide this he enlisted a fairy godmother: he persuaded Nancy Astor to invite the delegates to meet at Cliveden. Each night there were guests to dinner: J. L. Garvin, then editing *The Observer*, Geoffrey Dawson, editing *The Times*, Lionel Curtis, Philip Kerr, later to become Lord Lothian. At King's College the principal, Ernest Barker, was backing the movement, and it had the blessing of Albert Mansbridge. The C.I.E. meeting was addressed by Lord Grey of Fallodon. Before Macadam gave up his honorary post as organising secretary (he remained attached to the N.U.S. as an honorary treasurer and is still, in 1970, a trustee) he had secured the appointment of a paid secretary (Ralph May, who had been president of the student guild in Birmingham); he had won the confidence and support of people of great influence; and he had created the beginning of a sense of cohesion among university students in England and Wales, by regular visits to unions and guilds in all the constituent organisations which belonged to the N.U.S. This cohesion was improved by annual congresses (some of which we discuss below). The travel activities, which began with a trip to Cologne of six men students and one woman who was chaperoned by her mother, blossomed under May Hermes, ex-president of the Bedford College union, into a busy department in Endsleigh Street where, in co-operation with C.I.E., the National Students' Identity Card was issued – a sort of students' passport – and a handbook of student travel which, to this day, is for thousands of students the most useful service offered by the N.U.S.

The N.U.S. owes its birth to the determination of young men, many of whom had fought in the war, to take part in a European youth movement; and Strasbourg, which over forty years earlier had inspired the first S.R.C. in Britain, was the origin of this new step in the consolidation of student opinion in England and Wales. The present prosperity of the union rests upon an endowment of stability left by Macadam and the young colleagues who helped him.

In three or four years the first post-war generation of students had gone out into the world; their eager hopes for the future had become a little tarnished by reality, and a thin file of enthusiasts had to carry the N.U.S. through ten years heavily weighed down by disappointments and frustration. It was T. E. Lawrence who wrote:

We lived many lives in those whirling campaigns, never sparing ourselves: yet when we achieved and the new world dawned, the old men came out again and took our victory to re-make in the likeness of the former world they knew. Youth could win, but had not learned to keep: and was pitiably weak against age. We stammered that we had worked for a new heaven and a new earth, and they thanked us kindly and made their peace.

The student estate today, some of whose members display a cheap and ignorant contempt toward the N.U.S., owe more than they realise to that thin file of enthusiasts. From the very beginning they found themselves called upon to mediate between the nordic and gallic blocs of the C.I.E. More than once the N.U.S. council reaffirmed its desire to make the C.I.E. 'truly international'. The smaller European countries looked to English leadership in international student relations. In 1926 the N.U.S. delegation was instructed 'to work for the reconciliation of the French and German groups and the inclusion of all nationalities in the C.I.E.'.[3] A year later the N.U.S. council was urging that the C.I.E. should abandon its political activities;[4] but it was in vain; France still refused to agree to the admission of German students.[5] By 1931, ten years after the first congress in Prague, the conclusion was that the C.I.E. was 'on balance probably doing more harm than good in the field of international relations . . . and that the C.I.E. should be dissolved'.[6] Still the English delegations persisted in working for a European student brotherhood. By 1932 it seemed that they were beginning to have some success.[7] The C.I.E. had brought British and European students together in friendship. It promoted international athletics. It facilitated travel and exchange among students through the Students' Identity Card and in other ways. It is said that it even tried to protest against the rise of dictatorships in Europe. But it was too late. The storm clouds of nationalism gathered over Europe. Tolerance became equated to treason. The C.I.E. congress at Vienna in 1933 became an occasion for 'aggressive Fascist propaganda'.[8] For the second time in the twentieth century the lights were going out in Europe.

There were disappointments for the N.U.S. at home as well as abroad. One of the earliest acts of the executive was to invite Irish delegates to attend its meetings. But this was the time of the troubles. British troops were still in Ireland and although a political settlement was reached between Dublin and Westminster, it was a settlement on paper, not in the hearts of the people. It was not until 1944 that the N.U.S. constitution was amended to include student organisations from Northern Ireland. With Scotland relations were more genial. The Scottish universities, as we have already mentioned (p. 60), withdrew from the British Universities Students' Congress in 1912. The infant N.U.S. made no overtures to its elder sister in the 1920s, but there was a cordial, if cautious, sororal relationship during the 1930s and closer co-operation during the war. Delegates attended one another's conferences; there was a joint meeting of the executives of the two bodies for the first time in 1943; and in February 1945 the N.U.S. council resolved to investigate the possibility of establishing a regular interchange of delegates. One gets the impression that it was not so much tribal incompatibility as hard-headed realism (obstacles, as it was tactfully put, 'of finance and geography') which kept the N.U.S. and the S.N.U.S. on terms of acquaintanceship rather than marriage.[9]

The most difficult task of the N.U.S. leaders between the wars was to maintain loyalty and enthusiasm among their own membership in the universities and colleges of England and Wales. The dull beat of apathy runs through the records of councils and congresses in the 1920s, rising to hostility and defection from some member unions in the early 1930s. It was not until the leaders had shifted their emphasis from the international to the domestic concerns of students, and had worked out a student programme for university reform, that the N.U.S. again became an articulate and effective organ of the student estate. We describe below how this programme was worked out; but first we have to put on record how the N.U.S. survived the first ten critical years of its career.

Its attempts to create cohesion among the student organisations of Europe failed; but it was an honourable failure and an inevitable one: no youth organisation could withstand French arrogance and fascist fanaticism. Equally inevitable was a certain lack of confidence in the union's potential as a critic of the universities and as spokesman for students in Britain, for it was not backed by any strong S.R.C. or guild at Oxford or Cambridge universities, which at that time still enjoyed a prestige which overawed some of the less venerable and less complacent foundations. It is not surprising, then, that in 1922, when the president was asked to inquire into university entrance examinations, 'the meeting felt very strongly that it was no part of the functions of the National Union to concern itself in any way with questions touching the academic administration of Universities'.[10] Yet the union did in these early days score three successes on behalf of students. One, in response to an overture from the Association of University Teachers (A.U.T.), itself a very young body, was to form in 1927 a joint com-

66

mittee with four representatives from each body, to meet once a year, 'with the idea of carrying out an investigation into present methods of University education'.[11] The co-operation continued up to the end of the period covered by this chapter, and culminated in two quite independent, but notably similar, reports on university reform: *The future of university and higher education*, prepared by the N.U.S. (1944), and a series of articles adopted as policy statements by the A.U.T. council and published as a 'Report on university developments' in *The Universities Review* (1944-5). We discuss these reports on pp. 86-90. In the intervening years the joint committee met regularly and discussed such topics as the need for tutorial systems; curricular and examination reform; staff–student conferences in individual universities (these were successfully arranged in several universities, especially Birmingham); the obligation to attend lectures and the desirability – not enthusiastically received by the A.U.T. members – of circulating stencilled lecture notes; and freedom of speech. Over this last issue, raised in the tense atmosphere of Mussolini's attack on Abyssinia and amid propaganda for pacifism, the joint N.U.S.–A.U.T. committee walked on tiptoe. The view was expressed that the passing of political motions by student unions was undesirable; they should remain aloof from political matters. But 'the greatest freedom' should be allowed in political clubs and debating societies, and the A.U.T. representatives promised support if any student were to be penalised for his political views.[12] What was important was not anything which the joint committee achieved, but the fact that there was, in the very existence of this committee, a rudimentary recognition of the corporate body representing the student estate.

The second successful activity of the N.U.S. in the 1920s was to draw attention to the need for the universities to do something to minimise unemployment and misemployment among graduates. Although the student population in England and Wales varied very little over this period (it was about the same in 1930 as it had been in 1922) jobs were not easy to find and there was no efficient development of employment agencies. The N.U.S. deserves credit for continuing to publicise this (a whole congress was devoted to it in 1937) and for proposing some remedies such as the improvement in the ratio of teachers to pupils in schools. The third important service provided by the union was the travel bureau to which we have already referred and which, in addition to raising funds, was making a useful contribution to the union's original object, the promotion of international understanding.

But these efforts failed to silence the critics. When the executive met in February 1927 one of the vice-presidents, F. O. Darvall, opened a discussion on the union's policy. There was no large body of students in any university which was strongly in favour of the N.U.S. In some universities there was opposition; in most, apathy and distrust.[13] Similar dismal complaints were voiced in 1928 and 1929. By 1930 it was reported that at his own university, Reading, a motion for withdrawing from the N.U.S. had been defeated only by a casting vote.[14] There were similar signs of disaffection from other places; the representative from Swansea, for instance, said that the N.U.S. must meet the criticism that it concerned itself too much with international politics. The annual congress in 1931 was cancelled for lack of registrations. By 1933 Leeds and the Oxford Union Society had withdrawn from the N.U.S. and the annual subscription had fallen from £1033 to £892.[15] The constituent members, said one cynical representative from Manchester, should not have to pay a large sum every year for high ideals.

It is not difficult to diagnose the causes of this apathy and disenchantment. The prime reason was insufficient communication between the active enthusiasts and the rank-and-file of students. There was for a time a magazine, *The University*, with a circulation of as much as 3500,[16] but the mass of students either did not read it or, if they did, found nothing in it to arouse their support. A second reason was that the N.U.S. had little of interest to communicate anyway; the weary tasks of sending delegates to the C.I.E., collecting information about employment, drawing up agenda for congresses, discussing what at that time seemed unattainable dreams of tutorial systems and halls of residence, holding a congress on the art of living and the use of leisure: these did not make hot news. Thirdly, in the 1920s the 'average' student in universities and colleges affiliated to N.U.S. had a meagre corporate life in the university: no inducement to stay on the premises after lectures ended; a train or bus ride home, where he shed his college interests and had to resume his family obligations – being in time for high tea so that mother did not have to cook twice over, helping his younger brother over homework, hesitating, often, to disturb the household routine by bringing his college friends home. True, there were disturbing influences about: the emancipating novels of H. G. Wells, the aseptic social statistics of the Webbs, the iconoclasm of Bernard Shaw, the restless discontent of D. H. Lawrence, the brittle cleverness of Aldous Huxley. But the degree examination, the uncertainty of employment, the discomfort of swimming against the cur-

68

rent of orthodoxy, were sufficient to suppress in most students the dangerous thoughts raised by these writers. There were, by way of compensation, the comfortable essays of Chesterton and Belloc, the musical voice of Walter de la Mare, the solid chronicles of Galsworthy. One social upheaval broke the surface of student life between the war and the depression: the general strike of 1926. Today a strike of such dimensions would polarise student opinion, with a majority demonstrating in favour of the strikers. In 1926 nearly all those students who took any interest at all helped to break the strike; the handful of students who sympathised with the workers found themselves cold-shouldered by their friends, regarded as subversive rebels. The corporate social conscience of students had not yet been aroused. It is not surprising, therefore, that the N.U.S., founded under the influence of ex-servicemen and in pursuit of a vision of international fellowship to heal the hatreds of war, should have lost its appeal by 1930, when the universities were populated by young people whose memories of 1918 were distant and vague. Locally, individual student guilds and councils were strong – in Sheffield, for instance, there was a vigorous student group at this time – but national cohesion was weak. What is surprising, and praiseworthy, is the way a handful of young men – Darvall, Herklots, Ralphs, May, Simon, among others – worked imaginatively to keep the movement alive.

Apathy is still the chronic infirmity of student organisations. The estimate made at an N.U.S. congress a generation ago – that only about one in seven students takes a real interest and an active part in student affairs[17] – would now be regarded as optimistic. But this should not be a matter for despair; after all the number of citizens who take an active part in politics is comparatively small, too. What matters more is what the activists do and the degree of silent support which they get. Today, for instance, and on some issues, for every student who demonstrates there may be ten who silently sympathise with the demonstration, as some universities learn to their cost if they adopt repressive measures toward the demonstrators. Toward the end of the 1930s, although there were still complaints about apathy, the N.U.S. received much more support. There were two reasons for this, intricately connected: the first was that the N.U.S. turned its attention to university reform; the second was that events at home and abroad compelled thoughtful students to think beyond the degree examination, the safe job, the technical qualification. The depression, unemployment, fascism, the Jewish exodus, Stalin's Russia, the Spanish civil war: these stirred the conscience of the young and compelled the more sensitive among

69

them to make up their minds where they stood. And they were prodded by a new generation of writers who displaced Wells and Shaw and Galsworthy, including what A. J. P. Taylor calls 'the creation of a new element in the Labour party: the left wing intellectual'. Their media were the rows of pink-covered volumes published by Gollancz for the Left Book Club, and the scarifying articles which appeared week by week in the *New Statesman*. Isherwood, Strachey, Laski, Middleton Murray, among propagandists; Auden, Day Lewis and Spender among poets; Bernal and Levy among scientists, carried a more uncomfortable message than the socialists of the twenties. It was under these two influences that the N.U.S. sought and found its identity.

In search of an identity

This is not a history of the National Union of Students. If it were, we should have to trace the meanderings of its policies and the biographies of its leaders through the 'long week-end' between the wars. Our concern is solely with the rise of a student estate, and we therefore extract from the history of the N.U.S. only those events which have a bearing on our theme, which is the growth of a corporate opinion among students and its influence upon higher education.

We begin in February 1927, when a vice-president of the N.U.S. made his complaint about apathy and distrust among universities toward the union's work (p. 68). His diagnosis was that the N.U.S. was tackling problems remote from the interests of students. The executive concurred, and set up a sub-committee to investigate the role of the union in relation to the problems of universities. The committee's work was held up by what the annual report called the 'dispersal of personnel' and through lack of funds.[18] But it had one very happy outcome. One member of the committee was H. G. G. Herklots (who today holds high office in the anglican church). In 1928 he published a book, *The new universities: an external examination*, arising out of his experience on the committee. The book is an interesting social document, for although it was not an official document endorsed by the N.U.S. but a personal statement from a young Cambridge graduate, nevertheless it illustrates the temper of the time: Herklots was chosen by his peers to be a member of the sub-committee and he states that the views in his book had been discussed and criticised by students of many universities; 'the pickings', he called it, 'of many minds'.

The book is the testimony of a humane, sensitive man who accepts, perhaps reluctantly, the social framework of the age, and deplores some of the consequences: the attitude which regards a university course as a money-making asset rather than a sacrifice of money-making for spiritual and intellectual ends; which impoverishes the mind by restricting its range to the taught curriculum. And he deplores the effects which this attitude has on education in the civic universities: the undergraduate does not choose the lectures he wants to hear; he chooses a course, and then 'looks in the time-table to discover what lectures he is expected to attend'. Herklots found in the universities a complacent acceptance of the *status quo*; too little ferment of ideas, too few students asking what is wrong with the universities. But his own recipe for discontent is a mild one; certainly not revolution, not even any harnessing of the universities for social ends, but rather an aristocratic rejection of materialism, a concentration on quality, not quantity, in higher education. He saw danger in an expansion of higher education to produce an intellectual proletariat. The present decade (he was writing in 1928) should be one of retrenchment, not expansion: an advocacy, as he called it, of 'birth-control' among universities. The most illuminating passage in his book is one which advocates a serenity, a sort of lay quietism, as the proper spirit for study. It is right, he says, that the university should 'withdraw itself a little from the world that the world may be viewed in perspective'. For this to happen there must be physical detachment as well as intellectual detachment; universities must be made comfortable and attractive.

There is no doubt that in the 1920s this was the common mystique of a university, enjoyed by those fortunate enough to live in an Oxford or Cambridge college, envied by those commuting each morning into the grimy neo-gothic of Manchester or Leeds. And this is perhaps another reason why the first impetus of the N.U.S. had spent itself by 1930: withdrawal and quietism, even if only envied and not enjoyed, are inconsistent with an assertive corporate youth movement. You cannot conduct reform shut in an ivory tower. In the N.U.S. Herklots did not see a youth crusade which could change higher education and the society which supported it. He did see it as an influence to refine the prosaic life of the student in the new redbrick universities: offering opportunities for cheap travel abroad, encouraging student exchange, inquiring into appointments boards, loan schemes, and the organisation of student amenities such as unions and halls of residence.

All very worthy aims, but not enough to revive the fervour which founded the N.U.S. in 1922. Meanwhile the union's sub-committee, having ranged over the features of university life (lodgings and hostels, lectures and tutorials, examinations and employment, curricula and specialisation), resolved to give priority to a study of curricula, and issued to member organisations the customary questionnaire. The response was disappointing. The first attempt to design a students' policy on university problems foundered on the very apathy which had given rise to the attempt. By 1931 the N.U.S. was in a depression of morale.

It was the guild of undergraduates in Liverpool, Ramsay Muir's off-spring, which helped to dispel this depression. In March 1932 the guild sent a letter to all student bodies affiliated to the N.U.S., asking them to specify their discontents and to say what they expected from their national union. This goaded the council into action; it now realised that unless the N.U.S. transferred its attention to topics which touch the lives of individual students, its days might be numbered. At its meeting at Reading in July the council appointed a sub-committee to decide upon strategy. The sub-committee met three times and it appealed successfully to Ivison Macadam for advice. Its report, which recommended that the union should give greater emphasis to issues internal to the universities, was endorsed by the council in November. This was a dangerous corner turned in the fortunes of the union. Between 1933 and 1945 there was a steady crescendo of useful activity, coupled with an awakening of social conscience among students which took corporate form in some of the N.U.S. pronouncements. The interplay of concern for the university and concern for society brought its inevitable complications; in 1940 there was a serious split in the union over political alignments. But by the end of the war the N.U.S. was genuinely representative of the activists among British students, not only in universities but in teacher training colleges and colleges of further education. And its views were beginning to command attention from government departments and the press. The student estate enjoyed its first taste of influence.

There were two themes in the crescendo of activity. One was criticism of the university and requests (courteous in those days) for some participation in university government. The other was criticism of society and the beginning of a corporate view among students about social and political issues, and the rights and responsibilities of students to declare their corporate views. Criticism of the university began very *piano*. A University Life Group in Manchester issued a report which criticised the examination system. A delegate from Birkbeck suggested that the N.U.S. should try to exert some control over curricula.[19] Mr Kasz, a delegate from Manchester, proposed that students should be allowed to choose their courses, as in Germany, and the N.U.S. executive resolved that the possibilities of student migration from one university to another should be looked into.[20] There were the perennial complaints of too many lectures and too few tutorials. By 1937 the voice was becoming firmer. A report on student health was published, which was the outcome of three years of inquiry and which did much to stimulate the development of health services in universities. Students at Birmingham put it on record that promotion of academic staff on grounds of research alone was highly undesirable; 'since the primary duty of a University teacher should be to educate his students it is wrong that devotion to this duty should inevitably react unfavourably on his academic career'.[21] And the report of the president of N.U.S. in July 1937 contained the following forthright statement: 'There had been for many years a feeling of disquiet among students and a half articulate suspicion that the methods and conditions of many of our Universities were not conducive to that degree of intellectual discipline which a University training should provide. . . . It must be the task of the N.U.S. to assist and direct the effort of student criticism. . . .'[22] By 1938 the N.U.S. was asking its member organisations to lobby the University Grants Committee to press for an increase in the Treasury grant.[23] The annual congresses, too, were beginning to make corporate declarations; so much so that their reports (which were published and undoubtedly impressed some academics who read them at the time – Bruce Truscot goes out of his way to observe this in his *Redbrick University*) contain a cautionary sentence in a combination of heavy type and italics to preserve the freedom of action of the N.U.S. council, e.g.:

> . . . to avoid misunderstanding, however, it must be reiterated that the resolutions of the Congress are to be taken as, at the most, suggestions or recommendations *to* the N.U.S. and *not* as resolutions *by* or recommendations *from* the N.U.S.[24]

Clearly, participatory democracy did not appeal to the leaders of the N.U.S. in the 1930s! Nevertheless the proceedings of the congresses are important as early examples of articulation from the student estate and many of the recommendations were adopted by the council. In 1937, when the theme was graduate employment, there were among the resolutions some calling for university appointments boards.[25] In 1938 a commission on university curricula and teaching methods in relation to the needs of modern society had some hard things to say about the rigidity of degree courses and the need to include some kind

73

of continuous assessment, vivas and original work in examinations for degrees: comments some of which are as pertinent today as they were a generation ago.[26] And in 1939 another commission was applauding the staff–student lunches organised at Bristol and Liverpool and asking for closer relationships, 'collaboration . . . on the basis of concrete activities'.[27] The culmination of this decade of discussion was the paper for post-war reform which we discuss below.

Accompanying this growing criticism of teaching and curricula there were murmurs about participation in university government. They never became loud or insistent. As early as 1929 a student commission recommended to the N.U.S. council that 'the N.U.S. use its influence with the Committee of Vice-Chancellors to obtain representation of the undergraduate bodies upon University Councils'.[28] In Birmingham, it was reported, unsuccessful attempts had been made to get representation. Nottingham was trying but did not succeed. Only Birkbeck College, an institution devoted to adult students, had been successful: 'as a result of five years' agitation by the students, they had been granted representation on the Governing Committee of the College'.[28] The topic was discussed again in 1932. In Sheffield, it was stated, students could be represented on the governing body when student questions were under discussion; in Bristol close personal relations with the vice-chancellor 'attained the same ends'.[29] Six years later the item was still on the council agenda, though in the meantime there had been some successful examples of staff–student consultative committees, especially in Birmingham where, with the help of the Association of University Teachers, a joint committee of five staff and eight students was working 'most successfully'.[30] It is strange, after the agitations for representation put before royal commissions as long before as 1902, 1911 and 1916, that the N.U.S. did not stake a stronger claim for participation in university government. In its charter of student rights and responsibilities (p. 81 below) it did indeed include a right to a share in the government and administration of the universities. But this claim did not appear in its carefully considered policy for the post-war university. At the end of this phase of our story, when both the Association of University Teachers and the National Union of Students issued 'blueprints' for post-war development of universities, it was the A.U.T. which proposed that:

(a) The student body should be represented on the University Court.
(b) It should have the right of direct access to Council, Senate, and Faculties.

74

(c) The Guild or Union Council should bear a high degree of responsibility for student behaviour.[31]

And the N.U.S., in its 'blueprint', commented on these proposals as follows:

> Whilst agreeing with these points, the N.U.S. feels that they can be achieved most effectively if there are departmental staff–student committees. . . . Although much of value would result if students had direct access to the Faculty Board, they might not be able to participate in its work.[32]

It is noteworthy that the A.U.T. was recommending a cautious degree of student participation (its proposals were preceded by a guarded paragraph) at a time when junior university teachers themselves had all too little access to council, senate, and faculties. It leads us to ask to what extent students, through the N.U.S. or through their several S.R.C.s or guilds, were taking a lead between the wars in criticising universities and pressing for reform. A careful study of the records persuades us to conclude that the corporate student influence was imitative rather than original, hesitant rather than aggressive. Members of the educational establishment – at any rate the liberals among them – were well aware of the need for adaptation in universities. Men as distinguished as Norwood, Eustace Percy and Trevelyan were criticising examinations as roundly as any student. The University Grants Committee was, for that time, unusually frank about the need for reform in curricula. And at N.U.S. congresses it was not the angry student but his seniors who made the most subversive remarks. 'It might be no bad thing for students to approach the University authorities with the motto used by Mansbridge of the W.E.A.: "This is what we workers want to learn – it's for you to teach us how to learn it." ' This was spoken by Sir Bernard Pares in 1938, not by some member of the New Left in 1968.[33] 'The standard of University lecturing and teaching generally is too much dependent on the fortuitous circumstance of a research worker being also gifted with teaching ability.' This was Dr Lincoln Ralphs speaking to the same audience in 1938. And it would be an entertaining exercise to ask a panel of senior professors to identify the author of the following passage:

> Elsewhere [in other medieval universities] the students appointed the teachers, and could give them the sack if they did not give satisfaction. This was, perhaps, going rather too far, though it did show a commendable zeal to be taught the things that were thought to

75

be worth while, and to be taught them in a living and inspiring way. But, short of this drastic method, might it not be possible for students to demand certain kinds of teaching that they thought they needed, or even, if necessary, to provide it for themselves?

For example, you are all going out into a bewildering world, in which your lives will be profoundly influenced by political facts and political theories. . . . Yet no provision is made to help you to think clearly about these subjects, apart from the very few of you who take Political Science as a special subject. . . . Neither Aristotle nor Locke nor Rousseau were ever constrained to think seriously about, for example, such subjects as Nationalism, or Bureaucracy . . . or the working of representative democracy in very large States, or the relationship between civilised and backward peoples. . . . Why should not the student bodies demand and insist that guidance on such themes, and opportunities of discussion, should be offered to them? . . . I am convinced that if the universities are to be the seedplots of ideas . . . and if the students are to be capable of playing the part of leadership . . . they ought to be thinking about such questions, and insisting that, in one way or another, their needs should be satisfied during their university years.

Why didn't they do this? I think one main reason is that they have not been hitherto sufficiently organised as corporate bodies, with leaders of their own.

A speech from some Marxist at a session of a Free University? A harangue during a sit-in, translated into decorous English fit for spinsters? No. It is a version faithfully reconstructed from the *oratio obliqua* of sixty-seven-year-old Ramsay Muir, formerly professor of modern history in Manchester, when he addressed the N.U.S. congress in 1939.[34] He evidently stunned his audience, for the discussion afterwards centred on the causes of submissiveness among students. The agreed causes were economic pressure to concentrate on getting a qualification for a job, and the fact 'that in some universities and colleges, activities of the type indicated by Mr Ramsay Muir were frowned upon by the authorities'. The session ended with the opinion that students should examine the causes of the existing situation with a view to changing it and that the development of activities on the lines laid down by Ramsay Muir 'would do a great deal to effect such a change'. Thirty years later students are acting on Ramsay Muir's advice, though (as we discuss later) sometimes using techniques he would have deplored and sometimes for purposes he would have repudiated.

There is no doubt that those who took office in the N.U.S. between the wars were thinking earnestly and intelligently about reform in the universities. They were not alone in the solutions they proposed, nor were they in the van of those advocating reform, but this does not detract from the importance of their activities. They were supplying the elements of cohesion among student organisations in British universities, and in doing so they laid the foundations for a responsible and effective student estate. Their basic assumption was that the university was a society in which they were junior partners. Therefore their endeavour was to co-operate with the Establishment, not to range themselves against it. Not all students took this view. In 1936 a Miss Button from Sheffield suggested at a council meeting that the N.U.S. should model itself on the lines of a trade union,[35] and there was discussion of a report from her university which spoke of a 'militant defence of student interests'. But the president warned the council against this. In his report in July 1938 he indicated the ambivalence which still, in 1970, confronts the N.U.S. and its constituent organisations. He said, of the recent conferences and reports of the N.U.S.:

On the one hand they emphasised the value of the corporate life of the University and the desirability of closer co-operation with University staff; and on the other they proposed a programme for the N.U.S. which would make it closely approximate to a student trade union and which would inevitably alienate University staff. He thought the N.U.S. should guard against any such tendency.[36]

And so, hitherto, it has. The profit has been that the N.U.S., by 1969, carried considerable weight with governments, civil servants, the University Grants Committee and the Committee of Vice-Chancellors; though Miss Button's successors, the student militants, discount this profit by saying that the N.U.S. has sold out to the Establishment.

Alongside this growth between the wars of a somewhat respectful, hesitant interest in university reform, there appeared the first signs of a corporate student interest in social and political matters; a phenomenon common enough among students in some other countries, but new to Britain. As the upheavals of society piled one on top of another through the 1930s, some students began to feel that they, as a class, had special responsibilities; a burden-of-the-intellectuals, as it were. And if they had responsibilities as a class, they also had rights. The student estate began to be aware of its identity.

One example of corporate social concern occurred in July 1933, when the executive resolved to request the Committee of Vice-Chancellors to receive a deputation from the N.U.S. 'to discuss the granting of the fullest possible educational facilities to refugee students from Germany'.[37] Five years later this corporate social concern had crystallised into the enunciation of a specific principle of access to higher education. In 1938 the executive, exercising its prerogative to receive but not necessarily to adopt resolutions of the congress, made a statement symptomatic of the state of mind of the leaders of N.U.S. The congress had recommended 'that ability should be the sole criterion for University entrance'.[38] The council changed this to: 'that no person with the required ability should be precluded from attendance at a University'.[39] This was an important change, totally at variance with the 'birth control' hypothesis advanced by Herklots in 1928. In the following congress, after a somewhat patronising address from the former vice-chancellor of the University of Birmingham, Sir Charles Grant Robertson, the discussion was driven off course by a student who asserted that 'only one child in two hundred attending an elementary school can expect to benefit by university education. The possibility of achieving a secondary education is also limited by financial obstacles. There is a warped sense of values due to the structure of society and there will be no change in one without some change in the other.'[40]

For Robertson this must have been a stinging rebuke, for as long ago as 1930 he was an advocate of the 'more means worse' hypothesis of student numbers. He had, in a little book on universities, warned against the dangers of a 'highly competent mediocrity'.[41]

Was this the first Marxist shot from students across the bows of British universities? The 1939 congress must have been an encouraging meeting for reformers, for it included not only this interjection, and Ramsay Muir's incitement, but a splendid address from Reinhold Schairer, a refugee from Hitler, who said: 'The isolation of the universities as institutions for social advancement must go, and there must be a return to the ideal of Condorcet who saw in them the living centre of the whole learning of the nation.'[42] Here was a plea for the comprehensive university! After this the disquiet about society, and the universities' detachment from society grew more articulate. The elitism of writers in the 1930s like Julien Benda (*La trahison des clercs*) and Abraham Flexner (*Universities: American, English, German*) became abrasive to the conscience of the young. Expressions such as 'breaking down the barriers between students and youth generally', 'discovering how students can play their part in society', became common in the records of N.U.S. meetings. This emergence of a corporate social conscience was a natural consequence of the compelling events of the time. It was becoming quite widespread among leaders in the student movement and its protagonist was a man who became president of the N.U.S. His name is Brian Simon.

Simon is the son of a wealthy Manchester industrialist. Both his parents were liberal socialists of the mint of Tawney and the Webbs. He enjoyed all the advantages of an expensive education, and this made him, as it makes some young men with a similar background today, all the more angry with the social conditions of England which tolerated, and tried to forget, the fact that privilege was still very unevenly distributed. He became president of the N.U.S. in 1939–40 and dramatically raised the temperature of its deliberations. He also steered the council, as we describe below, into the rough seas of politics. His most effective contribution to the student movement was to offer to write a book, ostensibly to be based on 'material collected by N.U.S. from questionnaires and conferences of the last few years',[43] but which was in fact, the testament of a student with fire in his belly. He made the offer in 1938 but the dislocations of war prevented its appearance before 1943. In his foreword Simon makes it clear that his opinions are his own and not those of the N.U.S. Nevertheless they are important, to illustrate that the present current of protest among British students has its sources among men old enough to be the fathers of the present generation of protesters.

A student's view of the universities is an indictment of British society in the 1930s, and of the universities for being accessories in the corruption of contemporary society. Its theme is frankly Marxist and it employs the supercharged vocabulary of Marxist propaganda. It is 'hypocrisy' to speak of equality of opportunity in education. The educational system 'is essentially a class system'. Universities are adapted 'to the requirements of a small minority which wielded power in the present social order'. In accordance with the 'morality of capitalist society' success in reaching the university can be bought without reference to ability. The dominant social influences brought to bear upon students are a safe job and secure social status; the degree is a 'stepping stone to social preferment'. It is easy to see the temptation for a young don at Oxford or Cambridge to lose interest in the world about him, 'but modern universities have followed in his footsteps'. Simon, evidently inspired by Bernal (whose seminal book, *The social*

79

function of science, appeared in 1939), particularly attacks the view that the pursuit of knowledge should be divorced from the need for social action. From these premises it is natural to proceed to a condemnation of curricula, teaching and examinations. The curricula suffer from the lack of any purpose around which they can be planned. The teaching is dull and factual and impersonal. Examinations 'tyrannize' over the whole educational process. He quotes Mansell Jones in concluding that the formula for university education tends to become: 'Give instruction – test receptivity – classify results.'

Stripped of their Marxist overtones and assumptions, many of Simon's criticisms were correct. The response of the students to the condition in the civic universities was, as he said, either acceptance or revolt. And revolt carried students – and, if adopted corporately, would carry the student movement – into politics. Simon saw hopeful signs of this in the N.U.S.; there was an increase in political and social activity among the *Lumpenproletariat* of students. The academic neutrality of the previous decade was being increasingly rejected. 'The students' criticisms of the universities centre round the fact that the universities have a function in society and a duty to the people which, owing to the restrictions on entrance and the nature of the teaching, they do not fulfil.' It is of little value to reform the educational system if the need to reform society is realised only in an academic way: 'Direct work among the progressive forces in society has been, and should be, a fundamental principle for all members of the universities.'

The controversy still goes on in 1970: do universities better serve society by disinterested observation, experiment and criticism? Or do they serve it better by involvement and commitment? Simon's voice was smothered by the noises of war, and his following did not reach the critical mass which might have politicised the student movement. But he asked painful questions; not all of them have yet been answered.

This awakening of social conscience drew some students, and eventually the N.U.S. council, into politics. The early involvements were unexceptionable: a national student peace demonstration organised for armistice day in 1936; co-operation with the British Youth Peace Assembly in 1938; the presentation of an education bill to the National Parliament of Youth in 1939;[44] and a protest document about the government's call-up policy, called *Defend the universities*, in 1940.[45] But by 1940 there was trouble.

The trouble became visible to the public at the British Student Congress, which was held in Leeds in the spring of 1940. The whole mood of this congress was unlike the mood of any of its predecessors.

80

It was organised by the N.U.S. but six other student bodies, including political ones, were associated with it. There is, in the report of the congress, the usual caveat that its resolutions 'do not in any way commit the organisations associated with it'. Nevertheless the views of the 600 delegates cannot be regarded as totally unrepresentative of student opinion in the country. And, to judge from the recorded voting, these views were widely held.

The report of the congress, written by Brian Simon, pulls no political punches.[46] 'No real democratic system exists in this country.' The commission on problems of empire condemned imperialism, responsible for wars of 'conquest, aggression, and military occupation'. The resolutions carried 'are in themselves a manifesto against privilege'. The congress was opened by an address from H. G. Wells, whose socialism was evidently regarded by some delegates as disappointingly flabby. There was nothing flabby about the resolutions of the congress. By 378 votes to 19 it declared that 'the British Governmental system is dominated by those of wealth and position'; by 416 votes to 9, that 'the system of private production for profit is failing to utilise the potentialities of production for the needs of the people'; by similarly large majorities the congress called for improvements in school education and health services; it condemned, by 364 votes to 23, 'the present subjection of the colonial peoples by European commercial and financial interests, their consequent political and social oppression, and the destruction of their national life by the imposition of alien cultural and moral standards'. There was a somewhat ambiguous resolution in favour of ending the war forthwith (the Soviet Union had not yet been invaded by Hitler); but this was not endorsed afterwards by the N.U.S. council; the rule still held that the congress could not mandate the council. When the congress turned to universities it had similar strictures to apply. Brian Simon asserted that universities 'conceive their function to be the production of a limited number of trained individuals to fill the specialised functions of a complex industrial society' – precisely the charge still levelled by the New Left. A large number of resolutions on university reform were passed: student representation on all governing bodies, courses relevant to the needs of society, changes in teaching methods and examinations, expansion of universities 'to include a far higher proportion of students of working-class origin', an 'identity of interest between students and the people' (student unions, it was agreed, 'should be opened to townspeople at regular intervals . . .') and the congress adopted a *Charter of student rights and responsibilities* in the name of the 600 students gathered at

81

Leeds, which we reproduce in an appendix (p. 166), a sonorous document with unexceptionable rights but only two somewhat vague responsibilities, one of which was to defend the rights.

It was a stirring occasion and it undoubtedly created more solidarity and enthusiasm among the delegates than any previous congress had done. It was asserted, in a report in *The Times Educational Supplement*, that a chance analysis showed that 60 per cent of the students present did not belong to any student political organisation.[47] However, at an extraordinary meeting of the N.U.S. council in Birmingham on 12 May 1940 it was alleged – not without foundation – that the union was drifting into politics; that it was being labelled as left-wing and supporters of previous years were withdrawing their support; that it seemed to be more interested in opposing the government than in defending the universities.[48]

Some of the more conservative members of the N.U.S. were distressed by this turn of events. The trustees demurred. A further meeting of council was held in Sheffield on 6–7 July 1940, which resolved that it no longer had confidence in various of its officers (including its honorary treasurers, de Paula and Ivison Macadam) or in members of the executive 'who consented to the course of action adopted by the Trustees; and demanded their immediate resignation'.[49] The legitimacy of this meeting was challenged, and at the next meeting, held in the following November, a motion declaring it unconstitutional was lost by a hair's breadth of 29 to 30 votes.[50]

Injury to student organisations, like injury to the young, heals quickly, for there is a continual replacement and renewal of personalities. Macadam was elected a trustee. The incoming president declared that 'the NUS was not working for students against the whole of the community, but with students for all students and the community'.[51] But the momentum of the student movement was not lost. In the following year (1941) nearly twice as many students attended the congress, to discuss 'the student, his subject, and society'.[52] Concern with society was still the dominating theme, but the Marxist dialect had gone; it was replaced by the more conciliatory language familiar to those who frequent conventions. The N.U.S. council had protected itself against any repetition of the political fervour of the 1940 congress by deciding, in February 1941, that 'no political resolutions be permitted except such as contain specific and clearly defined references to student problems'. By 905 votes to 18 the congress condemned attacks on student liberties and deplored the action of those students who had 'attempted to prevent free political discussion by organised violence and hooliganism'; this was in response to a regulation made in May 1940 by the home secretary to curb undesirable propaganda. Most of the resolutions concerned educational matters and they were (as *The Times Educational Supplement* wrote in an editorial) 'framed in no spirit of self-interest but in the light of the wider interests of the community. . .'.

There was one important aspect of student rights in which the N.U.S. played a praiseworthy part, namely the protection of free speech and free assembly. It was shortly after the 1914–18 war that the vice-chancellor of Oxford is said to have prohibited the Labour Club, giving as his reason 'that he wished the junior members of the university to concentrate on the purpose for which they came to Oxford, namely the study of abstract principles'.[53] There are still dons at Oxford and Cambridge who would like to use this argument against student activists, but are dissuaded from doing so by the new techniques of dissent. In the thirties these techniques had not been discovered, and there were infringements of liberty which would nowadays precipitate a major crisis.

The most remarkable of these occurred in the London School of Economics in 1934. The Germans describe a professor as a man who thinks otherwise, and the professoriate at L.S.E. certainly fitted this description. Kingsley Martin recollects how in his time at the school 'war raged between the Socialists and the advocates of *laissez-faire*'.[54] The students, too, were said to be divided into a Proletariat and an Athletariat; and of course it is not surprising that in an institution where Laski taught, Marxism flourished. In the lent term 1934 the authorities organised a course of lectures on Marxism. The Marxist Society responded by arranging a parallel series of lectures and applied for permission to give them in a room in the school. Permission was granted but attached to it were the following conditions: they must be called meetings, not lectures; they must be confined to students of the school, and must not be reported or advertised outside the school, nor even posted on the ground-floor notice board; if held at 4 p.m. they must be over by 5 p.m.; and the room to be put at their disposal and the days for holding the 'meetings' must be determined with a member of the administration, a certain Mr Crotch. The L.S.E. students' union took umbrage at these restrictions, and asked to have them lifted. At the same meeting the union executive proposed a new code of practice for dealing with such problems, and this code was accepted by the union, and presented to the director of the school, William Beveridge.[55]

Beveridge was not the sort of man to accept codes from students.

He had even put Laski on the carpet for writing left-wing articles for the *Daily Herald*. He informed the union that any change in its constitution required his agreement and that a new code was being prepared by Mr Crotch.

On 27 February 1934 copies of the *Student Vanguard* were on sale in the school. A copy was brought to the director, who read in it what he considered to be a libellous statement about a member of the school's staff. The school's porters were instructed to prevent further sales of the paper on the premises. The president of the union, an American named Meyer, protested to the director that this censorship was a complete break with the tradition of the school. And over the Marxist Society meetings Meyer wrote: 'The fact that you have instituted a Code for meetings and are enforcing it before discussing the matter with the Union . . . seems to show an intention on your part to disregard the Union. . . . Against such an attitude I must strongly protest, and ask you to reconsider the action you have taken. . . .'

Beveridge was already somewhat rattled by Meyer. In some correspondence with him about a month earlier Beveridge had written: 'When you have come off your high horse and are better able to see the difference between your position in the School and mine, I shall be delighted to consider any further proposals affecting the welfare of the Union. . . .' Meyer was still riding his high horse and doubtless did not expect his protest to flatten the director. In any case he made matters far worse: on 28 February the *Student Vanguard* was again on sale in the school. The director sent for five of the vendors, including Meyer, and suspended them. That same evening the students' union called for their reinstatement. Meyer and his colleagues, 'after mature consideration', capitulated with an apology. On 6 March an emergency committee of the court of governors of the school met, summoned Meyer, who was permitted to say 'half of what he considered necessary' and was expelled. The chairman of the Marxist Society, Simons, was also expelled. Other offenders received milder sentences. The union passed another resolution expressing grave concern, appointed a deputation to interview the director, arranged to prepare a petition and to inform the N.U.S.

There were further resolutions and deputations. The emergency committee of the court of governors met again and confirmed the expulsions, but relented to the extent of leaving discretion with the director to decide whether Simons might apply for readmission. Whereupon the union resolved on an appeal to the full court of governors, and set up a committee to prepare a report for the Old

Students' Association and others. All this polarised opinion among the students. The committee decided to appoint representatives to the National Reinstatement Committee formed by universities' societies and other bodies outside the school, but their decision was later over-ruled. The union resolved that it wished 'to assure the Director in asking for clemency for Messrs Meyer and Simons, it in no way con-dones their action leading to their expulsion' and it again 'tried the personal touch' by sending the new president, who had replaced Meyer, to plead with him. This attitude was criticised by a writer in the June number of *The Clare Market Review*:

> It is a fundamental criticism of the Union that it did not prepare for action as soon as the Authorities took the step of suspending Meyer and the four other students. They should immediately have pressed for a full meeting of the Court of Governors, backing this demand with demonstrations and if necessary the other sanctions which remain to the students who are indispensable to the working of an institution.[56]

The affair ended with a whimper. The authorities, wrote one com-mentator, allowed the union to negotiate for as long as they pleased until every conceivable instrument of negotiation was exhausted – but the negotiations achieved nothing. Meyer did not return. The director's code, with a few modifications, remained. There had been a 'very serious break' in the liberal tradition of the school. There was not sufficient cohesion among students to make this incident into a major crisis. Thirty-five years later a very similar incident precipitated a con-frontation which is not yet over. The N.U.S., although it noted the incident at its executive meeting in 1934, was not able to intervene.[57]

There were other, more trivial incidents. In 1933–4 a poster against the officers' training corps – the English equivalent of American protest against the R.O.T.C. – was banned at Reading, and an anti-war demonstration was banned at Aberystwyth. It was reported also that there had been a refusal to recognise an anti-war committee at University College, London, and the October Club had been sup-pressed in Oxford. In 1936 the Oxford proctors were reported to have banned a procession of the Oxford Peace Council and in 1939–40 the authorities at Bangor restricted 'the sale of publications within the College precincts which enlighten students on present day affairs'.[58] It is impossible at this distance of time to assess the rights and wrongs of these episodes (we may be sure, from our experience of present-day episodes, that the reports received by the N.U.S. were likely to be over-simplified); but to each of them the N.U.S. made dignified and sensible protests.

All this helped the N.U.S. to find its identity. By 1942–3, on its twenty-first birthday, it had recovered its morale and earned widespread confidence. Membership was in the region of 50,000, with representation from all universities, and the union now admitted teacher training and technical colleges to full membership. Attendance at the congresses in 1941, 1942 and 1943 was a thousand or more. Representatives of the N.U.S. had had consultations with members of parliament, government departments, the Association of University Teachers, the National Union of Teachers, and the University Grants Committee; and there had been tentative, and somewhat unfruitful, contacts with the Committee of Vice-Chancellors. This phase of the union's history ends with the publication of the N.U.S. report on the reform of higher education in 1944, which we now consider.

Blueprint for the future

It was – apart from the declaration of student rights and responsibilities – the first considered manifesto from the student estate, a corporate statement agreed after drafts had been circulated to all constituent organisations of the N.U.S. It is a bland, almost apologetic, document, with none of the strident tones of Simon's book published in the previous year. But this deliberate use of the language of persuasion rather than the language of aggression is itself significant: it shows that the N.U.S. was prepared to use the techniques of academic diplomacy to further the interests of the universities of which its members were junior partners. The council had not found itself obliged to choose Simon's dichotomy between acceptance or revolt: it chose the middle way of patient negotiation. The fortunes of this choice is a theme of the next chapter.

If the manner of the N.U.S. report is modest, its matter is solid and sensible, and it adopts, in measured and even tones, most of the points made by Simon in his book. Indeed, though he would doubtless have repudiated the bourgeois style (now called 'Tio Pepe diplomacy'), he deserves credit for the impetus which led to the report.

The report was put into final shape after the Association of University Teachers and the British Association had published their views on post-war development in the universities, and it states in its opening paragraphs that it has taken account of proposals from these two bodies. It is a derivative document and it contains little which would have been regarded as novel at that time and still less which would have been regarded as unorthodox. Its importance for our theme rests on the way it was prepared and indeed on its very conformity with the views of more experienced people.

Toward the end of 1943 the N.U.S. circulated in a draft an *Outline for discussion on 'The reform of university education'*. It was a printed twenty-four-page pamphlet and was distributed to all member universities and colleges for discussion. In addition to general propositions about the functions of universities, the need for expansion, a broader-based schooling and an initial period of general education at the university before specialisation begins, the pamphlet has detailed proposals, which do not appear in the final report, on curricula and teaching in some specific subjects: engineering, medicine, pharmacy, geography, social scienc, eand education. These proposals were the outcome of a modest but interesting activity of the N.U.S. in the preceding years: the running of a number of faculty committees. In its search for points of cohesion around which the corporate life of students could be organised, the N.U.S. realised that the university union, unlike the Oxford college, was not a natural point of cohesion for most students in civic universities. But the subject of specialisation was, especially in those subjects where students gathered for hours every week to do practical work. It is true that these faculty committees 'talked shop' rather than the elevating themes of art, philosophy and religion which students are assumed, with very little evidence, to talk about over dinner in a college hall. But they talked about matters which did unite their common interests, and the views of these faculty committees were enlightened and useful. Even today some of them are very pertinent. Did the Royal Commission on Medical Education (for instance) which reported in 1968 know that the N.U.S. medical committee, a quarter of a century ago, was recommending that 'preclinical training should take place in a university faculty and not a hospital' and that 'in order to co-ordinate the hospital and the preclinical work both should be presided over as far as possible by the same Dean . . .'?

The final report is a somewhat blurred condensation of much of the thinking done by such faculty committees over the preceding years, and its style suffers from the determination of the authors to be tactful. But the discontents – and they were justifiable discontents – with the university are all there. The report insists, very politely, that universities

D   87 must be more closely integrated into society (a contrast to the withdrawal advocated by Herklots in 1928). A consequence of this is that the student should be given at the university an opportunity to understand 'the social and economic framework in which he will live and work'. There is a plea for what seemed to all academics at that time a massive increase in the student population: to be 50 per cent above pre-war level by 1950. This would require a massive system of grants to students: grants 'must be awarded to all who need them and have shown themselves able to benefit from higher education'. There is a suggestion – but the N.U.S. was divided over this – that everyone should do a year of social service before entering the university. There was a strong recommendation for a broadening of courses with some philosophy and sociology taught to all students, and other subjects 'having intellectual and social relevance to the central subject'. Universities should provide courses suitable for generalists, people going into such careers as administration and journalism.

The hardy perennials of dissatisfaction were there: objection to compulsory lectures and the need for more seminars and tutorial systems; halls of residence with staff living in; the use of audio-visual aids ('. . . it should be noted that recent progress . . . makes possible the use of films, radio, television and the gramophone to an increased extent for educational purposes': a sentiment which bore fruit twenty years later when the University Grants Committee issued a report on the use of audio-visual aids in universities); degrees to be awarded not solely on the results of written tests, but with the addition of 'oral exams, tutors' or professors' reports, laboratory and practical work, together with general class records'. 'Furthermore', the report says, 'it should be possible to include in each course some test of a student's initiative such as could be shown in a short thesis or piece of laboratory work.' The report suggests that academic staff should be encouraged 'to spend short periods in industry or in professional life outside the University'. There was a suggestion in the 1943 *Outline for discussion* that there should be special courses to train university teachers to teach, but in the final report the authors (who disarmingly say 'it would be impertinent for students to offer any detailed criticism of the present methods of selecting University staff') maintain a discreet silence on this point, though they do make it clear that students have to endure a good deal of poor teaching.

Over participation in university government the N.U.S. was, as we have already mentioned, more modest in its claims even than the A.U.T. in suggestions on behalf of the union. Voting membership of councils, senates, and faculties was not one of the N.U.S. priorities. But the report does advocate staff–student consultative committees; and Brian Simon, whose views doubtless represent the convictions of more radical students, goes further. 'It is essential', he wrote, 'that the student view should be heard. Therefore staff–student committees should be instituted based on the departments and linked up, first in faculty groups and finally on a complete college basis. They should have administrative powers, not being advisory only as at present. . . .' Another matter on which the report is emphatic is its insistence that students should have full self-government within their unions. It is a melancholy reflection on the obtuseness of some educational authorities that the N.U.S. was still having to press this point in a document on rights and responsibilities published twenty-three years later.

All this, it could be said, was in the air anyway in 1944, and it was not significant that students should join the chorus of post-war planners for higher education. We would disagree that it is not significant. First, although these ideas were in the air, no action was taken on some of them until over twenty years later. Only in 1969, for instance, were some universities announcing with satisfaction (and under pressures which we shall be discussing in a later chapter) that they had set up departmental and faculty staff–student consultative committees. Platitudes do not become stale until they are no longer true. Second, the very concurrence of ideas between the N.U.S. and the A.U.T. was evidence of a promising partnership between senior and junior members of universities. Both sides expressed appreciation of this partnership. Third, Samuel Johnson's notorious remark about women preaching ('it is not done well; but you are surprised to find it done at all') applied, in those days, to English students preparing educational manifestos aimed not just to preserve their own interests but for the public good. That scores of undergraduates in a dozen universities were prepared to spend hours discussing the *Outline*, and that the council should put in hours of work drafting and redrafting the report are, in our view, important signs of corporate responsibility in the student movement. Doubtless there were some dons who believed that student busybodies should not waste their time talking about problems which were the responsibility of their seniors (and, by implication, their betters). There are still a few dons who take this view. 'What right', they ask, 'has an undergraduate of eighteen got to criticise the curriculum, wasting his time and ours on consultative committees when he could more profitably spend it rowing or playing rugby or working?' This attitude denies the concept of the university as a corporation of masters and scholars; indeed it is an attitude inconsistent with many university charters. We shall, in a later chapter, be very critical of the ways in which some students interpret their rights of university membership; but we reject the attitude which excludes them from these rights; and it is certainly the right of a junior member that his voice should be heard over what he learns and how he is taught.

The N.U.S. report on the future of university and higher education was a declaration from the spokesmen for a student estate; it is this, more than its actual content, which was significant. Of course the spokesmen were a mere handful of enthusiasts. Of course the bulk of students continued to have little interest above attending lectures, passing examinations and getting jobs. But only a fool (and there still seem to be some) would dismiss the student estate on this account. In all democratic systems the representatives are more enthusiastic than the bulk of their constituents.

The first steps of the student estate into the post-war world were modest, unpretentious and amicable. The N.U.S. recognised its place as a junior, inexperienced partner, but a willing one, prepared to work. Individual student councils had established excellent working arrangements with individual vice-chancellors, though it was to be another twenty years before the Committee of Vice-Chancellors took cognisance of the N.U.S. But there was a gratifying gesture of response from some of the senior partners. On the initiative of the N.U.S. a joint public conference of the N.U.S. and A.U.T. was held on 13 October 1945 at Bedford College, to discuss the future of university education. Professors Brodetsky and Pascal were appointed to speak for the A.U.T. From this phase of growth over a quarter of a century came the opportunity for a flowering of the student estate. We now proceed to discuss the circumstances of this flowering.

5 The Flowering of the Student Estate

Post-war readjustment

On 8 October 1968, the national newspapers in Britain carried head-lines of the size and shape appropriate to a national event: 'Students' demands met by reforms' (*The Times*), 'Universities accept more student rule' (*Daily Telegraph*), 'Charter outlines students' role' (*Yorkshire Post*), 'Students win right to be considered adult' (*Guardian*), 'A plan to end revolt by the students' (*Daily Mirror*), 'Peace charter for dons and students' (*Mail*). At the end of this chapter we shall describe the important but not very dramatic document which prompted these startling headlines; but first we have to carry the reader from the conference of students and university teachers held in Bedford College on 13 October 1945 to the so-called 'peace charter' announced twenty-three years later. We cannot write history about events which are so close. All we can hope to do is to record some relevant facts and to suggest some tentative interpretations.

The indisputable fact which colours everything which has happened to the student estate since 1945 is the rate of growth of universities and colleges. In 1946–7 there were about 68,000 full-time students at university institutions in Britain. In 1968–9 there were about 200,000. This represents, since 1947, a crude average increase of nearly 10 per cent per annum (crude, because it has not been a steady annual increase over this period: numbers have gone up by fits and starts). This is unprecedented; the crude average rate of increase from the turn of the century up to 1939 was less than 5 per cent per annum. It is rate of change rather than absolute size which puts a strain upon an educational system. The student estate has not escaped this strain; indeed it has been intensified by two circumstances: first, the proliferation of universities (there were twenty-one, including five university colleges, in 1945; today there are forty-four), and second, the inclusion of non-university students in the organised body representing the estate. In 1969 the N.U.S. claimed a membership of over 407,000, of which only about 169,000 were in universities.[1]

It is a commonplace in biology that increase in size of organisms creates problems of adaptation which have to be solved if the organisms are to remain viable. The same is true of institutions. Everyone familiar with the university system is likely to agree that it has grown faster than it has adapted itself to the consequences of its growth. In this chapter we describe how the student estate has been affected by this growth. We remind the reader (and ourselves) that the expression 'student opinion' covers such a diversity of opinions as to be meaningless. The great majority of students, like the great majority of the public, have no opinion on many issues of great importance to them. But students, like the public, have articulate representatives (even if they do not want to be represented) who speak for them as a group. By default, if for no other reason, these articulate representatives become the voice of the student estate. So on one hand we anticipate and accept the criticism that we are recording the views of a handful of students who sit on the councils of the N.U.S. or guilds and committees of universities; on the other hand we defend what we record because this handful of students does create a corpus of opinion which influences university policy – indeed its influence already reaches beyond universities to other sectors of education and to some issues in politics.

There is a great difference between the circumstances of universities in the twenty years between the wars and in the twenty-five years since World War II. From 1920 to 1939 the total numbers at universities rose by less than 10 per cent; recovery from that war did not go on in an atmosphere of harassing expansion. From 1946 to 1969 recovery was complicated by a massive pressure for higher education – numbers at universities rose by 194 per cent – and by the dislocations due to war damage. But despite this great difference there were remarkable similarities in the fortunes of the student estate after the two wars. In 1946, as in 1921, ex-service students encouraged participation by the N.U.S. in international movements. This was followed by disillusion and withdrawal. At home there was emphasis on measures to improve the welfare of students: pressure for higher grants, better residential accommodation and the like. This was followed by a spell of disenchantment with student politics, reminiscent of the loss of confidence in the N.U.S. in the late 1920s. This in turn was followed by a renewed search for identity and purpose, from which student associations, both at national and at local level, have emerged with greater cohesion than they have had before, and with new ideals and ambitions.

The N.U.S. was founded so that British students could take part in the *Confédération internationale des étudiants*, a body which eventually

92

had to be abandoned because of its identification with fascism. After World War II the N.U.S. was one of the few national unions to survive and it took a lead in reassembling the students of Europe. At a conference held in Prague in 1946 the International Union of Students (I.U.S.) was born, and in 1947 the N.U.S. was affiliated to this international body.

A historian of the N.U.S. would have to disentangle the threads of idealism, intrigue and politics which have enmeshed all its relationships with international student movements. But this is not the theme of our book. Suffice it to say that within a year of affiliation with the I.U.S., the council was wasting time in bitter debates due to the increasingly partisan political character of its European fellow-students. In 1949 there was a flicker of hope. 'Standards of living and education throughout the world' (the N.U.S. council resolved) could not be raised without a constructive peace, and accordingly the council affirmed its resolve to strengthen the contact between the students of Britain 'and the youth and students of the world through the I.U.S.'[2] But in February 1950 the N.U.S., along with some other national student unions, broke with the International Union of Students (which was considered to have succumbed to communism), though it retained an associate membership with the I.U.S. to facilitate travel and exchanges with Eastern Europe. Even with this attenuated connection misunderstandings continued and in 1955 the N.U.S. withdrew completely from the I.U.S. Meanwhile another international body had been formed, the International Student Conference (I.S.C.), with a co-ordinating secretariat. This provided a new link for the international interests of the N.U.S., though – as we mention later in our chronicle – this, too, collapsed under the corrosion of international politics.

Over home affairs the N.U.S. was more successful. The 1944 report on *The future of university and higher education* established the union in the eyes of government officials as responsible, reasonable and sincerely interested in post-war reconstruction. The joint conference with the Association of University Teachers was given publicity (so the council minutes record) in forty-eight newspapers. It was agreed that a deputation including delegates from the A.U.T. and the N.U.S. should ask the government to consider the consequences of their policy on call-up and demobilisation, and in November 1946 the incoming president was satisfied that 'responsible relations with government bodies had increased enormously'. The leaders of the union reaffirmed their determination to keep the union's affairs out of politics. The occasion for this reaffirmation was a bus strike in Manchester when some students wished to get involved; the council 'whilst recognising the right of individual students to play a full part in political life . . . dissociates itself in its corporate capacity from any activity of individual students or student Unions which does not concern students as such'.[3]

On matters which did concern students the union's representatives worked hard. In the 1930s employment and health services were two of the prominent domestic preoccupations. In the late 1940s the domestic preoccupations were the provision of adequate grants to all students, the abolition of fees, and a minimum entrance standard. The students' spokesmen, many of them ex-servicemen and married, were finding it difficult to secure places in universities (before any building could be done, the student population exceeded by 28,000 the numbers for which there was, presumably, adequate accommodation in 1939); or, having secured places, they were inadequately financed. So in 1949 a 'Students' Charter' was drawn up, and a campaign was planned to promote it.[4]

The charter appealed (the word 'demand' was not yet a feature of these documents) for an expansion of universities and colleges, so that there should be a place and an adequate grant for everyone with the ability to benefit from it. Arising from the recommendations of a government working party which had recently been published, the authors of the charter asked for maintenance grants to cover fifty-two weeks in the year, allowances for dependants, and more help for various colleges of further education. The council called for 'the widest discussion of this Charter and an immediate debate on Higher Education by Parliament'. These themes – access to higher education and grants to students – occupied the N.U.S. to the practical exclusion of academic matters through the early 1950s. In July 1951 the council resolved to prepare a national campaign to press for more and better grants for students and more government assistance. It was not a propitious time for such appeals; the government had plenty of anxieties about the nation's economy, and spokesmen for the student estate showed a commendable restraint in pressing their views. But it seems that the government treated the students' spokesmen with a clumsy lack of tact, and by 1952 a note of impatience was audible in the N.U.S. council. The secretary reported that there had been a long correspondence with the minister of education (Florence Horsbrugh) 'but the replies had got us nowhere. . . . She had also consistently refused to recognise that the N.U.S. had any right to be consulted about matters which vitally affected the interests of students.' The council passed a long resolution which, among other things, expressed the belief that the union 'had shown a restraint which has been entirely unmatched by any corresponding sympathy or wish to co-operate on the part of the Minister'.[5] And in another resolution the council asked for a royal commission on the selection of students and their financing from public funds. The council was clearly determined to strengthen its negotiating power. The prime prerequisite was to get its facts right, and it set on foot in forty selected colleges a survey of students' income and expenditure. This increased sophistication in preparing its case was an important change in its mode of approach to governments, and it has been a feature of N.U.S. submissions ever since.

Whether or not the minister was as mulish as the council believed her to be is something which must await the verdict of history. But there is no doubt that her replies to the N.U.S. had conveyed an impression of obduracy which had two unfortunate consequences: among some students it sharpened a desire for a more militant approach, and among other students it aggravated a feeling of apathy about the N.U.S. and its activities. Attendance at the annual congresses fell off, and was not restored by the experiment in 1952, at Leeds, of combining the meetings with an arts festival. Membership of the union, which had expanded after 1945 by the incorporation of technical colleges, teacher training colleges and colleges for art and music, began to be eroded by disaffiliations. Disaffiliations for 1953–4 totalled twenty; King's College, London and Manchester University had withdrawn; there were estimated to be 25,000 students who stood outside the N.U.S. Yet the students' representatives were not willing to advocate a more aggressive policy. When in 1953 the council was pressed to plan a national campaign in view of the 'negative response of the Minister of Education to reasonable requests advanced by the Union', it was objected 'that the N.U.S. should show itself a responsible organisation' and the motion to have a campaign was defeated.[6]

This malaise, reminiscent of a similar malaise some twenty years earlier, led to a bout of self-examination within the N.U.S. Inquiries unearthed a diversity of criticisms. Delegates from some universities thought the union was being swamped by colleges of further education. Some delegates complained that meetings were packed by left-wing elements. This latter charge was denied as 'sweeping and unsubstantiated'[7] but a president in 1960 recalled that 'it was generally accepted in 1948, 1949 and 1950 that N.U.S. was not a Communist organisation but an organisation that was riddled with political factions, intrigue and conspiracies'.[8] Other delegates declared that their constituents were simply bored by the issues on which the council spent its time – international affairs, grants, and fees. It was clear that the rank and file of students would not continue to support the N.U.S. unless it changed its interests. But did the representatives know what sort of change their constituents wanted? At the council meeting in April 1954 there was set up a commission which gave a clear and interesting answer. 'It was unanimously felt', the commission reported, that more attention should be paid to academic matters. Unions in individual universities and colleges should gather information about syllabuses and curricula; the N.U.S., armed with this information, should develop its contacts with the Association of University Teachers. There was an interest, too, in the amenities and facilities of universities: unions, refectories, and libraries. This recalls a similar solution to a similar crisis twenty years earlier; the student estate again directed its spokesmen to give more attention to education, and less to 'trade union' affairs.[9]

Meanwhile a very welcome change had occurred in the ministry of education: David Eccles had succeeded Florence Horsbrugh. There was an immediate change of attitude from above and a spontaneous and generous response from below. A memorandum sent to the minister asking for representative status on all matters affecting students' welfare was 'courteously acknowledged by the Minister who, it was hoped, might prove more co-operative than his predecessor'.[9] David Eccles proved to be very co-operative; indeed he is said to have tried to have the means test on grants abolished so that students could feel independent of their parents. In the following year a senior representative of the ministry attended the council and assured the delegates that their resolutions and recommendations had been studied at the ministry 'with very great care and interest'.[10] And in April 1956 the parliamentary secretary himself, Dennis Vosper, gave an encouraging address to the council at Leeds.[11]

By the mid 1950s the N.U.S. had begun to recover its prestige. It did not have a large following among students, at any rate not an active or coherent one. It had not yet secured consultative status with the ministry of education or the U.G.C. or the Committee of Vice-Chancellors, but, among informed members of the public, it had earned respect for its restraint – a restraint which lost it support among some of its own members – through a season of bleak economic weather. It had developed useful contacts with the press and the B.B.C. And now, at the end of the decade 1945–55, it had the encouragement of a cordial minister of education and – most significant for its future – it had turned its attention again to issues of education.

The student estate, through its representatives, had not yet achieved 'consultative status' with those bodies which planned and financed higher education, but the door was ajar. In fact it was opened from the inside by academic mandarins, not pushed open by students. In 1955 a conference of European university rectors and vice-chancellors, meeting at Cambridge, passed the following ponderous resolution:

XVIII. The Conference,
considering that it is part of the educational function of the university to develop in its students a sense of responsibility,
recommends that students should be consulted, and accorded some measure of initiative in all questions relating to their welfare and their social life within the university;
expresses the hope that the academic authorities, whose right it is to make decisions about the curriculum and the conditions for the award of degrees and diplomas, will seek ways of making it possible for students to make known their point of view on these matters as well.[12]

The N.U.S. council was greatly encouraged by this resolution when it met at Birmingham in April 1957. It was further encouraged at this meeting by the address of welcome from the vice-principal of Birmingham University, who told the delegates that they belonged to a generation of students which was established as a third estate in the university, with the administration and dons as first and second estates (a classification of administrators which we ourselves would dispute), and that the third estate 'had great value to contribute to the growth of higher education'.[13] In the years that followed, the N.U.S. leaders worked hard and with an admirable spirit of responsibility to make this contribution. Their work was rewarded by an impressive growth of corporate opinion within the student estate and by an increasing degree of participation in discussions which have influenced the course of higher education. What began in 1955 as a sudden thaw in the ministry of education under the congenial influence of David Eccles culminated in partnership with the Committee of Vice-Chancellors in the joint statement in 1968. We shall select certain episodes in this progress toward partnership, to illustrate two themes: one, the growing interest in educational issues and the nature of this interest; and two, the emergence of demands for participation and the reasons for these

97

demands. At the end of this chapter we shall combine these two themes, to illustrate what influence the student estate has had on universities and what problems for the future arise out of the requests, which grew into claims and finally have become demands, for students to be incorporated into the government of universities.

There had not been a comprehensive statement of corporate student opinion since the report issued in 1944. In 1958 a *Policy statement* was approved, which brought together the familiar claims for improved amenities – abolition of the parental contribution in assessing maintenance grants, provision of residence halls and health centres, consultation over student awards. It reaffirmed the principle that much of the value of university and college life is the self-education of students outside the lecture room, through unions, societies and clubs; and that this principle should guide the future planning of higher education. There was still a great diffidence about student participation in academic affairs; the *Statement* goes no further than to repeat the resolution of the European rectors and vice-chancellors which we quote above. There was, however, one straw of dissatisfaction in the wind. The first article in the *Statement*, unanimously adopted by the council, was to urge the government again to set up a royal commission on higher education.[14] This idea was in the air at the time: Lord Simon of Wythenshaw had advocated it in the *Universities Quarterly* and it was thoroughly (and very competently) canvassed in a Fabian Society pamphlet a year later.[15] But the 'mandarinate' of higher education – vice-chancellors, the University Grants Committee – were not at that time contemplating, or even favouring, any such comprehensive inquiry into the course on which universities were set. Several voices were raised against the idea; sleeping dogs are better left asleep.

The N.U.S., encouraged by 'the first Minister to take the Union seriously', rose to the trust David Eccles put in it. It prepared evidence for the Albemarle Committee on youth services and the Anderson Committee on student grants. In November 1959 came recognition from an even more important quarter. The N.U.S. president was able to announce that the chairman of the University Grants Committee, Keith Murray, had agreed to address a conference of delegates from student unions on the preparations which his committee was making for the coming quinquennium (1962–7) and the ways in which student opinion could be conveyed to the committee. The union accordingly arranged a two-day conference in January 1960 which was attended by nearly 100 delegates. Keith Murray explained how his committee was glad to receive memoranda from representatives of students at each institution which it visited, and always met these representatives in the course of each visitation. He made it clear (and one of us, who served on the U.G.C. for eight years, can confirm this) that the student point of view was very much valued by the committee and undoubtedly influenced its opinions and some of its decisions.[16]

This response from the U.G.C. was a great and well-deserved encouragement to the N.U.S. and to its constituent unions. It resulted in a memorandum to the U.G.C. from the N.U.S. itself and it undoubtedly improved the quality of the submissions which came to the U.G.C. from individual universities and colleges. The representatives of the student estate could now feel assured that they would be consulted by the U.G.C., both collectively through the N.U.S. and separately in each institution visited by the committee, and also by the minister of education or his representatives. Only the Committee of Vice-Chancellors and Principals remained to be persuaded to recognise the N.U.S. (The union's minutes record an abortive attempt to meet representatives of the vice-chancellors over discussions on a 'clearing house' to solve problems of entrance to universities: the discussions which led to the establishment of the Universities Central Council for Admissions. The union's request was not granted).[17]

The two documents which most clearly express corporate student opinion at this time are the memoranda from the N.U.S. to the Hale Committee and to the Robbins Committee. The Hale Committee[18] was concerned with university teaching methods; the Robbins Committee[19] with the whole system of higher education. On both these topics the N.U.S. made statesmanlike observations. The memorandum to the Robbins Committee was particularly successful. It was a major preoccupation of the union's education and welfare department for six months; two conferences were held to discuss drafts and outlines; regional meetings were arranged so that the views of constituent unions could be incorporated into the memorandum. The memorandum received the honour of a full review in *The Times*. One interesting feature of this memorandum is the close resemblance between some of the forty recommendations made by the N.U.S. and some of the recommendations which the Robbins Committee ultimately made. We do not suggest that this is a case of simple causation, nor even that the evidence from the N.U.S. was more perceptive than that from other sources; but we are convinced that the students' proposals were arrived at through discussion and argument among themselves, and certainly are not merely reflections of the views of their elders. Those who think the Robbins report marked an advance in

99

educational thought must give the N.U.S. the credit for having had similar thoughts.

The publication of the Robbins report in 1963 is a convenient point to pause in our chronicle and to consider what proposals were being put forward by spokesmen for the student estate. Our data come from three sources: the N.U.S., the Scottish Union of Students, and submissions made to the U.G.C. by student representatives at individual universities and colleges. A study of these documents leaves two general impressions: in manner of presentation the best of them show a sophistication and care at least equal to that of similar memoranda from university teachers; in content the best of them show a mature sense of perspective and responsibility which is indistinguishable from the content of documents prepared by senior academics. They represent, of course, the views of very small groups of students speaking in the name of a large student population some of whom are indifferent to many of the issues, or inarticulate about them; but they nevertheless ought to be accepted as the voice of the student estate.

What is their content? Of course the submissions from individual student unions to the U.G.C. include requests for theatres, swimming baths, sports pavilions and psychiatrists on the campus. But these are clearly regarded as subsidiary matters, stuck into the end of the submission. Almost without exception pride of place goes to academic affairs. The opening paragraph of one submission runs: 'We feel deeply that we should remain a homogeneous and balanced university', and goes on to hope that, at a time of expansion, the university will not lose sight of its original aim, to provide a liberal education. Another submission deplores the retreat from the broad-based Scottish M.A. degree. Another asserts that the university must remain 'a community in which all members may pursue their chosen studies . . . in an atmosphere of learning'. The N.U.S. opened its submission to the U.G.C. in 1960 by firmly supporting expansion, and then adding these words: '. . . we are concerned lest, in the process of such expansion, there is a loss of quality in education. . . . There is a growing feeling that the nature of university education in this country is undergoing a radical and undesirable change. The universities are ceasing to regard their main function as "the cultivation of excellence". . . .'[20]

These are all unexceptionable sentiments of the sort emitted by vice-chancellors at degree ceremonies. But the students' memoranda then get down to detailed criticism. Lectures, they say, can be admirable as a means of conveying enthusiasm, but in some faculties there are too many of them and some merely transmit information which can be found in the library. They put up no arguments for easier courses or predigested information. Let the professor talk, they say, about what interests him, and let the student get the routine stuff out of books. Unanimously they ask for tutorials so that the learning process can involve active dialogue and not the passive taking of notes. The N.U.S. in its evidence to the Hale Committee, based on information collected from its constituent unions, shrewdly suggests that 'the existence of a tutorial system often depends more on the enthusiasm of members of staff than on the staff/student ratio'. One submission after another asks that university teachers should have some opportunity to acquire some training in teaching; the student representatives of one university propose that lecturers should be able to get leave of absence for this purpose. There are requests for week-end residential conferences between staff and students, a 'reading term' in the summer, and so on; and we have counted no fewer than fifteen student memoranda composed between 1960 and 1963 which suggest that appointments and promotions should depend on teaching ability as well as achievement in research. These are not the irresponsible impulses of busybodies; they are views worthy of respect from any don.

Beside these technical points about teaching, the chief dissatisfaction at this point of time (1960–3) was over what is ambiguously described as staff–student relations. The N.U.S. opens its evidence to the Hale Committee by saying: '. . . we believe that some form of real personal association with some member or members of academic staff is essential. . . .' The prime pedagogical problem in a university is how to bridge the gap between two generations. The evidence from students ten years ago, long before the present phase of turbulence, shows how commonly we failed to succeed. The student delegates to the U.G.C. from one university put in a dry comment about the futility of 'artificially contrived situations' such as sherry parties. Staff willing to entertain in their own homes, said another delegation, should be given an entertainment allowance. 'We desire', ran the students' submission to the U.G.C. from Sheffield in 1961, 'more intimate contact between staff and students, thus creating the relationship so essential to the student but which is denied him at present both academically and by virtue of the accommodation problem.' Birmingham students asked that staff should live in close proximity to students in the new halls of residence being built there; Newcastle students asked the same. The clearest expression of this view came from the students' union at Nottingham University in their memorandum to the U.G.C. It was written in 1965, two years after the publication of the Robbins report, but this makes it all the more significant for our theme. It runs: 'The idea of staff–student relations is not that staff and students should meet from time to time socially, or in other non-academic ways, and try as best they can to get on with each other. The idea in its true sense is fundamental to the concept of the University, it is common life. The stimulus to lead that life . . . must be academic. The root of this stimulus lies with the individual student and the individual tutor.'[21]

The University Grants Committee is a body not easily gulled by words. During its visitations it cross-examined the student delegates and was quickly able to test the sincerity of the assertions made in their memoranda. Occasionally – but only occasionally – the committee was disappointed. The cumulative impression created by these representatives of the student estate in dozens of universities and colleges was one of responsibility, earnestness and commitment to the idea of the university as a community. There is no doubt whatever that the U.G.C.'s advice to universities has been greatly influenced by the quality and consistency of these expressions of corporate opinion from the student estate.

We have gone to some length in giving these examples because we need to refer to them later when we discuss the present ambivalent attitude of students toward teachers: an end to paternalism, rejection of the odious Latin phrase *in loco parentis*, coexisting with this strong desire to unite with their seniors in one community, and to receive help and advice from an older generation.

At the national level the pronouncements made on behalf of the student estate were equally responsible and earnest. First among the forty recommendations made by the N.U.S. to the Robbins Committee was the policy statement the union has adopted consistently since 1938: 'All people qualified and able to benefit from a course of higher education should be able to do so.' Halls of residence were considered essential, not just to provide shelter but to prevent the student remaining enclosed 'in his own cocoon of specialisation'. Also, to combat specialisation, the N.U.S. proposed a two-year general course leading to a national diploma after which some students would enter advanced specialist courses – a notion which has recently been revived in a different form by Professor A. B. Pippard.[22] Other recommendations from the N.U.S. have become official policy: degrees in education available at colleges of education for instance, and more sandwich courses in industry. Throughout the document there is a sense of concern for society. Unless we meet the challenge to expand and change the pattern of higher education, 'the next generation of children will be educationally disinherited before they even see the light of day'.[23]

Participation

On educational issues the elected representatives of the student estate knew where they stood and they set out their standpoint clearly. Their policies were reasonable and moderate – far more so than the policy recommended in the report of the Labour Party's Study Group on higher education published about the same time,[24] which used as part of its raw material the N.U.S. memorandum to the Robbins Committee. In retrospect the most remarkable feature of the documents we have been discussing, both those from the N.U.S. and from individual universities and colleges, is what they omitted. Almost all of them, including the memoranda prepared by the N.U.S. for three major government committees, make no mention of student representation in academic government. The union had, for many years, pressed for students to control their unions, and to be represented on catering committees and in the management of halls of residence. In 1957 the union belatedly endorsed the view of the European rectors and vice-chancellors that students should be consulted over academic affairs; and in 1958 it was suggested, during the council's discussion of its policy statement, that 'students represented the consumer interest' and should therefore be able to make their views known on the curriculum.[25] The topic turned up again from time to time at council meetings. In November 1960 there was a plea for student representation on all planning bodies in institutions of higher education,[26] and in April 1961 the council urged that 'all universities should allow student representation on their non-academic committees and in particular, planning committees'.[27] This was at a moment of great opportunity for the reform of higher education. Planning committees for universities in York and East Anglia had been set up in 1960 and committees for universities in Essex, Kent and Warwick were about to be set up. The council was especially concerned that the student view was being so little consulted in the planning of these new universities. Yet pressure for participation was still weak. Student representation on academic boards and committees was no part of the N.U.S. submission to the Robbins Committee in June 1961, and in November 1961 there was a discussion at the council meeting which revealed the mood of the spokesmen for student opinion. It was resolved: 'Council believes that

103

student opinion should be effectively considered by the committees in Institutions of Higher Education which determine academic policy.' The word 'considered' was deliberate. Mr MacArthur, a delegate from Leeds, said 'they had had enough experience of consultative committees in which student opinion was rarely significant'. So the motion was expressly framed to exclude the word 'consult'. 'The idea behind the motion' (we quote from the minutes) 'was not that students should be present when salaries and staff appointments were discussed but that students should have some say in the content and structure of courses and the amount of lecture time.' They were not asking for 'representation' but 'consideration'.

This was the state of opinion among student leaders at the end of 1961. For people concerned with higher education the year 1962 was a year of 'waiting for Robbins'. The N.U.S. held its usual council meetings in April and November; the issue of participation was not raised. But at the council meeting in April 1963 there was another significant discussion which revealed the mood of opinion. D. Piper, from Birkbeck College (which specialises in the education of mature students), moved:

> Council calls upon the Executive to promote the principle that students should be represented on the effective governing body of institutions of higher education. Council further requests that such student representatives should be present when staff appointments and salaries are being determined.[28]

He at once agreed to delete the second sentence in response to amendments from Goldsmith's College and Manchester University; he then proceeded to defend the remaining motion by claiming that it was 'not as radical as it might appear' and that it was silly to put people of equal intelligence (the staff and the students) into a semi-hierarchy. But he did not get enthusiastic support from some of his fellow-delegates, and a representative from King's College, London, opposed the motion as an unjustifiable demand. Students, he said, were privileged persons; many of them had a free hand in running college societies; many colleges had staff–student committees which admirably served their purpose. The proposal, in his view, was tantamount to accepting a job and then demanding the same status as the employer. 'A ludicrous proposal', he called it. In the end Piper's motion was diluted into the following form and passed with seven votes against it and five abstentions: 'Council calls upon the Executive to promote the principle that students should be represented on the effective governing body of institutions of higher education by a member of the students' union.' This decision registers a slight build-up of pressure since November 1961, when it was only 'consideration' which was asked for, not 'representation'. But the mood in favour of participation was still one of pious hope rather than insistent demand. Following the council's resolution the N.U.S. distributed a questionnaire to its member organisations and received from 140 universities and colleges evidence of 'a strong belief in responsible student representation at all levels'. This was reported to the council at its meeting in November 1963. At this same meeting the council debated the Robbins report (which had been published in October 1963), and noted some of its shortcomings. But in composing its list of shortcomings the council said nothing about the omission in the report of any reference to student representation. Even more indicative of the mood on representation is the tenor of the commentary on the Robbins report issued on behalf of the N.U.S. by its executive in April 1964. Although the report had recommended many measures which coincided with those advocated by the N.U.S. in its evidence, nevertheless some discords of criticism were considered necessary. Thus, the report scarcely considered what higher education was *for*; it had too little to say about 'relevance' of courses (a word which was to have a kaleidoscope of meanings between 1964 and 1970). But on student participation? Nothing except a reassertion, tucked away in the summary, that students had a vital role in the development of higher education and should be included as equal partners in planning, especially of student housing.[29]

But during 1964 the mood began to change. The first sign of the change was in a policy statement presented to the N.U.S. council in November 1964.[30] This statement was designed to set the course for the student movement before marching into a 'post-Robbins world' of higher education. It was the culmination of ten years of debate by spokesmen for the student estate, for it was in 1954 that the union set up a commission to rescue itself from its post-war malaise. 'Policy', wrote the N.U.S. president in his foreword, 'which was once visionary and revolutionary is now current practice or legal requirement. This statement is again visionary and revolutionary.' In fact it is not as visionary and revolutionary as its authors believed. Compare it with the post-war blueprint issued by the N.U.S. in 1944, prepared under the influence of student leaders now in their forties, and one is struck by the similarities: opposition to compulsory lectures, need for a fuller use of teaching aids, extension of tutorial systems, closer contact between staff and students, broader-based courses, full control by students of their own unions. But the policy statement for 1964 does urge the case 'for formal representation of the student body on all committees or similar bodies' which make decisions about the form, structure and content of the academic curriculum.

The spokesmen for the student estate were possibly not aware that men old enough to be their fathers had marched into the post-war world under a banner of aspirations not very different from their own. But they were aware of instances – both in individual institutions and at national level – of resolutions being passed into a vacuum, submissions being made without response. The evidence for this awareness was a note of irritation, swelling occasionally into militancy, which was audible at student conferences. In diagnosing the present mood of the student estate it is important to recollect that some proposals put forward by the N.U.S. in 1944, and generally admitted to be sensible, had to be repeated in 1964. MacArthur in 1961 expressed his disenchantment with consultative committees whose views were disregarded. The Hale report on university teaching methods, published in 1964, confirms MacArthur's opinion, for the report states: 'It is indeed a fact that the views now put forward by the student organisations do not differ much, in their main outline, from those expressed in . . . the report of the University Grants Committee for the period from 1929–30 to 1935–36.'[31] And the N.U.S. memorandum to the Hale Committee (published as an appendix to the report) ends with a good-natured gibe hoping that the committee's report will not swell the file marked 'NO ACTION TO BE TAKEN'. Even a reasonable student might be excused for displaying impatience at a delay of thirty years in making some simple improvements in teaching methods. There were moments when it seemed that impatience would break out. At an N.U.S. council meeting in April 1963 Mr Swindlehurst, a delegate from Bradford, is reported to have moved that 'Council empowers N.U.S. executive to adopt a more militant attitude in pursuing its policies where other means are proving unsatisfactory' and he spoke of strikes, civil disobedience and the distribution of literature. Another delegate recalled that in Italy students locked themselves in lecture rooms in an effort to get better courses. Mr Swindlehurst's motion was clearly defeated on a vote. And there were two or three other occasions when the assembled council rejected proposals for 'active implementation' of the council's policies, in favour of persuasion by publicity and discussion. This restraint was praiseworthy but it had to be exercised against a growing pressure for active participation in decision-making. If recommendations get lost in the upper strata of the academic hierarchy, then student representatives must themselves climb into these regions to sponsor their recommendations.

There were other reasons, too, for the change of mood. Some lay outside the world of higher education altogether. There was disillusionment with both major political parties, sliding into contempt for the whole parliamentary system. The very affluence and security of the welfare state bred discontent which found its outlet in violence: gangs with flick-knives, mods and rockers disturbing seaside towns on bank holidays, a malaise clearly described by T. R. Fyvel in his book *The insecure offenders*. Among some students this discontent with society has taken the form of doubt about the values implicit in higher education (in the ears of these students 'success' is a dirty word and degrees are irrelevant). One more form of discontent is guilt about the privileges which students enjoy in Britain; an embarrassing dilemma because on one hand it is the policy of student leaders to demand grants without means tests in order to ensure freedom from parental control; and on the other hand it is their policy to compensate for this privilege by erasing all symbols of elitism: they ask, for example, that the public should be welcomed into their libraries, hostels, gymnasia, meeting halls and theatres.[32] This discontent bred of affluence is one ingredient of the student conscience which we discuss in the next chapter.

Another cause of the change in mood was a growing sense of strength and cohesion in the student movement. It united a great diversity of students across administrative frontiers which still separate institutions of higher education. There is still no integrated system of higher education in Britain. Universities retain their autonomy, under the loose surveillance of the U.G.C. Colleges of education are now on the fringe of the university world but are independently managed. Polytechnics, technical and commercial colleges, colleges of art are controlled by a great variety of authorities. At every level except that of the students there is no common direction and no nerve-centre of organisation. At the level of the students the N.U.S. was emerging as a body with a common purpose. It was, moreover, a body which had at last secured recognition. Thanks to the initiative taken by David Eccles in 1954 (against the advice of his civil servants) the union had easy access to the secretary of state for education. When interviews were sought with the U.G.C. they were readily granted. *The Times*, in a leading article, graciously announced that the N.U.S. 'was carving out a niche for itself'. And early in 1965 the union was awarded the accolade of recognition: the prime minister invited members of the N.U.S. executive to dine with him at 10 Downing Street.

A movement of such strength and cohesion cannot allow its energy to run to waste. It has to find causes on which to exercise its powers. Already there were signs of spontaneous activity over some of the dilemmas of society. On 30 November 1964 more than 5000 students from forty British universities and colleges marched through London to protest against apartheid, and a few months later 800 students protested at the American embassy against military activities in Vietnam. It was more difficult to find justifiable campaigns within the university system; but there was much to be done in the public sector. Some colleges of education had rules of discipline which might have been borrowed from a convent. Some colleges of art would not countenance unions run by the students themselves. And even in the universities the rights of students were sometimes challenged. In Trinity term 1964 the Oxford proctors dispensed what was regarded by the N.U.S. as hasty and ill-considered punishment on students who had taken part in a demonstration to express displeasure at a visit by the South African ambassador. In Cambridge there were murmurs against the wearing of gowns after dusk on the ground that students did not want to be differentiated from young people in the town. Besides, nothing much was being done about some long-standing complaints, despite lip-service to reform. Curricula were still too specialised; university teachers were still not being trained to teach and their promotion still depended too heavily upon the research they had done; tutorial systems were still too infrequent; access to higher education was still not democratic enough. A few senior academics listened and diagnosed the change of mood;[33] the majority were unaware of it. Spokesmen for the student estate, accustomed now to being consulted by ministers of the Crown and government committees, still failed to catch the ear of the Committee of Vice-Chancellors and Principals.

Partnership with the Establishment

In 1965 the N.U.S. was presented with an opportunity to try its strength over a major issue of academic policy. The colleges of advanced technology were being transformed into universities. This necessitated a complete scrapping of their hierarchical structure (they were run more like schools than universities) and the substitution in its place of royal charters appropriate to autonomous universities. The governing bodies of these colleges were busy during 1964 preparing draft charters and statutes. The drafts had to go to the Privy Council for approval, and the University Grants Committee was given an opportunity to comment on them first.

This was a phase of transition when old constitutions were dissolved and new ones were put in their place: a phase reminiscent of the constitutional reforms to the Scottish universities in 1887–9. On that occasion (we described it on pp. 27–39) the Scottish student councils pressed for statutory recognition and succeeded in getting it. In 1965 the N.U.S. woke up to the fact that some of the colleges of advanced technology were drafting new constitutions without consulting students on matters of the utmost importance to them: disciplinary procedures, autonomy of unions, and machinery for participation in university government. It was disclosed at the April council meeting that the draft charter and statutes for the University of Surrey (the new title for the Battersea College of Technology) were about to go to the Privy Council for approval. A delegate from Battersea asserted that the students had only managed to acquire a copy of the draft surreptitiously. The executive, as soon as they heard about this, had lobbied leading members of the Parliamentary Labour Party's education committee, and had written to the secretary of state for education and science. The council resolved that it 'deeply regrets the lack of consultation with student bodies prior to the drafting of the charters of new universities appearing or shortly to appear before the Privy Council for ratification'.[34] The executive was mandated to press for three matters to be incorporated in the constitutions of the new universities: (i) fair disciplinary procedure, (ii) autonomy of students' unions, and (iii) representation of students on decision-making bodies in the universities. A month later the N.U.S. submitted a printed pamphlet (which had a wide circulation) of *Recommendations for the amendment of the charter of the University of Surrey* to the Privy Council.[35] This, together with criticisms from the Association of University Teachers and interventions by a number of M.P.s, had the required effect. The draft was held up pending discussion and submitted for comment (this was common practice) to the University Grants Committee. One clear outcome was an undertaking that the Privy Council would consider N.U.S. evidence in respect of all charters for the new universities to be created out of colleges of advanced technology. Meanwhile the N.U.S. kept up the pressure. A press conference was held on 13 January 1966 to publicise the University of Surrey (Battersea) case. On 17 January a letter was sent to the prime minister as chancellor-designate of one of the new universities (Bradford) whose charters were under consideration. The next day the president of the

N.U.S. received a hand-delivered letter from the secretary of state for education and science, written on the Privy Council's authority, to say that the Privy Council was:

> putting to the sponsors of these Charters the desirability of making the following provisions in their Charters, wherever they have not already done so:
> 1. The Senate and the Council of the new universities should be expressly empowered to establish joint committees of themselves and representatives of the student body.
> 2. Provision should be made whereby a procedure will be laid down for a right on the part of a student suspended or expelled to be formally heard by the Senate or by a body appointed by the Senate before the decision becomes final.
> 3. Provision should be made for an association representing the student body.

This went some way toward satisfying the requests of the N.U.S. But not far enough; and the N.U.S. circulated to every member of parliament a pamphlet entitled *Outside the law*, which exposed the shortcomings of the letter from the secretary of state, and reiterated the proposed amendments to the charter for the University of Surrey. There was further correspondence over several other charters, and the outcome was that the provisions proposed by the Privy Council were everywhere adopted; if they had not been it is doubtful whether the charters would have been granted.

Let us pause for a moment to consider precisely what were the complaints which at this time so exercised the minds of spokesmen for the student estate. The first was simply that student unions in the colleges seeking charters had not been consulted, and had not had an opportunity to comment on drafts. The other complaints referred to provisions (or the lack of them) about discipline, the union, and representation. The draft for the University of Surrey illustrates these complaints. Statute 5 (5) B gave the vice-chancellor power to suspend or exclude any student without assigning any reason, and the senate, under Statute 18 (30), was empowered, on a report from the vice-chancellor, to confirm the sentence or to expel the student. There was no provision for a court of discipline and no right of appeal. The statutes were subsequently amended to meet this objection.

A second objection to the draft constitution was that it gave the university authority to prescribe the constitution, powers and functions of the students' union and 'to take such steps as it thinks proper for controlling organisations of students'. The N.U.S. maintained that the last phrase could be used to prevent the right of free association, and – in the hands of clumsy administrators – this could well be true. But the clause was neither modified nor withdrawn. Over the provision to determine the union's constitution the students' objections were unconvincing and again they were overruled. They maintained that the union should be completely autonomous and yet they expected the union to be recognised as an official body in the university, with access to other official bodies such as council and senate, whose constitutions *are* prescribed by the university. Why, among the constituent bodies in the university required by the constitution – academic assembly, senate, council, students' union – should the union alone not be subject to the university's supervision? What a contrast this is to the attitude of the Scottish students in 1888! In their memorial to the government they specifically asked that the bill before parliament should be amended to empower the commissioners 'to fix the constitution and manner of election, and to regulate the powers, jurisdictions, and privileges of the Representative Councils' on the grounds that if these bodies were to be recognised by parliament and assigned a definite part in the government of the universities, it would be 'only just' that they should submit to statutory regulation. We observe here the first signs of an ambivalence which is at present clouding discussion of the status of the student estate. Is it to be integrated into the other 'estates' of the university, as one community? If so, there is an arguable case for some student representation on councils and senates; and (a point overlooked by the students) an equally strong case for staff representation on the students' union and the editorial board of the student paper and, for that matter, on the N.U.S. executive; and on this assumption unions, along with other assemblies of university members, must be willing to submit their constitutions to the university's sovereignty. Or is the student estate to be separate from the university, a trade union organised to protect its interests against what may be the conflicting interests of the academic staff? If so, there is no case for student representation on councils and senates. We believe that the student estate must choose between these alternatives: it cannot expect to get the privileges of both. The present constitutions of universities, in which students are designated 'members' in the charters (or, as in Cambridge, are part of a corporation of chancellor, masters, scholars), assume the first of these two alternatives; and indeed this was the assumption behind the rectorship of the Scottish universities until 1858, for up to that date the rector was supposed to represent the whole body corporate of the university, not the students alone (p. 29). There are, however, spokes-men for the student estate who use the jargon of trade unionism ('a dispute has been declared at . . . University', wrote one student official) and who would clearly prefer the student movement to take this line; the line taken by Miss Button of Sheffield as long ago as 1936.

The N.U.S. leaders were somewhat embarrassed about this ambi-valence, for, when they came to their third objection to the charters of new universities, they wrote (in their submission to the Privy Council, para. 25): 'Although in the previous section we have laid claim to the autonomous nature of a Students Union we do not think that we are introducing irrationality by detailing also the case for student repre-sentation at all levels of policy formulation and implementation within the University Structure. (A similar interpretation will doubtless be advanced by the A.U.T. and A.T.T.I. on behalf of their membership.)'

The view of the Privy Council was that staff–student consultative committees were desirable, but to oblige universities in their constitu-tions to have student representation on their main executive bodies (particularly if the representation were to come from a union whose constitution was not acceptable to the university) would be undesirable. But it was a notable advance that ministerial blessing had been given to joint committees to deal with academic business.

The N.U.S. did not get all it asked for, but it had won something of a diplomatic victory over the charters of the new technological uni-versities by sensible negotiation which had enhanced its prestige. But the campaign had still to be carried into the existing universities whose charters and statutes were not under review; and the militants were not satisfied with mere consultation over academic matters: they pressed for representation, 'a long term campaign to advance the democratic rights of students to participate in, rather than receive, higher educa-tion'.[36] This was in April 1966. In the following October the union issued a pamphlet entitled *Student participation in college government* which summarised, institution by institution, the state-of-play on student representation on governing bodies and senates and committees, and which reaffirmed its belief 'that full student representation can make a vital and positive contribution to solving the problems created by expansion. . .'.[37] These views were reiterated in the memorandum which the N.U.S. submitted to the U.G.C. for the quinquennium 1967–72.[38] But the main point of attack for this campaign had to be the Committee of Vice-Chancellors. The executive was accordingly instructed to seek a meeting with representatives of the committee, and the N.U.S. reported that in September 1966 'the first ever joint meeting took place' between themselves and the committee.[39] Since 1966 there has been close contact between the two bodies, but it is remarkable (and in the light of history it seems unfortunate) that forty-four years had to pass before two bodies so deeply involved in the welfare of universities met officially to discuss common problems.

The last citadel of the Establishment had welcomed the N.U.S. to its conference table. Over discipline, union autonomy, and consultative staff–student committees it was obvious that the Privy Council's views would sooner or later be adopted throughout all colleges and universities. But 'sooner or later' was not good enough for the N.U.S. By now the shock wave generated by the disturbances at Berkeley had reached Europe. The techniques of civil disobedience, unlike the techniques of industrial protest, proved to be admirably suited for forcing issues in student politics. At the same time – this is a question we discuss in the next chapter – the walls which had insulated the domestic affairs of universities from political passions were breached and the two could no longer be kept apart.

Political movements among students have been studied and described by experts and we have nothing useful to add to these studies.[40] The N.U.S. council had always included a minority which wanted to politicise the student movement. The majority had always successfully resisted this. The N.U.S. constitution as revised to 30 November 1966 still required that its objectives 'shall be pursued in entire independence of all political and religious groups or propaganda'. At council meetings the chairman would rule out of order motions and discussions which infringed this rule. From time to time the rule was challenged: e.g. in 1940, when the management of affairs was in the hands of some ardent socialists; in 1953, when King's College, London, disaffiliated on the ground that the N.U.S. was becoming a political forum; and again in 1960, when a motion to amend this part of the constitution was defeated. In 1963 the clause was amended to allow wider scope for discussion (some educational problems had become inseparable from politics) but still 'it shall not be the role of the National Union to provide a general political forum'. But those who wanted the union to take sides on political and social issues, such as the Vietnam war, kept up the pressure, and those who put educational issues first found themselves on the defensive. Every opportunity was taken to embarrass those student leaders who had patiently and doggedly sought, and gained, a partnership with the Establishment. One opportunity was provided by disclosures that the International Student Conference, to which the N.U.S. was affiliated, was receiving funds from the notorious United

States Central Intelligence Agency. This was disclosed in a muck-raking publication called *Ramparts* in 1967. It was doubtless correct, but the N.U.S. executive took the view that the union should not leave a sinking ship; it should rather try to rescue and resuscitate the I.S.C., which was giving useful service to student unions in developing countries. The New Left used this opportunity to try to discredit the leadership of the N.U.S. The issue was debated by the council in 1967–8 and in November 1968 the N.U.S. decided to withdraw its membership.[41]

The New Left had other opportunities to embarrass those who were successfully establishing the prestige of the student estate through the legitimate processes of a democratic society. They advocated confrontations, demands, non-violent direct action, in place of negotiation and bargaining with the Establishment. Every sign of delaying tactics on the part of vice-chancellors or heads of colleges, every instance of clumsy handling by the authorities of a dispute, every episode which could be interpreted as a denial to students of their democratic rights was seized on as evidence that the N.U.S. was weak, compromising and betraying its constituents.[42] In the autumn of 1966 a group of twelve students signed a manifesto establishing a Radical Student Alliance, with declarations about student rights (no different from the objectives of the N.U.S.); education and society (the conventional New Left approach, with emotive phrases like 'collective action', 'democratically composed' college authorities and 'solidarity with those who are victims of oppression'); and the assertion that student society is not closed and should co-operate with trade unions and other local and national organisations. 'Lack of militancy and perspective', states the manifesto, 'have so far prevented student organisations from achieving these aims.' The movement, now incorporated in the Radical Socialist Students' Federation (R.S.S.F.), utterly rejects the philosophy and tactics of the N.U.S. in favour of 'politicizing' universities and colleges by deliberate provocation, in ways which we describe in the next chapter.

The R.S.A. and its successor the R.S.S.F. have not succeeded in discrediting the N.U.S., though their activities have done damage to the public image of the student estate. But the constant abrasion of a militant minority has, of course, prodded the N.U.S. into more aggressive tactics to secure its ends. To their great credit the leaders of the N.U.S. have not allowed their movement to be steered into a collision course with the authorities. They have been obliged to sharpen their demands and to quicken the pace of negotiation. Outbreaks of protest, beginning with the distorted and malicious charges brought by some students against the director-designate of the London School of Economics in 1966, and spreading among a dozen or more universities in Britain, sensitised the universities to pressures from the student estate. The N.U.S. on the whole played a role of conciliation. On 28 February 1968, for instance, it is recorded that 'the good offices of Mr Geoffrey Martin, President of the National Union of Students, were helpful in promoting' informal discussions between the vice-chancellor and the president of the Leicester students' union, then engaged in a sit-in. Geoffrey Martin's mediation was successful, and at the April council of the N.U.S. in that year he reasserted that to raise the stakes of student participation into student power was not the policy of his union. 'We believe', he said, 'in involvement and in solving problems, one with another, in an orderly way. . . . Violence as a solution to any problem has never had a place in this National Union. . . .' Martin stood for the university and college as integrated communities, with common aims, needing much more co-operation between senior and junior members than had existed in the past. He did not believe in a struggle for power between senior and junior members. But his constituents were becoming impatient. Mr Harper of York University spoke of the dangers of unions being 'bought off with token representation' and he moved a resolution asking for support for 'direct action to attain their ends' when university authorities failed to respond to their demands. The resolution was passed after the addition of the words 'non-violent' in front of 'direct action'. This pledged the N.U.S. to support sit-ins and other demonstrations of protest if the circumstances justified them.

In the feverish atmosphere of the summer of 1968 the N.U.S. was obliged to take the initiative or to lose at one stroke the following of its constituents and the confidence of the Establishment. In June 1968 the Committee of Vice-Chancellors, after a week-end meeting at Cambridge, issued a statement severely condemning the unrest but plainly welcoming student participation.[43] Meanwhile the N.U.S., realising that the concessions granted in the charters and statutes of the technological universities must now be extended as quickly as possible to all institutions, drew up a ten-point programme of educational reform and issued a campus reform manual to every constituent union, concentrating on participation, union autonomy, discipline, and the consequences of the Latey report, which recommended that the age of majority should be lowered to eighteen.[44]

But unilateral statements, coming either from vice-chancellors or the representatives of students, were not likely to calm the summer turbulence of 1968. The Sorbonne had been under siege; Columbia was humiliated; the Free University of Berlin was in thrall to the S.D.S. With the complicity and active promotion of the mass media, student heroes had emerged: Cohn-Bendit, Dutschke, Hayden, Rudd. In Britain (as Cohn-Bendit himself admitted) there were none of the grave reasons for protest which were to be found in America, France, and Germany; so protesters had to fall back on relatively trivial reasons, or mere pretexts. Student militants might harangue union meetings by saying that they were 'determined to unmask the repressive structure of what goes by the name of a university but is, in fact, nothing but a mire of intellectual corruption';[45] but their audiences could not be persuaded that things were quite as bad as that. Mob resonance, however, is a very real danger, and there were signs that British students might be swept into the cyclone of protest which was sweeping through universities from California to Tokyo.

Where unilateral statements could do no good, a joint statement, demonstrating that senior and junior members of universities were co-operating in common aims and not mobilising against one another in civil war, might calm the waters and keep channels open for the flow of reforms. To this end representatives of the N.U.S. and the Committee of Vice-Chancellors met during the summer of 1968, originally to discuss the ten-point programme. But out of this discussion, and after hard bargaining, there was produced a joint statement which was published on 7 October 1968. It was accorded prominence in the press, as we have illustrated by the headlines with which we opened this chapter. It is a document of historical importance, not so much because of its content (which is inevitably hazy beneath the mist of compromise) as because it is an affirmation on behalf of senior and junior members of universities that they are partners in the educational system under a voluntary discipline of scholarship. Students are not customers purchasing degrees, nor wards under guardianship, and certainly not enemies.

The concordat traverses familiar topics and we shall not analyse it in detail.[46] Beneath the bland sentences there flow two currents of opinion which are important for the theme of this book. One is the quickening realisation by the vice-chancellors that the student estate must be taken into partnership and has – in its corporate opinion – much to offer the universities. (It was amusing to hear the president of N.U.S. tell his council in November 1968 that 'the problem we face is not any longer with the Vice-Chancellors . . . it is the fuddy-duddiness of backward-looking university teachers'.) The other current of opinion was the faster-flowing conviction on the part of students that British universities, despite their high quality compared with those of most other nations, were in need of reforms of the kind not touched upon in the Robbins report.

Pride of place in the concordat went to student participation in university decision-making, with a demarcation of areas where students should have clear representation, areas where 'the ultimate decision must be that of the statutorily responsible body' but where it is essential that students should be consulted, and areas 'where student presence would be inappropriate'. It is made clear that the N.U.S. seeks for its members representation on councils and senates, and that it welcomes the staff–student committees attached to senates, faculty boards, and departments, which were already functioning in some universities.

And how would the student estate wish to use the participation for which it asks? Discussions at N.U.S. meetings and submissions from individual unions to the U.G.C. for the quinquennium 1967–72 give a pretty clear answer to this question. Spokesmen for the estate press, first, for a complete change of attitude over discipline. Encouraged by the Latey report (and overlooking the emphatic statement in that report that to reach the age of majority does not exempt a student from the rules of a society he has voluntarily joined – no residential college can tolerate, as the report puts it, disturbance by trumpets or strumpets in the middle of the night) the student estate would insist that all surveillance of moral behaviour should be abandoned, all rules which do not bear on the academic activities of the university should be rescinded; the student should suffer no constraints save those required by the law of the land or mutually agreed between students and staff to promote academic work. Furthermore any action for breach of discipline must accord with the principles of natural justice, with the right to be legally represented at courts preferably including student members, a right of appeal and an assurance that no senior member of the university acts as accuser and judge. Paternalism must go. The don has no authority except the expertise he commands over his subject. And yet (and we return to this theme) the student estate still wants the don to do more than simply to sell knowledge. He wants informal talk, tutorial supervision, concern with the student's welfare. Perhaps what he wants is *fraternalism*.

On academic affairs spokesmen for the student estate would press for research into examinations and drastic reforms in the common practice of end-of-year three-hour written papers as the prime assessment for a

degree. There is pardonable impatience among students about the reluctance of some academics to listen to these pleas; for although the
common conclusion, after such inquiries as have been made, is that the
present examining system is the least of a diversity of evils, nevertheless
we have known for a long time that examinations are unreliable. It is
thirty-eight years since Hartog and Rhodes published their classical
Examination of examinations, and recently the *Universities Quarterly*
devoted a whole issue to critical essays, by academics, on the present
system.[47] Secondly, on academic affairs, participation by students would
sharpen the criticism of patterns of courses offered in some universities,
and encourage the cultivation of fresh fields of study which universities,
through inertia or indifference or lack of resources, may at present be
neglecting.

The concordat with the vice-chancellors was followed by another
concordat, for colleges of further education, with the Association of
Education Committees. On behalf of the student estate the N.U.S.
had achieved an honourable partnership with government, the U.G.C.
and the vice-chancellors. It was a partnership which involved no
capitulation to the Establishment. Agreements were reached by hard
bargaining; differences were not papered over. The episode of history
which we have traced from the early nineteenth century ended in a
flowering of the student estate in 1968. For there is no doubt that the
student estate did, in 1968–9, have a profound effect on the universities
of Britain. Hardly a month passed without an announcement that one
university or another had revised its disciplinary procedures, or set up
staff–student committees, or admitted student observers to the senate,
or elected student members to its council, or set up commissions to
review participation throughout the university or to consider examination techniques. Whether the effects will be good or bad for universities
is a matter of hard, sometimes bitter, controversy. We reflect upon this
question in the next chapter.

Before passing on to that chapter, we have one footnote to add. The
flowering of the student estate has been followed by a sudden east wind.
The meeting of the council of the N.U.S. in November 1968 (now to
be called 'conference') might have been expected to be an occasion for
celebration and self-congratulation. It was nothing of the sort. About
1000 persons attended. The sessions were described as a shambles.
'From the outset' (we quote from the official record) '. . . conference
was peppered with hoots, boos, guffaws, guerilla procedural tactics,
points of order (forty in thirty minutes), two votes of no confidence in
the chair. . . . One cause of offence to the vociferous dissidents was the

presence of a banner over the platform saying "Education – reason not revolution." ' It was an attempt by the militants to take over from the moderates. It did not succeed, but the pressure created something of a crisis mentality for the next meeting of the conference, in April 1969. On that occasion the conference rescinded the concordat between the N.U.S. and the Association of Education Committees, and criticised severely the concordat with the vice-chancellors. It mandated the executive to renegotiate these concordats, and it laid down:

> as the basis of all future NUS policy on representation:
> (i) that on all governing bodies of colleges and universities there should normally be *one-third student representation*, with effective representation also of non-professorial academic staff, and democratically elected representatives of national and local interest outside the colleges.
> (ii) that as far as internal government is concerned the institutions should be under the control of all who work in them, including students, academic and non-academic staff, with representation on the principle that any decision-making body shall be composed, *equally*, of all interested sectors.
> (iii) that in the departments, academic and departmental questions should be dealt with by committees with *decision-taking powers*, and with 50–50 staff/student representation. These committees should be advised, where applicable, or practical, by a general meeting of all members of the department.
> (iv) that committees of solely student concern . . . should *normally* be under student control. . . .
> To this end Conference believes that mandating on principles is essential for democratic representation on all committees.[48]

The conference further 'accepts that the strength of NUS is in its membership, not its press image and *therefore*' (our italics) wants the union and its executive to support constituent organisations which take action in any non-violent form to press their claims so long as the claims are in line with N.U.S. policy.[49]

Finally – and this is bound to weaken the influence of the student estate on educational policy – the conference decided to delete the clause in its constitution which specifically precluded political discussion.[50]

Some of these resolutions, if pressed, would certainly damage the partnership between the student estate and the rest of the community of higher education; they would be what is now called counter-productive of reform. One can only hope that the wording we have quoted is as unpremeditated and irresponsible as some of the comments made from the floor during the conference. 'Never again', said one delegate, 'will we be deluded into thinking that one or two tame students on a tame sub-committee is anything more than a token of impotence.' The bizarre proceedings were considered by some people to be due to the preponderance of 'underprivileged' students from non-university institutions. But this is not the explanation. The official record quotes one girl delegate from a college of education (soon, presumably, to be entrusted with the education of children) as contributing to the debate on representation with the words: 'Why the hell do the b——— universities have the floor all the time?'[51] We hope that parts of the conference's mandate on representation will be consigned to the oblivion where these two comments from the floor belong. For the student estate is developing a corporate conscience which among some of its members is deep and sincere. Our universities and colleges, and our society, need this conscience. In our next chapter we reflect upon it.

6 The Conscience of the Student Estate

'A conscience of society'

The future, wrote de Tocqueville, is 'an enlightened and upright judge, but one, alas, who arrives always too late'. Only the future can judge whether the turbulence in the student estate during 1968–9 will improve or damage higher education in Britain. But parliamentarians, journalists, television commentators, and persons who ventilate their views in letters to *The Times*, do not wait for the enlightened and upright judge. Their observations, sometimes wise and perceptive, sometimes ignorant and prejudiced, sometimes downright distorted and mischievous, have confused what is already a very complex episode. We make no claims in this chapter to dispel this confusion. All we do claim is that our comments are based upon some understanding of the historical roots of the student estate, and some first-hand experience of the present turbulence; but we remind the reader that in the following pages we are not recording history, we are reflecting on contemporary events. We shall not anticipate the verdict of the enlightened and upright judge, but we shall venture to speculate about the future of the student estate, and our speculations are of course coloured by our convictions.

The National Union of Students is the recognised spokesman for the student estate in England, Wales, and Northern Ireland (the Scots still retain their own independent union). Its corporate views carry weight with the Committee of Vice-Chancellors and Principals, with government officials, with parliament. This, of course, does not mean that the 407,000 students affiliated to the N.U.S. present a solid block of opinion; on some topics they appear to speak with one voice only because very few of them speak. A question such as grants versus loans commands massive support (in favour, of course, of grants); quasi-political questions, such as the concordat made between the N.U.S. and the Association of Education Committees, can (and this one did) lead to repudiation of executive action by the annual conference. Moreover there are thousands of students who do not recognise the

N.U.S. as their spokesman; some, who belong to more militant groups such as the Revolutionary Socialist Students' Federation; others – a much greater number – who are simply not interested in student movements at all. But all students are part of the broad generic category which the press calls *students* when it is reporting 'student demonstrations', 'student residence' or 'student grants'; they are, whether they are conscious of it or not, the student estate.

The mass media have created an identikit of the student who speaks for the student estate, and defenders of students are constantly reminding the public that the 'typical' student is not like this mass media image at all: he is among the tens of thousands of students who neither demonstrate nor demand, but contentedly attend lectures and pass examinations. Both these generalisations are incorrect. We shall now try to replace them with something less simple but more accurate.

In 1967 the council of the N.U.S. had before it a draft statement of rights and responsibilities.[1] The statement differs from the manifesto issued at the student congress in 1940 (p. 81) in that it is less strident about rights and more specific about responsibilities. It contains one paragraph which serves as a text for this chapter:

> After all, students act as a conscience of society. Hence in developed, as in developing countries, the great issues of peace and progress often first crystallise in the dialogues of the academic community. The fulfilment of this role is one of the major responsibilities of students toward society.

Collective rights, collective responsibilities: these are not impossible to define. But a collective conscience? To define this is virtually impossible. There is no doubt that something which could be described as a student conscience has influenced national policies about the Vietnam war, civil rights, chemical warfare, and military training; but this is a generalisation which conceals rather than illuminates the truth. The validity of the generalisation is that students of all shades of opinion and all levels of commitment now have the feeling that they are a power to be reckoned with; they have a corporate identity. Student activists (we do not use the word in a defamatory sense) exert their influence, inside universities and beyond, by appeal to this corporate identity. This is the strategy of activism.

Conscience is an attribute of persons, not classes. The strategy of activism is to mobilise individual consciences. The student estate has no internal corporate discipline – there is no 'party line' to which its members must adhere – so individual consciences have to be mobilised for each campaign. Success in a campaign depends on the range of consciences which respond to the appeal. We begin, therefore, with an attempt to describe some categories of student conscience.

Categories of the student conscience

This book is about the influence of students on universities, and throughout the historical chapters it has been easy to discuss this theme without getting it entangled with another theme: the influence of students on society. Except sporadically (as, for example, around 1940) the two themes could be kept apart. It is impossible to keep them apart in any discussion of what is happening today, for the pressures which some students are directing against the university are really protests against society; they are being delivered to the wrong address. But the circumstances are such that the university cannot redirect them; it must accept them and respond to them. We omit from our discussion protest about genuine domestic grievances such as tasteless food in the refectory and overcrowding in the library; or genuine 'trade union' issues, such as inadequate grants and squalid lodgings. These grievances concern amenities or rights rather than consciences. The present turbulence in the student estate has much deeper causes than these.

At the centre of the turbulence, in practically every university, there is a small group of dedicated students. They have one thing in common: they hate the consumer society. Their dedication has one aim: to destroy it. Associated with them are others who hate society but respond by withdrawing from it rather than confronting it; the weapons they would use for defence are flowers, not flagstones. The sociologists call these groups alienated and there are shelves of books analysing their origins (upper-middle class from permissive homes is a common description); their subconscious disorders (the Oedipal Rebellion against all father-figures is one hypothesis); their contempt for all constraint ('Clothes are a constraint; razors are a constraint; courses and examinations are constraints; ... refined language is a constraint');[2] their rejection of the cumulative and consecutive structure of knowledge as practised in universities in favour of spontaneous emotional surges of self-realisation; their resemblance, in their uncompromising and apocalyptic denunciation of society, to some early fanatical christian sect out of the pages of Gibbon. Scores of observers have remarked that these students have no constructive programme for society: their faith is that something unpredictable will arise from the debris of revolution. Meanwhile these students are prepared to be parasitic on the existing order which they profess to reject. As for the universities, they would have to be 'restructured' through non-stop seminars (in which suitable members of the staff would be allowed to join) about what the university is *for*, run by students and on the unexamined assumption that the participants will always remain students. The one positive article of faith which students in this group seem to share is that now, in an age of plenty, utopias need no longer be dreams in books: they can become realities; though how this will be done if expertise in the universities is liquidated, they do not presume to know.

Revolutionaries are no new feature of student society. Students manned barricades in 1848 and fought in Spain in 1936. But there is a contrast between the revolutionaries of the 1960s and those of the 1930s. In the 1930s the revolutionary was under the discipline of an international movement controlled by adults. He embraced a severe orthodoxy. The plan of campaign in which he enrolled went beyond temporary disruption to an ultimate reconstitution of the State. His beliefs were built on history and at their pinnacle there was hope. The modern ultra-left student has no reverence for the past and little hope for the future, despite his assertions about utopias. He submits to no party discipline. He accepts no orthodoxy. He does not look to adults for leadership. His heroes – Ho Chi Minh, Mao, Ché, Castro – are (as Edward Shils put it) 'remote in space or dead'.[3] He has even discarded Marcuse who taught him the philosophy of rejection. He has no predictable ideology: there are innumerable ways of rejecting society. H. L. A. Hart, in a perceptive essay buried in a report on student affairs at Oxford, summarises the mood of this group. There is a rejection of all political parties, including Soviet communism, as 'repressive oligarchies committed to the maintenance of the established order which is managed in the interests of a few'. The classical technique of revolution – appeal to the repressed workers to rise against their masters – fails because the workers are disinclined to feel repressed; but this is due to their ignorance: they are dulled 'by the opiate of relative prosperity'. All forms of organisation and authority, including representational democracy and communist bureaucracy, are repressive (the very tolerance to be found in western democratic societies being a subtle weapon of repression); so direct democracy by general assemblies, similar to a New England town meeting or the deliberations in an Ibo village, is the only valid procedure for government. The truth having been revealed to students in this group, it is their special responsibility to 'politicize' and so to redeem society.

They constitute themselves an elite minority (despite their hatred of elitism), rejecting votes, referenda and other democratic procedures on the indisputable ground that at the beginning of a revolution the majority, by definition, is always wrong. They know that many adults regard them as juvenile delinquents. Their reply would be that they are confronting, like David against Goliath, 'the mature delinquency' (the words are Marcuse's) 'of a whole civilisation'.

The consequence of this attitude for the universities is best told in Hart's own words:

> In the perspective of this movement the universities appear both to sustain the structure of a corrupt society and to reflect it . . . in spite of pretensions to political neutrality, freedom of discussion, and the claim to develop critical as well as informed minds, the universities are centres of indoctrination in which criticism of society is confined to discussion of marginal improvements of the present social system. As much as by what they fail to teach as by what they teach, the universities, in their present form, close the minds they profess to open. In this situation the university becomes, for the student activist bent on social revolution, a base, a pulpit, a target, and also at times a sanctuary.[4]

This is unlike the attitude of militant students towards their universities a generation ago. Curricula, teaching and examinations were all condemned in those days as they still are; but the nature and function of the university were not questioned. In 1940 Brian Simon, having denounced the state of society which isolates universities from the people, and the prevailing conceptions of higher education, called on his audience at the students' congress in Leeds 'to defend the universities against all attacks'.[5] This is not the modern militant's view. In 1968 the *New Left Review* issued advice on the techniques of persuasion to be used in student disputes. 'What we should do', the writer says, would be:

> to behave as provocatively as necessary and to effectively sanction the University to the extent that they *need* to use force, probably the police. Complete occupation of offices rather than corridors will achieve this. It is at this stage that the administrations commit their ultimate folly, and it is at this stage that the staff and less political students will feel encouraged to enter a situation already politically structured.[6]

In any serious assault upon a university the primary source of turbulence is likely to be students who hold views like these. There are very few of them, but very few are enough. They are not interested in university reform – indeed reform is an embarrassment to them because they use issues of reform as a way to mobilise a much larger group of students. The N.U.S. is another embarrassment to them. They sneer at its successes and exult in its weaknesses. The university for them is (as Hart put it) primarily a base and a sanctuary; their declared aim 'international, extra-parliamentary and returning militant politics to the street'.[7] Their objective is not votes on the senate but barricades at the gates.

Very few students, unless intolerably provoked, itch to build barricades, but a great many students look with distaste upon the values of the modern state and fear that they will be sucked into a consumer society which can offer them no motive for living except success. These form a large group, much larger than is realised, because the group is not continuously and stridently articulate. Many of them do not believe that the remedy is revolt, but it is a serious mistake to suppose that they are complacent about either society or universities. They see (as one American Rhodes scholar wrote) 'a hypocritical society which condones the use of napalm but not marijuana'. They believe that students, being privileged, should cleanse this society but they agree – many of them – that the best way to do so is to enter it equipped, as doctor, engineer, economist, to bring about viable and effective reform. Students in this group are interested in university reform too, and are prepared to work for it, preferring the 'proper channels' though, if these fail, they will adopt non-violent but unconventional means. 'The skills a university teaches', wrote one of them, 'may be taught in such a way as to encourage smugness and resistance to social reform. If this is the case, dissenters have a duty to protest – but not in the name of the vision of a politicized university nor in a manner inconsistent with the democratic, humanist vision of a community of scholars.'[8] This is a group whose members are, on the whole, prepared to submit to the disciplines of learning and being examined, though many of them feel strongly that they should be drawn into the decision-making which determines what they are taught and how they are examined; and some of them leave the university after successfully graduating, resentful about the irrelevance (some call it futility) of the knowledge and techniques they have acquired, convinced that the authority which plans their courses is unaware of their frustration. They are therefore prepared to press for much more student participation on councils and senates and boards. Although they are willing to regard themselves as *in statu pupillari* for

126

their academic work, many of them reject the style of life which was symbolic of the elite status of students: gowns, college ties and scarves, sporty clothes, a refined accent and (as they call it) 'sherry diplomacy'. (The sherry party, as one observer of this scene ironically remarks, is 'the major sacrament of counter-revolutionary apathy'.)[9] They reject, too, constraints upon their private lives and especially upon their relations with members of the opposite sex. Students with these views, as Richard Hoggart suggests, may be engaged in 'one of the most important secular changes in attitudes of the last two or three hundred years . . . the beginning of the end of the Protestant Ethic in its two main forms of expression: in its attitude to the importance of work and in its attitude to the sexual life'.[10] If this is so we do well to observe it attentively. It may turn out to be another unforeseen consequence of technology, much more severe than other side effects of technology, such as the effects of automation on work and of the pill on women.

The mood of this group of students comes closer than that of any other group to the present corporate mood of the National Union of Students. Moods in the young change quickly and it would be fool-hardy to predict what the mood may be even a couple of years ahead. But today (1970) it would be correct to say that the great majority of those students who take an interest in corporate opinion in the student estate share in varying degrees the attitudes of this second group. If we were looking for labels for them, we should call them legitimate activists.

There are, in the crude classification we offer, two more groups in addition to the two we have described. The third group, in Britain the biggest of all, is composed of students who have come to the university with clear-cut intentions. They know what they want to do (to get a good degree, to get into the cricket eleven, to produce plays). They are reasonably satisfied with what the university offers and with what they expect society to offer them when they graduate. They want nothing to do with student politics inside or outside the university. They disapprove of militants and will oppose what they consider senseless disturbance of the university's life. By the activist they are regarded as the great apathetic lump, which cannot be relied upon to back causes, make complaints, issue demands. But there is one cause to which many of them will respond. If the authorities behave repressively or unjustly toward activists, particularly if the police are called in to quell trouble, a surprising wave of loyalty to their generation – a solidarity of youth – sweeps through members of this group, and their sympathies flow swiftly to the support of fellow-students whose views

E 2

they reject and whose techniques are repugnant to them. And this, as militant organisers know well, can change the scale and purpose of a student protest. This latent tolerance among the *majority* of students is a very important feature of the student estate.

Finally there is a fourth group which reveals itself if there is serious unrest in a university. This group comes out in favour of militant opposition to activists and provides a backlash – sometimes a violent one – if the authorities seem too compliant. Of course this taxonomy of students does not cover all types. There are some whose interests lie so far outside the academic and social activities of the university that they scarcely belong to the student estate at all; their loyalties are to churches, athletic clubs and the like. And there are many students who remain unattached to any group at all, including some who are to be found at sit-ins and protests for purely frivolous reasons, not out of conviction but 'for kicks'. If they have shaggy hair and bizarre clothing, it is imitative, like the patterns on harmless insects which look like wasps.

Individualism, fortunately, is encouraged in universities, and it would be totally misleading to imagine that our artificially separated components of the student estate do really constitute discrete categories. Human nature defies pigeon-holes. Individual students are constantly flowing from one category to another. Individual issues which affect the student estate are constantly changing the boundaries of the categories. But there is, throughout the whole student estate in Britain, a new awareness of its corporate identity. It is too early to understand all the reasons for this but we remind the reader of some of its contributory causes: (i) The fact that students are organised into institutions of their own – the S.R.C.s, guilds, and N.U.S. which are the main topic of this book. (ii) The fact that freedom from parental control and the responsibilities of adult life no longer arrive simultaneously. There is now a stretch of three to four years during which hundreds of thousands of the more intelligent of our youth possess unprecedented freedom (financial, social, sexual) with no corresponding responsibility. This, as Raymond Aron has said, is a socio-biological problem. Certainly in our experience it produces novel effects: sometimes guilt (a student told one of us, as this book was being written, that his dislike of Cambridge was due to its comfort and its beauty); sometimes an impulse to fill the 'responsibility gap' by assuming premature responsibility for managing the university or putting right the wrongs of mankind; sometimes an escape from the student estate, till the gap closes by flux of time, into an unreal world induced by the deafening discotheque or the more sinister diversion of drugs. (iii) The fact – which loses none of its truth by repetition – that students, being more sensitive and perceptive than most others in their generation, respond to the instant visibility of violence, injustice, poverty, offered by mass media; and are aware, in a way older people are not, that time may be running out. One academic has put this last point well. It will be a triumph for this generation of students, he wrote, 'if it simply arranges that there is another generation after it'.[11] And even today the only boast which millions of men and women can make is 'I have survived'.

The strategy of protest

The present phase of student turbulence in British universities can be superficially diagnosed as follows. It is due to the confluence of three circumstances: first, the presence of students' organisations which mobilise and media which publicise corporate opinion; second, the presence, mainly outside the universities but to some extent inside them, of issues worth protesting about; and third, novel and effective techniques of protest.

Student protests are as old as universities, and one does not have to go back to the middle ages to find examples of them. The history of American colleges in the nineteenth century includes lurid examples of murder, assault, and arson by students in such respectable places as the universities of Virginia, North Carolina, Harvard, Yale, and New York.[12] Nearer home, in 1818, pupils at Winchester College demanded the dismissal of a tutor whose manners met with their displeasure. The headmaster declined to do this, whereupon the pupils, led by the prefects, barricaded themselves into the school, took over the kitchens, manned the walls, armed themselves with stones, and defied the authorities, the constables, and even the military; until finally the headmaster gave in, and the offending tutor disappeared and was never seen again.[13] And we have in earlier chapters of this book given examples of turbulence in British universities during the nineteenth century. But these were sporadic outbursts which did not have much lasting effect upon the institutions where they occurred: they were, as someone has said, like the spasmodic eruptions of violence in a medieval ghetto; they evaporated or they were crushed. During the twentieth century there has been perpetual unrest in the universities of some countries, India for instance;[14] but this has been associated with the politics of liberation, usually in backward communities where students were the spearhead of nationalist movements. It is noteworthy that in these communities it is the relatively privileged who are the revolutionaries, not the peasants; and this is true of affluent countries too. We are witnessing in some universities attempts at revolution by fragments of the elite, who have, so far, failed to persuade the proletariat to follow them.

To dismiss student protest as the mischief of a lunatic fringe, or to condemn it indiscriminately as a species of hooliganism similar to the wrecking of trains by football fans, are attitudes too irresponsible to merit serious comment. Let it simply be said that no changes in the structure of society, good or bad, peaceful or ugly, from Galilee to Cuba, have occurred without pioneers labelled as lunatics. Some of the most vehement critics of student protest call themselves protestants. Student protest may be a mere ripple on the surface of society, or it may be the ground swell of major change. What is certain is that some student protest is admirable and even heroic: South African students opposing apartheid, Czech students in Wenceslas Square, American students defending civil rights in Mississippi. It would be a dull conscience which was not stirred by demonstrations to call attention to the homeless, the hungry, and the victims of oppression. It is not the strategy of student protest which is itself evil, it is the way this strategy is manipulated by some student groups for ignoble ends, or directed into paths of violence.

Abuse of the student conscience

It is this abuse of the collective student conscience which we now discuss. It damages the reputation of students, whatever their views, and weakens the influence for good of their leaders. We emphasise, therefore, that in the following pages we are not discussing legitimate protest (which is occasionally necessary, even in British universities, as a sort of enema to cure a blockage in the academic administrative tract or insensitivity to students' genuine needs). What we are discussing is deliberate disruption for disruption's sake or to secure by the short cut of ultimatum concessions which could be secured by legitimate means.

First, a few words about the origin of the modern technique of protest, for this has done for the student estate what the phalanx did for the Greeks: it has given students, for the time being at any rate, a tactical advantage over those against whom they choose to use it. It is not really novel (one of us witnessed a sit-in in the administration block of the University of Hyderabad in 1951). It was refined as a technique by American blacks to support civil rights in the Southern States; then adopted on the campuses of a few American universities, from which it has spread all over the student world.

As it has spread, the strategy has changed. In its early forms it was non-violent and it did not seek violence. One rudimentary form of it was the peaceful marching and sitting of campaigners for nuclear disarmament. In Britain it has – but for a few untypical incidents – remained non-violent. The main sophistication in the strategy of British student protest is the campaign of words which accompanies a 'happening'. Some of the most effective student revolts are waged not with petrol bombs and crowbars but with typewriters and duplicating machines.

Chronicles of some of the more spectacular student revolts are now on the market.[15] But, for the theme of this book, it is the modest eruptions which are more instructive. In Britain there is no evidence that they are the result of sinister foreign conspiracies, though there is undoubtedly a good deal of revolutionary mimicry. Militants at the University of Essex visit Paris; students 'occupying' buildings are entertained by films of the revolt at Columbia; and there is, of course, fraternal co-operation between comrades of the New Left in different universities and they attend one another's sit-ins.

Raymond Aron has described the complete spiral of protest as: provocation–repression, repression–revolt, revolt–repression.[16] In any deliberately planned operation it is the aim of the militants to mount the spiral; and it should be the aim of the university authorities to prevent this. The militants cannot mount the spiral without massive support from sympathisers (members of groups two and three described above). To ensure this they must – and this is a point worthy of serious reflection – choose a cause with a moral content, or one which can be transformed into a moral issue.

And so it begins. At the London School of Economics it was an allegation that the newly appointed director had a record of race-prejudice (totally without foundation, but truth is an early casualty in these episodes). At Essex it was chemical warfare (symbolised by a visitor who had come to give a technical lecture on chemistry). At Bristol it was a contrived and disingenuous indignation at delay in a decision to allow less privileged persons who were not students at the university to use the union building. All moral causes: to reject racial discrimination; to condemn war; to renounce privilege. If the first cause has less moral content than these, then it must proclaim some denial of rights, such as representation on university boards or committees, though the danger about these is that if the demands are reasonable the rights may be negotiated and the protest will collapse. So the demands must be in the form of an ultimatum (representation to be granted within a week) or must be certain to be rejected ('equal and democratic staff–student–worker control of all college and university organisation', as one manifesto put it).

The next step is the provocation. This takes various forms: insulting visiting politicians or diplomatists; breaking up meetings; occupying buildings. Any unambiguous and intolerable challenge will do. The non-violent sit-in has proved to be the most effective, because it can have several effects, all favourable to the dedicated revolutionary: it provides the maximum embarrassment to the university authorities; it creates easy publicity; it becomes the opportunity for a teach-in attended by large numbers of innocent students who come out of curiosity and who may be victimised by the authorities or even converted; and its psychological influence, depending on the issues involved, varies between that of a carnival and an evangelical revivalist meeting. It is worth while to pause to consider all four of these factors.

The embarrassment to the university authorities is complex. There is an immediate polarisation of opinion among the academic staff. Some advocate tough action: call in the police, expel the ringleaders, deal with it as though it is mutiny at sea. Others disapprove but declare 'we must maintain communication with them', and they visit the sit-in to reason with the 'action committee' of rebels, which by this time will have been set up. Still other members of the academic staff positively approve the cause (which may indeed be one which deserves approval) and – confusing the ends with the means – they collaborate with the sit-in and address some of its sessions. A second embarrassment is the weakness and slowness of any legal sanctions. In Britain the laws regarding trespass and the issue of injunctions to restrain people from occupying property are designed to give the maximum protection to the trespasser and the minimum of sanctions to the owner. This is something Britain should be proud of. It is one of many examples of the great liberties we enjoy, and it is ironic that advantage should be taken of it by young people who shout about the repressive, intolerant, victimising society into which they have had the misfortune to be born. They are doubtless secretly comforted by the assurance that confrontation with the authorities will not lead to Siberia, a Chinese gaol, or a Cuban firing squad.

But advantage is taken of our liberty and the university authorities have got to devise a counter-strategy which does not override liberty. If at this stage they take a step which could be regarded as repressive, if they arbitrarily and suddenly punish 'ringleaders' or even threaten to do so, the issue of the sit-in will immediately change and the occupants may increase tenfold. Race prejudice, chemical warfare, will be forgotten. For now there would be a more immediate moral issue: victimisation, suppression of free speech. It is a far cry from the battle of Gower Street (pp. 13–16), but the succession of events is very similar; except that the escalation in 1830 was spontaneous; now (as our quotation on p. 125 demonstrates) it may have been deliberately contrived. The university authorities have therefore to realise that the objective of those who engineered the sit-in (we remind the reader that we are considering campaigns of disruption, not legitimate protests) is not to improve race relations, nor to abolish chemical warfare, nor to allow non-students to enjoy the union; it is (let us repeat the words of the *New Left Review*) 'to behave as provocatively as necessary and to effectively sanction the University so that they *need* to use force, probably the police'. For once force is used emotive words like 'brutality', 'fascist thugs', 'outrageous intimidation' can be used; and this mobilises more support.

It is, in fact, a campaign of words, using a deliberate double talk which demonstrates that hypocrisy is no monopoly of the older generation. The primary weapon of all sit-ins is the inexpertly duplicated flysheet. (A facsimile monograph of these would be well worth publishing, as a study in this peculiar form of psychological warfare.) Double talk is an old technique of revolution. Ché Guevara's comrades were 'brutally murdered by thugs', but when his own comrades had to commit murder it was put this way: 'We then had to proceed to his physical elimination. The execution of anti-social individuals . . . was, unfortunately, not infrequent in the Sierra Maestra.'[17]

Similarly to throw a stone at a window is malicious damage. To throw it at the bourgeois mentality within is 'an act of spontaneous moral revulsion'.[18] There is the singular logic of anarchy: 'the institutions our resistance has desanctified and delegitimized . . . have lost all authority. . . . Since they are without legitimacy in our eyes, they are without rights.' Violence is not smashing gates or assaulting members of parliament or battering at the police: it is the violence done by a repressive curriculum in capitalist economics and the 'intolerable assault on the mind' of the examination system; for these constrain personal development. (Curricula and examinations *do* need reform, but not by this sort of cant.) So the manifestos are churned out, peppered with paranoid phrases: 'Are we for police repression or are we against it?' 'Join the struggle against victimisation.' 'We are denied even common justice.' 'Free speech crushed.' Meanwhile, if the university is wise, free speech flourishes, there is no sign of police, no one is victimised, and the university's statutory disciplinary procedures (if not too rusty or outdated, as some of them have proved to be) are quietly put into operation. If the university is unwise the spiral defined by Raymond Aron reaches its second phase; 50 occupiers become 500.

Warfare by words requires effective publicity. The action committee accordingly welcomes press and television into the sit-in. Press conferences with the action committee are eagerly reported in the press; the public are told how orderly the occupation is: litter swept from the floor, lavatories clean, offices undisturbed; and how intransigent the university is: demands ignored, injustices perpetuated, grievances unanswered. This builds up the drama and provokes the critical backlash – 'authority abdicates'; 'students a new danger to society' – all of which helps to sell copies of the newspaper. The vice-chancellor may call a press conference to put the university's point of view; but this is not likely to lead to any coverage in the press: what vice-chancellors say on these occasions is not news.[19] Television teams distort the picture even more, for, by telecasting carefully selected, or even deliberately staged, incidents, they create news of non-events.[20]

The sit-in has two fascinating features which deserve careful study. One is the kaleidoscope of demands, becoming less and less negotiable as the occupiers realise the strength of their position. Thus in one university a demand for the reconsideration of examination results (which appeals only to those likely to fail) changed into a demand for representation on senate and council 'within eight weeks of the date of this meeting' (which appeals to a much larger group). In another university resentment because a non-permanent member of the staff did not get her contract renewed (which was of interest only to students in the sociology department) was soon transformed into 'the acceptance in principle of equal student–faculty power in the hiring and firing of professors'. The other fascinating feature is the effect of the sit-in on those who take part in it, particularly some of those who come purely out of curiosity. Unless there is fear and danger, the whole atmosphere is one of carnival. Everybody knows the sit-in has no future; it is like a cruise at sea: for a few hours hundreds of young people (some of them lonely, some of them shy) find gaiety and companionship. Although it is in a densely overcrowded room, sleeping-bags on the floor, graffiti

134

on the walls, beat music on the gramophone, there is a sort of Arcadian euphoria. An American observer has this to say about it: 'Dozens of this group (from different campuses) have said in effect, "The Sit-in was one of the deepest experiences of my life. We were packed in those rooms and corridors with hardly room to breathe, talking the whole night through. We came to no agreement but it was a great experience just the same." Said others, "It was a *religious* experience" . . . "I didn't know you could feel that way." '21 In one university the action committee issued a regular bulletin of features: '1.30: Discussion on reactionary sociology; 4.00: Seminar on radical film-making; 5.00: Open discussion on what does student power mean; 8.00: Blues jam session and maybe a dance.' In another the news-sheet declared: '. . . everybody's taking their girl to the sit-in. Couples in evening dress make the late night scene.' And the authorities are wise to allow this to happen, for there is no surer way to mobilise generational tolerance in favour of the sitters-in than to prevent them from coming in and out of the 'liberated' building.

So a carnival – or a religious experience – is offered to hundreds of innocuous and law-abiding students by organisers whose real objective is quite different, but who cannot attain this objective until they have mobilised either the conscience or the enthusiasm of hundreds of their unpoliticised fellows. If the university authorities have played it cool, they will on one hand have avoided any acts of repression or retribution (they will in any case be accused of committing such acts), and on the other hand they will have avoided any concession under duress. But the university must defend its integrity, and there is no way to do this except to punish those who disrupt its activities. Therefore ringleaders of the kind of unjustified disruption we are discussing must be identified, charged, and punished. Identification is difficult and it will provoke cries of victimisation. The answer to this is to invite any who wish to be charged with complicity to subscribe their names. Finally, if disciplinary action is taken, there will be a demand for mass amnesty for all who took part in the occupation. Amnesty, declared the occupants of the administration building in the University of Chicago, should be granted 'not as an act of mercy, but as a point of political principle'.

It would be impertinent on our part to suggest how universities should react to episodes like these, apart from making the generalisation that the spiral of provocation–repression, repression–revolt . . . must be interrupted as early as possible. But we have two reflections to offer. One is that those universities which have not remained silent under the shower of words from student militants are the ones which have managed to retain the initiative during attempts at disruption. The other reflection is that British universities will be in a stronger position to deal with mischievous unrest when they have clarified their response to some of the sincerely (and often silently) held views of students about authority and power in universities, and about what is called student participation; until, in fact, universities have re-examined their relation to the student estate. This brings us full circle back to the theme of this book. We now turn to these two reflections.

'Aggressive tolerance'

The first we dell with very briefly. The cascade of propaganda which issues from dupicators during sit-ins may be – it usually is – composed of lies, innuendo, and the stale rhetoric of revolt. But it is a mistake to dismiss it as harmless trash. It puts the Establishment on the defensive and if the Establishment responds with nothing but silence or pompous resolutions, the thoughtful critical student may well begin to wonder whether the Establishment has a convincing defence to put up. The New Left declare that tolerance is repressive; their aim is to provoke an act of intolerance. Silence from the Establishment may create the impression that tolerance is weak. The proper response is not intolerance; it is (if we can give it a label) *aggressive* tolerance. Aggressive tolerance means that a university, threatened with some act of disruption, does not suppress it by force but by moral condemnation. This of course takes time. The prime tactic is to circulate continually, to staff and students, accurate and uncoloured facts, and also frank comment, preferably written by young members of staff known to have liberal views, about the relation between disruption and the articles of faith of a liberal university. The most notable example of this technique comes from the University of Chicago, which had a serious disruption in 1969. The university had not renewed the contract of one of its assistants (who was not on tenure) in sociology. It was alleged that this decision had been prejudiced by the assistant's political views. On 30 January students occupied the administration building and issued demands to the president, including one for the immediate re-hiring of the assistant, and one which read 'Amnesty [for themselves] with the understanding that we consider our actions legitimate and not subject to discipline'. The same day, and almost every day thereafter until the sit-in was over, the university issued an hour-by-hour 'Chronology of developments', reporting, in flat black and white, what the sitters-in were doing, what various committees were doing, what disciplinary steps were being taken. Everyone on the campus was aware (for instance) that by 10 p.m. on 30 January 115 students had been summoned to attend the disciplinary committee; that at 6 p.m. on 2 February demonstrators in the administration building elected a new steering committee; that at 10 a.m. on 12 February a thirty-page report was issued on the case which had precipitated the sit-in; and that at 4.50 p.m. that day 'four truck loads of garbage were removed from the administration building, on grounds that the garbage constituted a fire hazard'. This bulletin neutralised much of the material being published from the demonstrators. But this was not all. Almost every day flysheets were issued, written by members of the staff or groups of students, commenting on the affair. Thus, as a riposte to the demand for amnesty, the chapel deans and the chaplains of the Episcopal, Roman Catholic, and Methodist churches signed a flysheet with these words:

> When Martin Luther King, Jr. supported civil disobedience, he did so by reminding us that '. . . an individual who breaks a law that conscience tells him is unjust . . . willingly accepts the penalty. . . .' We do not find this spirit prevailing in the present call for amnesty. On the contrary, the demand for amnesty indicates a lack of moral seriousness about the relation between acts and their consequences.

Other flysheets critical of amnesty were issued by members of the teaching staff. The demand for amnesty was (wrote O. J. Kleppa) 'a confession of moral impotence, an unwillingness to accept one of the basic ingredients of adult life'; and H. S. Bennett, in another flysheet, wrote '. . . I have recollection of the loud and heroic sounding trumpetings from persons entering the administration building for the sit-in. . . . Now they whine for amnesty, implying that they want to do away with all risk.' The cumulative effect of these flysheets and the daily chronology was to cut the demonstrators down to size, so that they appeared to be adolescents seeking a painless martyrdom; to reassure the public that the university had never lost the initiative, to minimise the risk of an emotional right-wing backlash (a danger in British universities too); and to build up a conviction in the minds of staff and students that tolerance, which allowed the students to occupy a building for over two weeks, without ejection by force and without calling in the police, was not a negative thing, an absence of convictions: it was a passionately held faith in human values. At the end of the affair the disciplinary committee announced its unanimous decisions over 126 students summoned to appear before it, and the *Chicago Tribune* ran a leading article headed 'A great university is true to itself'.[22]

Power and participation

We digressed from our theme to describe in some detail the manipulation of the student conscience by those who wish to disrupt universities not in order to improve them but to discredit them. We think it is important that this activity, which is a tumour in the student estate, should be clearly distinguished from the student conscience itself. The tumour is dangerous and must be eradicated, but the surgery must be delicate enough not to injure the student estate. For the social issues which mobilise student opinion into a collective conscience – apartheid, the homeless in Britain, the state of the Third World – are the concern of us all. It is arguable whether putting weed-killer on a rugby pitch to disconcert South African footballers, or squatting in a house in Piccadilly, or marching through Grosvenor Square, are the most effective ways to demonstrate concern; but there is no doubt that the British people would be less concerned about these issues if students did not sometimes do these extravagant things.

Inside universities there are similar areas of concern. All university teachers know that some curricula need revision, some teaching is poor, some methods of examination are capricious. Students do not know much about the skills needed for reform on any of these issues. But they are consumers of education; it is not essential to be a producer to judge the quality of the play. These issues are, or ought to be, a matter of common concern to teachers and students alike, though students can make only a limited contribution to their improvement. And again, the suspicion remains that some (not all) of the demonstrations of discontent which occurred in 1968 have quickened the concern of university authorities in these issues.

The issues of discontent inside universities, like those outside them, take extravagant forms. The invariable outcome of a demonstration on any of these issues is a demand for participation, which is a woolly word covering consultative committees at one end and 'student power' at the other. The *Union Nationale des Étudiants de France* mean by student power a student veto on all committees.[23] The Canadian Union of Students (perhaps in an aberrant moment) seems to share this interpretation.[24] Richard Atkinson, a student at the London School of Economics, interprets student power as 'parity of representation'.[25] The National Union of Students, at its conference in April 1969, mandated its executive to negotiate on the basis 'that on all governing bodies of colleges and universities there should normally be *one-third student representation. . .*'.[26] So 'student power' can mean anything from minority representation to majority control. Behind all its meanings there are unexamined assumptions about power in universities. If there is to be a stable understanding between universities and spokesmen for the student estate these assumptions about power must be examined.

For the assumptions at present are totally misconceived. Jack Straw, when he was president-elect of the N.U.S., delivered a lecture on student participation in higher education.[27] He did clearly distinguish between the three broad areas of participation: consultation, minority representation, and majority control, and came down clearly in favour of representation. He reviewed the arrangements for participation which followed the joint statement (we described it in Chapter 5) of the Committee of Vice-Chancellors and Principals and the N.U.S. in October 1968, and condemned them. Why? Because the participating students had experienced no 'transfer of power' to themselves or their constituents. Throughout his lecture the word 'power' recurs like a drum beat in a tattoo. 'The few who reign in our universities are so blinkered by the desire to maintain their own areas of power . . . Universities are engaged in a power retaining exercise.' 'But why', he says, 'have all these concessions not resulted in any change of power, in any real reform? Very simply, because the concessions have been based on the idea of student consultation, a concept which does not involve any transference of power from those who at present hold it. . . .' And: 'One of the ways in which university and college authorities have deluded themselves is by believing that reform is possible without a change in power.'

Straw appeals for 'straight talk and discussion' on the problems of control in educational institutions. There must have been a good deal of straight talk in a score of universities in the year 1968–9. Some of it has indeed been published.[28] But Straw's complaint is justified. Demands for student power are commonly countered by arguments – some sound, some dubious – to dissuade students away from voting membership of certain boards and committees. But the arguments do not, so far as we have discovered, dispel the misconceptions about power which practically all students (who are interested in the matter at all) seem to hold: namely that there are intense concentrations of power in universities.

Hence the common disillusionment. Straw puts it well:

> It is true, of course, that many student unions have gone beyond membership of mere consultative committees, and in an increasing number of cases are now directly represented on the governing body, academic board, university senate, or university council and their committees. But with a very few exceptions student members are few in number – rarely more than two on a board of thirty or more – and soon discover that the body upon which they sit, whilst constitutionally having power as the supreme decision maker, does not make decisions.

This statement is correct. But Straw's interpretation of it is incorrect. The disillusion is genuine (it was one of the wisest of academics, and one of the most sympathetic to students, Northrop Frye, who wrote: 'It takes patience to grant students everything that can be granted in the way of representation on decision-making bodies. . . . The reward of the patience is that students soon come to realize that these things are not what they want. . . .'). But this is not just because there are 'rarely more than two' students on a committee, nor is it because there is some crafty decision-making junta behind the façades of senates and councils. It is for a much simpler and more profound reason: that the power to make the decisions upon which universities really depend is so dispersed and diluted that no one, whether student or vice-chancellor, can get his hands on it. In a word, to talk about the power of the 'few who reign in our universities' is poppycock.

Consider what these decisions are. Universities exist to preserve, transmit and advance knowledge. To discharge these functions there require to be four basic categories of decision-making: what is taught? in what directions is knowledge to be advanced? who is to be taught? who is to teach? There are, in addition, important but supplementary decisions to be taken, such as certification for degrees and diplomas, the distribution of scarce resources such as money, buildings, and sites, and the provision of shelter, food and housing for those who belong to the university.

It is the first two categories of decision-making which are crucial. The central covenant on which universities stand is that it is the individual teacher and no one else who decides what he shall teach and in what direction he will advance knowledge. Any vice-chancellor or dean or committee who issued directives on these matters would be breaking the covenant. To entrust these two categories of decision-making to committees, whether there were students on them or not, would not be a 'transfer of power', it would be imposing power where none has existed before. This freedom has been won after centuries of struggle, from Galileo to those who refused to teach Lysenko's genetics or Hitler's theories of race. We know that some of those who reject the values of modern society also reject 'the tradition of liberal scholarship and academic freedom' and question what they call the 'legitimacy' of traditional university studies.[29] By all means let the content of courses be criticised by students; teachers are as responsive as anyone else to criticism. But to suggest that power over these activities should be exercised by committees of any sort would be implacably opposed; it would be the turn of the professors to make non-negotiable demands.

The other two basic categories of decision-making are who is to be taught and who is to teach: admissions and appointments. In neither of these matters is power concentrated. Admission in a big university rests with dozens of different departments (and in Oxford and Cambridge with dozens of admissions tutors in different colleges). There is no central co-ordination, or practically none. The criteria which determine whether one candidate is admitted to read chemistry and another to read English (or whether one candidate is admitted to Clare College and another to Peterhouse) are subject to no central constraint except the minimal entry requirements to the university. Accordingly, though little pockets of power, of a sort, are dispersed in dozens of corners of the university, they are limited to a very narrow segment of decision-making and are deliberately (for this is the ethos of university government) out of reach of the administration and its central committees. Over academic appointments there is a similar state of affairs. Since teachers, once appointed, have a freedom to think and teach and write which is unusual among persons receiving salaries from public funds, they have to be chosen with care. It is again part of the ethos of university government that while some central body (council or senate) may formally appoint a university teacher, it is done only on the initiative of one of what may be scores of small, independent and unco-ordinated committees of experts. In some universities (Cambridge is an example) the independent committees have the final say in most appointments. Electors to professorships, for example, simply write out after their meeting an announcement of the election and have it pinned up on the notice board. No 'authority' in the university – senate, council, or board – is required to approve the election.

No wonder students in search of power fail to find it. Of course the central bodies on which they sit, or demand to sit, do make decisions, some of them important decisions. But they are made always on the advice of experts. It is a basic principle of university government that initiative for decision-making begins at the grass roots, among individual teachers, or small consultative committees with (so it is thought) no 'power', and decisions seep upwards as recommendations to be approved, not downwards as directives to be obeyed. Councils and senates, like the house of lords, can delay legislation; they cannot originate it or (usually) even amend it. Their strongest sanction is to send it back for reconsideration.

We do not want to create the impression that these governing bodies never do anything that matters and that a student therefore should not wish to sit on them. They provide the stage props but they are not the play. They have to decide between competitive claims for inadequate funds and this may well determine whether (for instance) scarce resources should be used to establish a department of sociology or strengthen the department of physics. But since the members of the governing body may only fortuitously know anything about either of these subjects, the body will inevitably depend upon the advice it gets from experts. The members of the governing body therefore have to act in a judicial capacity, not as representatives of interests, still less as mandated representatives. Of course a few fail to live up to this responsibility; bias is not unknown on the senate any more than it is on the bench; but it is rare. And of course some professors play at academic politics, just as some divines play at politics in the church; but that is rare too. Straw quotes the (hypothetical) chairman of the committee on priorities who asserts that 'no-one represents *anything* on this committee'. Straw calls this a 'patently hypocritical argument', which 'reflects the façade but not the reality of university life'. He is wrong, because he does not know. This, paradoxically, is the strongest argument for including a student on a committee of priorities: it would dispel ignorance; and to do this is, after all, one of the purposes of a university.

So we return to our theme. The student estate can, in our view, contribute usefully to university government. But, despite nearly a century of growth of corporate student opinion, students still have much to learn about how this contribution can be made. It is partly the university's fault that they have not learnt sooner. The first lesson to be learnt is one we have already mentioned: that effective participation – whether it is by teachers or taught – is not through power, it is through influence; not by counting votes but by weighing words.

Student participation, in one form or another, goes back to the middle ages, and we have described its halting growth from the nineteenth century. During the years 1967–9 there was a leap forward: all British universities made arrangements for participation or extended the arrangements they already had. The concordat between vice-chancellors and the N.U.S. defined what was believed to be the extent and kind of participation on which the two sides could agree, but it was a pragmatic document which did not examine the nature of authority in universities and hence did not give reasons for the grounds on which students could or should share in this authority.

The precondition for running a hospital is that the beds should be occupied by patients who come to be treated, and that the medical and nursing staff should be competent to provide the treatment the patients need. The status of a student in a university differs from that of a patient in a hospital; but there is something in common between them. The precondition for running a university is that the places should be occupied by students who come to learn, and that the teaching staff should be competent to provide the education the students need. Both the doctor–patient and the teacher–student relationship require at the minimum a voluntary consensus about the purpose of the institution they have voluntarily entered. And this presupposes a clear and limited demarcation of authority; clear, because if doctors and professors do not know more than patients and students, there is no point in having hospitals or universities at all: patients and students might as well stay at home. And a limited authority, because the only expertise of doctor or professor which patient or student is obliged to acknowledge is in the expertise which brings the two together. Outside this expertise neither doctor nor professor can claim any authority.

Beyond this, the analogy between patient and student breaks down, for all the patient wants from the doctor is a cure, whereas the student wants to acquire the expertise of his professor. This is a peculiar expertise, comprising two components. It is necessary to be familiar with the orthodoxy of the subject – in plain words, to know a lot about what has been written – and it is necessary to apply to this orthodoxy a disciplined dissent, questioning facts and assumptions, and so transforming yesterday's truth into tomorrow's discarded hypothesis. A student cannot be taught this art of dissent unless he is encouraged to stand up to his teacher, even to resist his teacher's views. It is not for nothing that medieval universities taught through disputations. It follows that students have rights and responsibilities resembling those of an apprentice in a guild. This, as we wrote in our introduction, is

143

reflected in the charters of universities. There is, therefore, a responsibility upon students to accept the purpose of the university, as a place which exists so that those who know more can transmit knowledge and the techniques of scholarship to those who know less. And, provided the responsibility is accepted, there is a corresponding right to dispute in the university not only about knowledge itself, but about the way it is taught, examined, packaged, and stored.

So we come to the case for participation. We remind the reader that we are now not considering the students who wish to use the university as a base for mini-revolutions or extra-parliamentary opposition, nor the students who cherish misconceived ambitions of power, nor even the busybody student politician who relishes committees in the way other students relish music or chess; we are considering students who, having been told at matriculation addresses that they are joining a community of scholars, take this announcement seriously. Some of their unscrupulous fellow-students are – as we have already described – anxious to mobilise their conscience for ends which would damage the university. It is up to the university to secure their confidence and to enlist their loyalty.

The case for participation by students like these can be stated simply. First, it benefits the university, because it provides clear and swiftly flowing channels of communication which help teachers to teach better and students to learn better; this is the experience of every teacher who has encouraged feed-back from his students. Second, to take part in some decision-making is a valuable education, and the university should not let this opportunity run to waste; most senior academics who have run staff–student committees testify to their educational value. Third, it is folly to pretend that any constraint except self-constraint will, in the long run, preserve cohesion between the student estate and the universities; the perpetual threat of disciplinary sanctions would be intolerable. To draw students into the decision-making process achieves two ends: it gives them the information without which consent would be meaningless; and it is an initiation into the democratic process.

But participation is an art and it must be practised according to conventions and rules. This is a statement which arouses deep suspicion among students. So it is not sufficient to enunciate the conventions and rules: they must be explained. The first point which needs to be explained is why university business – and student union business for that matter – cannot be conducted by open democracy, with 'unstructured' meetings of staff and students, listening to speeches designed to coerce rather than to inform, and then reaching policy decisions often by no more than a show of hands, which mandate their leaders. The reader may be surprised that this mode of government should be proposed at all for academic communities. But it is already the practice of some unions (e.g. that at the London School of Economics); it commands wide support among left-wing students and staff; and it was adopted at the Sorbonne in the summer of 1968.[30]

The attraction of open democracy is that all members of the community are involved and, if they reach a consensus, they experience the exhilarations of mass solidarity and corporate responsibility.[31] But open democracy 'presupposes equality of competence to judge of issues concerning the common welfare, equality of access to information, etc. ... Its prerequisites would seem to be a relatively large area of implicit and unquestioned agreement, and a limited complexity or frequency of issues requiring resolution. ... Its difficulties are to elicit a consensus of rational judgement ... to sift inequalities of judgement, experience, commitment, responsibility. ... Its dangers are confusion and loss of coherence ... inconsistency from decision to decision, irresponsibility or apathy, control or manipulation by an ideologically homogeneous or organised or vocal ... or tenacious minority.'

University communities are not consistent with these presuppositions and prerequisites. The issues are extremely complex; there is not, as between students and teachers, a large area of implicit and unquestioned agreement. And – as we have already emphasised – the basic responsibilities in universities are so widely dispersed among individuals that they should never come before open meetings for decision at all.

Lesson one, therefore, is that university government cannot effectively be conducted by open democracy. The alternative democratic process is indirect, representative democracy. This also seeks to achieve agreed rational ends by participation. But it assumes that there exists in the group a great diversity of desires and a great inequality in judgement and experience. Its machinery 'aims to elicit, implement and maintain coherent rational decisions on common welfare ... out of that multi-levelled aggregate of discontents, desires, demands and purposes, some widely shared, profound, reasoned or powerful, some narrowly sectional, momentary, fashionable, irresponsible or unreflective'. In this pattern of democratic government the electorate acknowledges that its representatives are better informed than are their constituents. It entrusts to its representatives some degree of autonomy and discretion of judgement. It realises that there has to be consistency and coherence of direction and pace in the development of policies. The prerequisites for this form of government are mutual trust between the electorate and its representatives, and the assurance that from time to time (but not so frequently as to destroy all sense of direction) the representatives can be ejected and replaced by others. Its dangers are 'that feelings of identification, participation, and commitment are relaxed, and may be diminished to the point of apathy or alienation'; in short, a 'we-and-they' attitude may be driven between the electorate and its representatives.

In the last two or three years it has been said hundreds of times that a university is not a mini-state, and the patterns of political institutions do not apply to universities. This is true, but there is nevertheless a similarity between the problems raised by the inequalities acknowledged in indirect democracy and those raised by the inequalities acknowledged in universities. The minister of health knows more about the health service than his constituents, but his constituents have the right to criticise hospitals and the minister fails in his duty if he disregards the criticisms. The professor of economics knows more economics than his students do, but they, too, have the right to criticise and he has the duty to take account of their criticisms. For the exercise of these rights it is not enough to have channels of comment – deputations bearing petitions and the like: there must be channels of action. It is the lack of these channels of action which has provoked students (in some art colleges, for instance) to cut channels for themselves. On these grounds (and for the purely educational reasons we have already mentioned), we believe that government by representative democracy, modified to take account of the peculiar structure of authority inherent in the purpose of universities, is the best way to conduct academic government; with one reservation: that since most students come to the university to study, not to participate, they must not be under any obligation to participate. Apathy is to be preferred to misinformed or reluctant participation. So students must be free to opt out of student government, and the university must guarantee this freedom. But, with this reservation, representatives of the student estate should have the opportunity to take some responsibility for decision-making in academic affairs.

This much is already commonly conceded. But there remain several difficulties about student membership of boards and committees which need to be resolved. One difficulty is the widespread belief among students that their representatives must be mandated and should be recalled if they do not achieve the purpose for which they were elected. This belief arises from a misconception of what governing bodies and their committees actually do, and (as was evident from the comment which we quoted from Jack Straw on p. 140) a misjudgement of the capacity in which other members of governing bodies and committees serve. Thus a student (or for that matter a teacher) who is elected to, let us say, a university senate, must understand – and his constituents must understand – that he serves the university, not any section of it. Although he must be familiar with the views of his constituents, he must remain completely free to contribute his own views, based on his own judgement, to the senate.

Another difficulty is the contrast between the way business is conducted on a university senate, and the way some student representatives want it to be conducted. A comment made by two student representatives after they had attended their first senate meeting was 'we were suppressed by the agenda'. It is easy to understand what they meant. A typical senate agenda might run to 100 or more pages. It includes reports from faculty boards; recommendations from appointments committees; requests for supplementary allocations to pay for an additional technician and a *Lektor* in German and a computer-programmer; funds to be authorised for the conversion of an office into a dark room for an electron-microscope; and a 'background paper' to help the senate to decide whether geology or economics should have priority in the building programme. This is not what the students hoped for at all. They would like to plunge into discussion about what sort of economics should be taught, what use computers should be put to, and whether students can switch from history to law, or migrate to other universities for part of their undergraduate course. In brief, they hoped for something between a debate, a seminar, and a commission on the pattern of higher education; and they have to learn that if the senate spends time discussing 'fundamentals', then the *Lektor* will not be appointed, the faculty board reports will not be acted upon, the dark room will not be made, the building programme will collapse. The statutory boards and committees have to discharge masses of business, much of it dull and trivial, but essential nonetheless; there is no time to raise matters not on the agenda, or points of procedure, and certainly no time to wallow in philosophical dialogue about what the university is for. This is not to say that these matters do not need to be discussed; on the contrary, one of the weaknesses of senates is that they too rarely plot their course by the stars. But day-to-day business has to be done; that is what senates and faculty boards are for, and this swallows up all the time which most academics are prepared to give to boards and committees. What students want is a continuing commission in which the university continually checks its course to the far horizon. Hence one frustration among student representatives.

A further frustration and difficulty arises from the conventions which senior academics – often unwittingly – follow at meetings of boards and committees. If everyone were to speak the business would never be concluded. Therefore many members remain silent. They may remain silent even if some proposal is made which is profoundly distasteful to them, knowing either that it is not a 'starter' or that if it comes to a vote it will be turned down. Student representatives may therefore put up a suggestion (one of us has often witnessed this) which *appears* to be acceptable; only to find out afterwards that most senior members of the committee would not entertain it for a moment; and yet they remained silent. Or the chairman, realising that a proposal may become less controversial if a decision on it is postponed, will (deliberately) refrain from putting it to the vote; or a clear-cut plan may be trimmed and modified so that it is agreed by consensus instead of being forced through in its original form on a majority vote. These are all conventions, perfectly well understood by experts, which are often necessary if the conduct of business by boards and committees is to be tolerable at all. But the conventions are not familiar to students, who suspect sharp practice, and who want the members to accost one another in argument and to vote on every issue. Students, in brief, reject the diplomacy of evasion and the tactics of ambiguity. They demand that differences should be emphasised, not covered by an icing of genial urbanity. So (as one of us recollects) a joint staff–student meeting which reaches a consensus on some issue (such as a new disciplinary code) without a vote and without much wrangling is considered by some inexperienced student representatives to be far less 'successful' than a head-on collision of views ending in an impasse!

Student representatives on academic bodies, therefore, must agree not to be mandated, to serve the whole university and not their constituents only, to submit themselves to the heavy agenda and to keep 'fundamental' discussions for special *ad hoc* committees appointed for that purpose. They must not expect that much will be decided by votes. Power, in so far as there is much of it on committees, resides in the convincing statement, not the number of hands raised. So to condemn the presence of two students on a board of thirty as 'token' representation is nonsense. One of us recollects a student representative on the governing body of the University of Sydney who was so persuasive, and so well informed, that ten minutes' advocacy from him was worth a dozen votes.

It is therefore both honest and proper for universities to insist that it is quality of representation, not quantity, which matters, and to resist pressure to put up the bids (as the N.U.S. has recently done) for numerical representation on committees.[32] Pressure of this kind is damaging to reform. It looks like a bid for 'power', and it generates from some senior academics a counter-pressure of compromises: to insist that students should be present only as observers without votes, or that student representatives should be excluded from a good deal of the business. These compromises are as objectionable and as short-sighted as the pressures for more numerical representation, for two reasons. First, they are bad educationally, for they confer on students a right (to attend meetings) without a corresponding responsibility (to be involved in decisions). Second, they are bad politically, for they resemble episodes during the twilight of colonial rule, when responsibility was given so grudgingly that even its benefits were resented. Much better if the university begins as it means to end, giving the student estate such rights and responsibilities as are compatible with the university's authority (we turn to this topic in a moment) and holding student representatives as responsible as any other committee members for the consequences of their decisions. But, if student participation is to be successful, academics will have to anticipate the difficulties we have described, and others too; and, once and for all, myths about the location of power in universities will have to be dispelled. How to solve these difficulties is a matter of controversy. Our own view (based on the experience of student participation which one of us has had for thirty years in four universities) is that students derive little benefit from membership of the central statutory bodies which have to trans-act the university's day-to-day housekeeping; but they may derive much benefit, and have much to contribute, by full membership of committees which have authority to act and to which matters within their experience are delegated. And we do well not to be patronising about what is 'within their experience'. The naïve question sometimes strips from the adult mind deeply rooted assumptions. And there is no doubt that as one grows older and more experienced one asks fewer naïve questions.

Authority in the university

The essential powers inside a university are, or ought to be, so dis-persed among its academic staff that they cannot be concentrated into the hands of a few. A university's powers *outside* its own walls are not the theme of this book, but we digress for a moment to make one assertion, namely that the price which a university pays for acquiring power outside its walls is loss of freedom. If the university, as a corporate body, puts its weight behind any pressure group in society or any political party (as both our ancient universities have done in the past) it compromises its freedom.[33] There may be times when it is necessary to do this (the attitude of the Open universities of South Africa to apartheid is a case in point). But the price has to be paid all the same; their freedom is in jeopardy.

The exercise of power is repugnant to a university, both in its internal business and in its external relations. But not the exercise of authority. Authority is an essential attribute of a university; and if the present crisis in universities were to be described in one sentence, it would be this: Universities are victims of the world-wide revolt against all authority; they suffer more than other institutions because this is a revolt of youth, and universities specialise in youth; and, finally, their suffering is aggravated because universities are not clear just what the limits of their authority are. Let us examine these propositions.

The revolt against authority surges around our everyday life: wildcat strikers defy trade unions, priests dispute the ruling of the roman church, students protest against universities, football crowds stampede referees. Those entrusted with authority find themselves in a dilemma; they know that the right way to deal with the revolt is to discover and expose its deep and invisible causes, but they have to deal with the immediate and visible problem of preserving law and order. And the psychological effect on those in authority of having to preserve law and order in universities may take two forms, both undesirable: it may harden them to resist any change, or it may drive them to make unpremeditated changes under duress in order to restore peace. All universities which have experienced revolts against authority know that the main embarrassment is not the revolt (we can now plot the course of that and we are beginning to know how to control it): it is the polarisation of the dons into hawks and doves; in other words, it is an ambivalence about authority within the academic profession itself. One institution issued a leaflet of advice on sit-ins which ended with the wise words: 'Listen patiently to your hawks and doves but do not be influenced by their advice.'

The revolt against authority is a treasure-trove of research for sociologists; they could almost be forgiven for relishing a sit-in in the way a botanist could relish the volcanic eruption of Krakatoa. But sociologists

150

are not competent to solve that aspect of the problem which is the most important for academics, namely how to redefine the nature of the authority in universities against which students are revolting. We have discussed at length the rights and responsibilities of the student estate. But a university is a society of masters and scholars. The masters have rights and responsibilities too, and their prime responsibility is to uphold the authority of the university.

The authority of the university rests on two articles of faith, the supremacy of reason and disciplined imagination for solving intellectual problems, and (as Raymond Aron called it) the moral code of liberalism. Both these articles of faith are under attack; the New Left challenges what it calls their legitimacy. They are illegitimate because they seem to have failed to make the 'civilised' world a just and loving community. The urgent problems of society, some of the young say, are not intellectual and therefore reason is 'irrelevant' for their solution. The moral code of liberalism, they say, has not saved society from massive immorality. Hence the search for activities which do not require the austere exercise of reason or technique, through spontaneous self-expression in drama and art and in free or anti-universities. Hence, too, the rejection of the moral code of liberalism and the denigration of tolerance.

Revolutionaries denounce political systems, but they are really fumbling for a new ethic, not a new party. Their indictment is against the values of western society. They are not much concerned about the way universities are run; they are concerned with what universities stand for. They believe universities stand for values which have betrayed mankind; they would be content to see universities, in their present form, go the way of the monasteries (tourists visiting the empty skeletons of Magdalen or Trinity as at present they visit Fountains Abbey).

If universities were to abandon these two articles of faith this is precisely what would happen to them. Reason and the moral code of liberalism cannot alone save society. Passion, compassion, wisdom: these are essential but they are acquired by living in society, not by listening to lectures. And it is on these lines that universities must defend their authority. It is not their duty to provide moral panaceas for a sick society; they cannot be all things to all men. Their limited function is to remain dedicated to an activity which has already proved to be of incalculable benefit to mankind, namely the exercise of reason and imagination upon intellectual problems. This is their essential contribution to society and they should be implacably opposed to pressures to deflect them from this function. Universities are specialised institutions competent nowadays only to cultivate the intellect. (We write 'nowadays' deliberately, for this has not always been so. When universities and colleges were religious foundations they had a double function and chose their teachers accordingly. Today piety is not a quality which counts in the appointment of teachers.)

The rejection of the moral code of liberalism is also something which universities should implacably oppose. The code stands for a critical detachment from the immediate purposes and values of society, toleration of diverse points of view, recognition of a pluralism of values. It is alleged by some left-wing critics that universities have already broken this moral code by attaching themselves to the 'military industrial complex'. Universities (these critics say) are not detached; they share the assumptions of a consumer society. They are not disinterested; they accept tied funds for research. They allow diversity, but only a marginal amount which will not rock the academic boat. Their tolerance is a flabby acquiescence in the ills of society: it allows deviationists to talk but not to act. And so on; all (in our view) a travesty of the state of affairs in British universities, which although of course they are influenced by the values of the society they serve, have preserved their critical detachment with great vigour.[34] Other left-wing critics do not accuse universities of breaking the moral code of liberalism: they reject the code itself, and seek to impose on the university a socialist-value monism in place of a liberal-value pluralism. They would, if they had their way, shackle the university with rigid ideologies, refusing to allow intellectuals to have, as it were, visas to cross the frontiers of some new orthodoxy. Even in communist countries the moral code of liberalism gains a foothold in universities: no Soviet politician would now dare to declare that relativity or genetics are heretical.

Reason, and the moral code of liberalism. Faith in these values means that a university works on the hypothesis that the minds of any of its members, senior or junior, can be changed, without compulsion or duress, by evidence, reason, and logical argument. This constitutes what Northrop Frye, in a brilliant essay, has called the educational contract.[35] Authority in the university rests on the educational contract. Its purpose is not to preserve the *status quo*; it is precisely the opposite: it is to leave the options open for change. Universities *as institutions* often show deplorable inertia, but the really first-class scholar is a pacemaker for change. He creates a controlled revolution of thought in his own subject. This in turn may create a controlled revolution in society, as Einstein's work did, and Freud's. To choose reason and the moral code of liberalism as articles of faith for universities is not a matter of making the best choice among several systems; it is inconceivable that the accumulation, transmission and advancement of knowledge could go on in any other way. Hence the need for academics to defend the authority of the university in society without compromise. A university which does not assume that it has this kind of authority will lose the confidence of its students. A student who is unwilling to recognise this authority has enrolled under false pretences.

But it is a limited authority; professors are clever men, but often only in the subjects which they profess. They have no special authority in political or public affairs. ('Better to be governed', said one cynical don, 'by the first hundred persons in the Cambridge telephone directory than by the faculties of the University.') Nor is wisdom more likely to be found among professors than among plumbers; possibly less likely, for wisdom is inhibited by pedantry and plumbers are never pedantic. Nor have professors any special authority in establishing moral values, and this brings us to the unsolved problem with which we end this book. Some of the sincere revolt against authority is a rejection of present moral values and a search for new ones. Guidance in this search lies outside the legitimate authority of the modern university. Yet it is a search which becomes the first priority for some of the most gifted undergraduates. It determines their attitude to academic issues. For instance, much of their objection to specialisation and single-subject honours degrees, when they are cross-examined about it, is seen to be a complaint not against specialisation, but against a curriculum which does not put academic studies into their human context. It is twenty years since Moberly criticised British universities because they would, as he put it, teach students how to make bombs or cathedrals, but would not teach them which of these objects they ought to make.[36] It is arguable that this is something students should be left to decide for themselves, not to get at second-hand from their teachers. But Moberly's criticism is still valid. One hidden cause for frustration in the student estate is that many teachers have not made up their own minds on issues like these. Perhaps this is what the Paris students meant when they scrawled the slogan 'ears have walls'. It is not a negligible fact that it needs a moral issue to precipitate a serious student protest.

Moberly's criticism is not easy to meet. The days are long past when a university teacher believed that what he taught should be not only accurate but edifying; in any case experience of life cannot be transmitted between generations. But there is a case, much stronger than it was when Moberly wrote, for universities to do something; for today some students are asking whether this kind of help can be integrated into the academic tradition. It was reported in the press in 1968 that in one of the new British universities a group of students were demanding to be taught 'life' instead of literature, history or science. On the face of it, a puerile and silly remark, which was sneered at by critics. But it is a remark worth pursuing, for to pursue it may be to compel the students who make it to do some clear thinking. The very assertion (which we quoted some pages earlier) that traditional university studies have lost their 'legitimacy' presupposes that the concept of legitimacy is accepted. What studies, then, *are* legitimate? We listen, so far in vain, for a reply. But the remark is a sign of hunger: a demand that during these three years between school and the responsibilities of life the university should offer something more than an aseptic diet of knowledge and technique; hunger for a diet which cannot be defined.

What can be done? By individual university teachers who have themselves wrestled with Moberly's question, a great deal, especially by listening. But what can be done by universities as corporations? Nothing very dramatic or very original, but three modest things could be done:

(i) Students feel more secure when universities assert their authority over the limited field where they can claim sovereignty, that is, over intellectual matters. In this field they must be uncompromising about the need for detachment in scholarship; impatient with those who choose to come to universities and yet who profess to despise the intellectual approach; relentless against any who try to resolve issues by disruption or force and not by reason and persuasion; unforgiving toward intolerance and bigotry. So in this field the university should declare its authority.

(ii) Students can be shown how they can acquire some moral principles from the curriculum, whatever the subject. For the very discipline of scholarship carries its own ethical values. To follow the facts where they lead requires courage, for the scholar may be obliged to jettison some cherished belief in the face of new facts. To have to submit one's work to an international community where it may be upset by a junior colleague or by someone in a far country, black or yellow, christian or hindu, requires a sense of equality which disregards seniority or race. To see one's own work become outdated and regarded by one's own pupils as error requires humility. These are the virtues of authority in scholarship. And they are virtues not imposed by the old upon the young. They are inherent in the structure of

154

modern science and scholarship; learning could not be organised in any other way.

(iii) These two measures alone will not satisfy the conscience of the student estate. There has to be a third, the most difficult: an assurance that intellectual detachment is not inconsistent with concern for humanity. 'What we have to determine', wrote Northrop Frye, 'is to what extent concern is a scholarly virtue, and whether or not it is, like detachment, a precondition of knowledge.'[37] The conscience of the student estate may already be determining this for us. It is concern which unites the more sensitive members of the student estate to the rest of their generation. They will not break this tie. Practical evidence of their concern for society is of course something for students to work out for themselves; they must not expect paternalism on this any more than on other issues. There are welcome signs that the National Union of Students may act for the student estate by organising large-scale community action.[38] But the students who display this social concern still need to be assured that the scholarly virtues of objective study and intellectual detachment can coexist with concern for humanity. They fear that detachment really means indifference and objectivity means impersonality. If this fear is not dispelled mistrust and cynicism about the educational contract may spread into an epidemic of anti-intellectualism. It is an essential task of university teachers to dispel this fear. The authority of the university for the rest of this century may well depend on the concern for humanity among its teachers.

Documents

Memorial of the students' representative councils of the Universities of St Andrews, Glasgow, Aberdeen and Edinburgh to members of H.M.G. on the Universities (Scotland) bill, 1888[*]

    i. Hon. secretary, S.R.C., University of Edinburgh, to the marquis of Lothian, secretary for Scotland [S.R.O.: GD 40/16/20 f. 41]

My Lord   10 May 1888

The Representative Councils of the Scottish Universities hoped for an opportunity of formally approaching your Lordship by deputation, on the matter of a Memorial anent the Scottish Universities Bill. Having been informed that your Lordship will not visit Scotland during the Whitsuntide Recess, they desire to formally approach the Lord Advocate, if an opportunity can be got. At the same time they desire that your Lordship, as our Lord Rector, should have brought personally before you the grounds of the memorial which we propose to submit to the members of Her Majesty's Government connected with the Scottish Universities. I am therefore desired to request the favour of a brief interview with your Lordship on Thursday the 17th inst, at which date I hope to be in London.

I have the honour to be
Your Lordship's obedient servant
[sgd] S. William Carruthers
Hon: Secretary

Minuted: Telegraphed will endeavour to grant interview between one & two on Thursday 15. May. 1888.

    ii. President, S.R.C., University of Edinburgh, to the marquis of Lothian, secretary for Scotland [S.R.O.: GD 40/16/20 f. 44]

My Lord,   15 May 1888

I have now the honour to enclose for your Lordship's perusal the Memorial of the Students Representative Councils of the Scottish

★ See above, p. 26.

Universities with respect to the Universities Bill, referred to in the letter of the Secretary of this Council to you dated the 10th inst.

The Memorial is the outcome of much anxious deliberation on the part of the councils whose unanimous opinion it now embodies. Without desiring unduly to push forward students interests they have thought it best to frame a complete statement of the amendments on the Bill desirable from a student standpoint. The desire to make the Memorial clear and complete has necessarily made it somewhat lengthy but the Memorialists trust it may receive your favourable consideration.

They are the more encouraged to hope for this since they recognize that the express recognition already accorded to the Representative Councils in the Bill is due to you as its author, and the kind consideration your Lordship has displayed to the Students of Edinburgh University as their Lord Rector gives the Edinburgh Students Council the greater confidence in appealing to you in this matter so vitally affecting their interests.

I am, my Lord,
Your obedient Servant
[sgd] A. H. B. Constable
President, Edin. Univ. S.R.C.

Minuted: Ackd 17.5.88.
Enclosure:

TO THE RIGHT HONOURABLE

THE CHANCELLOR OF THE EXCHEQUER, THE CHIEF SECRETARY FOR IRELAND, THE SECRETARY FOR SCOTLAND, THE LORD ADVOCATE, AND THE SOLICITOR-GENERAL FOR SCOTLAND

THE MEMORIAL

OF

THE STUDENTS' REPRESENTATIVE COUNCILS OF THE UNIVERSITIES OF ST. ANDREWS, GLASGOW, ABERDEEN, AND EDINBURGH.

WHEREAS a Bill intituled 'An Act for the Better Administration and Endowment of the Universities of Scotland' has been introduced into Parliament by Her Majesty's Government,—

AND WHEREAS the said Bill very deeply affects the welfare and interests of the present and future Students of the Scottish Universities,—

AND WHEREAS the Memorialists, while expressing their cordial approval of the enlightened spirit in which, upon the whole, the demands for University Reform have been met by the provisions of the Bill, and while especially expressing their satisfaction that in the Bill the Students' Representative Councils have for the first time received express recognition, are nevertheless humbly of opinion that the interests of the Students have not been sufficiently recognised or safeguarded by the provisions of the Bill,—

AND WHEREAS the practical working of University Institutions is a matter of at least as great and direct importance to the Students of the University as to the General Council, upon which important powers were conferred by the Universities Act of 1858, and which powers are by this Bill sought to be confirmed and increased:—

The Memorialists therefore desire respectfully to call the attention of the members of Her Majesty's Government connected with Scottish Universities to various respects in which they submit the Bill should be amended, especially with a view to securing, by providing for direct election of Students' representatives, a more truly representative character to various bodies in the University whose constitutions are proposed to be altered by the provisions of the Bill, and also with a view of securing to the Students' Representative Councils, to be regulated as hereinafter suggested, the right of access to, and of having laid before them the Ordinances framed by, the various bodies to whom, by the Bill, the future government of the Universities is to be entrusted. For these reasons, and with these among other objects, the Memorialists beg respectfully to suggest that the Bill should be amended in the following respects:—

I.—By providing for increased Student Representation in the University Court.

Of the University Courts as at present constituted, Students' representatives form in no case less than one-fourth part. By the new Bill the number of members of each of the Courts will be more than doubled, and the Memorialists submit that the Students are entitled to a proportional increase in representatives. The Memorialists would therefore suggest that, in addition to the Rector and his Assessor, as provided for in the Bill, two Assessors should be directly elected by the Students' Representative Councils, their term of office to be three years, and to be so regulated that one election shall be held in each year in which no Rectorial election takes place.

II.—By providing for Student Representation on Standing Committees.

By Section 6, Subsection 7, of the Bill, the power is conferred upon the University Court of appointing one-third of the members of any Standing Committees charged by Ordinance of the Commissioners with the immediate superintendence of any libraries or museums, and by Section 7, Subsection 2, power is conferred upon the Senatus of appointing the remaining two-thirds. While not wishing unduly to interfere in these matters, the Memorialists submit that there are many minor details which, while not worth separate representations from the Students' Representative Councils, are cumulatively of great importance to Students, by whom the Museums and Libraries are mostly used, and these might be brought before such Committees by Students' representatives sitting thereon; and they therefore suggest the addition of a new Section to the Bill after Section 8, giving to the Representative Councils the right of appointing one-sixth of the members of all such Committees.

III.—By defining the relations between the Commissioners on the one hand, and the Students' Representative Council and Students generally on the other.

(a) *The Commissioners should be empowered to fix the constitution and regulate the powers of the Representative Council.*

In view of the recognition of the Representative Councils in the Bill, and the advisability, as herein suggested, of assigning to them a definite part in the Government of the Universities, the Memorialists consider it would be only just that these bodies should submit to Statutory regulation. By Section 14, Subsection 3, of the Bill, the Commissioners are empowered to regulate the powers, jurisdictions, and privileges of various bodies in the University, among which the Representative Councils are not included. The Memorialists therefore suggest that a new Clause should be added to Section 14 of the Bill empowering the Commissioners to fix the constitution and manner of election, and to regulate the powers, jurisdictions, and privileges of the Representative Councils.

(b) *The Commissioners should be expressly empowered to examine Students.*

By Section 14 of the Bill the Commissioners appointed under the Act are empowered to call before them certain members of the University to examine them before making Ordinances for certain purposes, and among these Students are not expressly included. The Bill no doubt seems to contemplate the Representative Councils making direct representations to the Commissioners; but the Memorialists submit that, considering the vast importance to Students of regulations, for example, regarding the organisation of studies or conditions of graduation, it would be more satisfactory were Students expressly inserted among the members of the University to be examined with a view to the framing of such Regulations by the Commissioners.

(c) *The Commissioners should be required to communicate Draft Ordinances to the Representative Councils.*

By Section 17, Subsections 2 and 3, of the Bill, it is provided that the Commissioners shall submit Drafts of proposed Ordinances to the Court, the Senatus, and the General Council, who shall within three months thereafter have the right of lodging objections or amendments thereto. The Memorialists submit that such Ordinances, which must in almost all cases affect Students' interests, should also be communicated to the Representative Councils, and a like power conferred on them of lodging objections thereto.

(d) *The Representative Councils should have the right of petitioning Her Majesty in Council.*

By Section 18, Subsection 2, of the Bill, it is provided that within one month of the publication of any Ordinance in the Gazette, the Court, Senatus, General Council, or other body or person directly affected thereby, may petition Her Majesty in Council to withhold her approval from such Ordinance. Upon the same grounds as those given above, the Memorialists submit that a similar right of petitioning should be conferred upon the Representative Councils.

IV.—By defining the relations between the University Court and the Students' Representative Council.

(a) *The Court should be specially empowered to consider all Overtures made to it by the Representative Council.*

By Section 6, Subsection 2, of the Bill, power is conferred on the Court to take into consideration all overtures and reports made to it by the Senatus and General Council, and return deliverances thereon. The Memorialists gratefully acknowledge the courtesy recently extended by the University Courts to the Representative Councils in this direction; but they submit that the right of bringing matters affecting Students' interests before the Court in this way is too important to be left to the courtesy of the Court, and should be expressly recognised in the Bill.

(b) The University Court should communicate Draft Ordinances to the Representative Council.

By Section 19, Subsection 2, of the Bill, it is provided that upon the expiration of the powers of the Commissioners the Court shall have power to frame Ordinances which shall be submitted to the Senatus and General Council, whose opinion thereon, if returned within one month, shall be taken into consideration. The Memorialists submit that it should be provided that such Ordinances should also be communicated to the Representative Councils, with a like provision, for their opinion being taken into consideration.

V.—By defining the relations between the Senatus Academicus and the Students' Representative Council.

The Senatus should be specially empowered to consider all Overtures made to it by the Representative Council.

The Memorialists, while also gratefully acknowledging the courtesy hitherto shown by the Senatus, submit that, for reasons similar to those given above, a new clause should be added to Section 7 of the Bill (which defines the new powers of the Senatus), making the same regulations with regard to overtures and reports to be submitted to the Senatus by the Representative Councils as they have above submitted should be inserted with regard to overtures made to the Court.

VI.—By referring to the consideration of the Commissioners to be appointed under the Act the body by whom Professorial appointments should be made.

By Section 6, Subsection 4, of the Bill, power is conferred upon the Court of appointing all Professors whose Chairs are, or may come to be, in the patronage of the University, and also of appointing Examiners and Intra-mural Lecturers, and of recognising Extra-mural Lecturers. While expressing no opinion as to the University Court being or not being the best possible body in which to vest the power of making such appointments, the Memorialists submit that on account of the paramount importance of securing the best qualified men to fill the University Chairs and other posts, the mode of appointing Professors, Examiners, and Lecturers, should not be absolutely fixed by the Bill, but that it should be left as a subject of inquiry by the Commissioners whether the appointment to each Professorial Chair, Examinership, Tutorship, or Lectureship, whether at present vested in the Crown, Curators, corporate or other bodies, or in private individuals, should not be vested in a Board specially selected and qualified to judge the merits of candidates, both as teachers and as specialists. The Memorialists therefore suggest that a clause to that effect should be added to Section 14 of the Bill, which defines the powers of the Commissioners, and that Subsection 4 of Section 6 of the Bill should be deleted.

In the name and by order of the Students' Representative Councils of the Universities of St. Andrews, Glasgow, Aberdeen, and Edinburgh,—

For the St. Andrews University Students' Repersentative Council,
[sgd] Thomas Patton Milne, President
For the Glasgow University Students' Representative Council,
[sgd] Chas. E. Robertson, President
For the Aberdeen University Students' Representative Council,
[sgd] William Mackie, President
For the Edinburgh University Students' Representative Council,
[sgd] A. H. B. Constable⎫
Wm Lyon Mackenzie⎬ Presidents
Daniel J. Kuys⎭

Statement by the Students' Representative Council of the University of Edinburgh to the Scottish Universities Commission, February 1890⋆

THE STUDENTS' REPRESENTATIVE COUNCIL OF THE UNIVERSITY OF EDINBURGH desires to call the attention of the SCOTTISH UNIVERSITIES COMMISSIONERS to the following points, viz.:—

I. The aims of the Council are—
1. To represent the Students in matters affecting their interests.
2. To afford a recognised means of communication between the Students and the University authorities.
3. To promote social life and academic unity among the Students.

II. The constitution of the Council is laid before the Commissioners for their consideration.

The Council desires to petition the Commissioners on the following points, viz:—

I. That a revenue be provided for the Students' Representative Council, whether by increasing the Matriculation Fee to

⋆ Enclosed in a letter from the joint honorary secretaries of the S.R.C. to R. Fitzroy Bell, secretary to the Scottish Universities Commission, 17 Feb 1890 [S.R.O.: ED 9/37]. See above, pp. 26–7.

£1. 1s., and devoting the additional 1s. to the purposes of the Students' Representative Council, or by such other way as the Commissioners may deem desirable.

II. That draft ordinances of the University Court be submitted to the Students' Representative Council, so that it may have an opportunity of expressing its views.

III. That in the election of the Lord Rector's Assessor the Students' Representative Council submit names to the Lord Rector, one of which he shall select.

IV. That the Rectorial Elections do not take place till after all the Faculties have met. It often happens that the election takes place before one of the Faculties is opened. The change suggested is considered desirable, in order that all Students may have an opportunity of exercising their right of voting.

V. That there be a Matriculation Examination for all Students entering the University with a view to graduation, and that at least four compulsory subjects be passed at once.

VI. DIVINITY.—That in the Faculty of Divinity, such special subjects as Apologetics and History of Religions, be treated under separate Chairs.

VII. MEDICINE.

1. EXAMINATIONS—We do not think that the present regulations regarding the *First Professional Examination* require alteration. With regard to the *Second Professional Examination*, however, we are strongly of opinion that a candidate should be allowed to appear for examination in Anatomy and Physiology at the end of the second year of medical study, provided that the candidate has dissected the human body at least once—no Student being allowed to pass the whole Second Professional Examination at a period earlier than is at present allowed.

With regard to the *Final Examination*, we are also strongly of opinion that this examination should take place twice a year, as is the case with the First and Second Professional Examinations.

At present, if the Second Professional Examination is passed in July (under existing arrangements), the candidate must appear for his Final Examination in the May following—a period of ten months—or else he must wait for another year—a period of twenty-two months. An examination at the beginning of the Winter Session seems to us to be reasonable.

2. EXAMINERS.—(*a*) We are of opinion that candidates would be more satisfied with the results of their examinations if the Oral

Examination of each Student were conducted by *two* examiners, the one to assign values to the answers returned to the questions of the other—a plan which is not at present generally carried out. (*b*) We would also recommend an increase of the Examining Staff. This is especially called for in *Clinical* Surgery, where two examiners have to examine upwards of two hundred candidates, whereas in Clinical Medicine the work is divided among five examiners. It is generally considered that the examinations in Clinical Surgery are conducted in an unsatisfactory manner.

3. OVERCROWDING OF CLASSES.—The authorised teaching staff bears a very small numerical relation to the educational work to be done—(one Professor to about three hundred students)—and Professors are under no obligation to teach for more than one hour daily. In consequence of these two circumstances, the classes are so crowded that it is impossible that a large proportion of those present can obtain any benefit from much of the objective part of the lecture, and obviously all genuine individual teaching is impossible. We are of opinion that an increase in the University teaching staff, and a wider recognition of extra-mural teaching for purposes of graduation, is essential.

4. CLASS LECTURES.—In order to allow more opportunity for practical demonstration and teaching, we should suggest that the regulation that at least one hundred *lectures* be delivered during a Winter Session, and fifty in a Summer Session, be held to mean that the Professor shall *meet his class* for the purpose of instruction at least one hundred or fifty times respectively, and that Practical, *viva voce,* and Clinical Instruction be given much greater prominence in medical work.

5. CLASSES.—We are of opinion that considerable overlapping of subjects occurs in several classes, and that more time might be devoted to the teaching of these subjects if an arrangement were adopted whereby this overlapping could be eliminated.

(*a*) *Embryology and Histology.*—In this connection we would call attention to the fact that Embryology is taught in the classes of Natural History, Anatomy, Physiology, and Midwifery, and that Histology is taught in the classes of Anatomy, Physiology, and Practical Physiology, all of which classes are in the regular curriculum.

We would suggest that Histology should be omitted from the systematic courses in Anatomy and Physiology, and be entirely taught in the Practical Class of

Physiology, which should also include more instruction in Physiological and Clinical Chemistry.

(*b*) *Materia Medica*.—In the department of Materia Medica, the physical characters and appearances of drugs are taught both in the systematic and practical classes. We suggest that the consideration of the physical characters of drugs and pharmacy should be limited to the practical class, in which a more extended course of pharmacy be included.

(*c*) *Midwifery*.—We are also of opinion that in the class of *Obstetrics* more prominence should be given to the Diseases of Women and of Children.

(*d*) *Surgery*.—We would also suggest that the institution of an (optional) Elementary Class in *Surgery* (say, during the Summer Session) would relieve the Professor's winter course of much of its elementary matter, and thus make it more adapted to the wants of senior Students. We are also of opinion that a course of *Operative Surgery* should be compulsory, and completed before the commencement of the Final Professional Examination.

(*e*) *Optional Special Classes*.—We recommend that there should be optional courses of not more than six weeks' duration, at a fee of not more than £1. 1s., in Embryology, Bacteriology, Diseases of the Eye, Diseases of the Ear and Throat, Diseases of the Mind, Diseases of Children, and Diseases of the Skin.

(*f*) We think that the fees for practical classes should be reduced after two years' attendance on the classes.

6. RESEARCH.—We consider that research should be promoted by affording much greater facilities for Students and graduates using the University laboratories, also that facilities should be given for private research.

The present fee is considered excessive, more especially as the attention each individual receives is exceedingly slight.

We would recommend a considerable reduction of the fee paid for laboratory instruction, and the appointment of special University assistants to superintend these departments.

VIII. SCIENCE.—That a Faculty of Science be created.

IX. ARTS.

1. That there be a Degree of Music in Edinburgh. At present,

although there is a Professor of Music, there is no degree granted, and therefore, Students are not encouraged as they are in England to prosecute studies in this department.

2. That for the Degree of M.A. there be optional subjects. There is a keen desire among Students that the present system of granting degrees in Arts be radically changed, by a choice of subjects being allowed.

3. That English Language and Literature be included in one of the examinations for honours in the degree of M.A.

4. That in the Faculty of Arts, Professorships of Modern Languages and History be founded. This is felt to be a great want at present, and if the system of granting degrees in Arts is changed, it is considered that the founding of these Chairs will be necessary.

IN NAME AND ON BEHALF OF THE STUDENTS' REPRESENTATIVE COUNCIL,

W. CAMPBELL LAHORE,
HARRY G. MELVILLE,   } *Presidents*
A. STODART WALKER,

L. CLARENCE D. DOUGLAS,   } *Honorary Secretaries*
ROBERT G. SCOTT,

Charter of Student Rights and Responsibilities, 1940*

600 STUDENTS gathered at the British Student Congress at Leeds, DEEPLY CONSCIOUS of the inequality, the poverty and the destruction of human life and values which characterise our society, BELIEVING that the Universities, Colleges and Training Colleges of Great Britain have an indispensable part to play in the advance towards a new, peaceful and just society, AWARE that they are not at present fully playing that part, REALISING that British students have the responsibility of ensuring that the knowledge and culture of the universities are used in the interests of the people as a whole, of ensuring that University education is not the privilege of a class, and of working with all sections of the people to this end, CONFIDENT that the students of Britain will contribute their share to the efforts of progressive humanity, inside and outside the universities, to secure peace and justice for all peoples,

* N.U.S., *Report of the British Student Congress, 1940* [1940] pp. 2–3; endorsed by N.U.S. council, 12 May 1940. See above, p. 81.

FIRMLY CONVINCED that freedom, liberty and democracy within the Universities and Colleges are essential if they are to implement their responsibilities towards the community,

And having heard evidence of recent encroachments upon student liberties:

WARN the students of Britain of the danger of further attacks,

AND CALL UPON THEM to work in unity and with all their strength for this Charter of Student Rights:

THE CHARTER

THE RIGHT to the free expression of opinion by speech and Press.

THE RIGHT to organise meetings, discussion and study on all subjects within the University and College precincts.

THE RIGHT to belong to any organisation, whether cultural, political or religious.

THE RIGHT to participate to the full in all activities outside the universities, and to collaborate with extra-university organisations.

THE RIGHT to a share in the government and administration of the universities.

Given these Rights,

WE PLEDGE ourselves to fulfil our responsibilities to the community,

AND CALL on all students to defend them by their united action, and all sections of the British people, for their support.

References

Introduction

1. *Higher education, dept. cttee, evidence,* pt I, vol. A, pp. 216–48; 1962–3, Cmnd 2154–VI, xiii.
2. Cf. A. B. Cobban, *The King's Hall within the University of Cambridge in the later middle ages* (Cambridge, 1969).

Chapter 1   *The Latent Estate: 1815–50*

1. [J. G. Lockhart] *Peter's letters to his kinsfolk* (1819) I, 202, 208.
2. Cf. Sheldon Rothblatt, *The revolution of the dons* (1968) pp. 86–7.
3. Henry Wall, fellow and bursar, Balliol College. *Oxford Univ., R. com., rept,* evidence, p. 146; 1852 [1482] xxii.
4. [John Wright] *Alma mater; or, seven years at the University of Cambridge* (1827) II, 146.
5. Duncan Mearns, professor of divinity, King's College, Aberdeen. *Univs of Scotland, R. com., evidence,* IV: *Aberdeen,* p. 57; 1837 [95] xxxviii.
6. Patrick Forbes, professor of humanity, King's College, Aberdeen. Ibid., p. 14.
7. Alexander Grant, *The story of the University of Edinburgh during its first 300 years* (1884) II, appx S.
8. *Quarterly Review,* XXXVI (1827) 240.
9. H. Hale Bellot, *University College, London, 1826–1926* (1929); F. J. C. Hearnshaw, *The centenary history of King's College, London, 1828–1928* (1929).
10. George Jardine, *Outlines of philosophical education,* 2nd ed. (Glasgow, 1825) p. 13.
11. Thomas Thorp, *The students' walk* (Cambridge, 1840).
12. Thomas Whytehead, *College life: letters to an undergraduate* (Cambridge, 1845).

168

13. C. A. Bristed, *Five years in an English university*, 3rd ed. (1873).
14. John Venn, *Early collegiate life* (Cambridge, 1913).
15. Ref. 3, evidence, p. 43.
16. Ibid., p. 148.
17. Mark Pattison, ibid., p. 42.
18. Adam Sedgwick, *Four letters to the editors of the Leeds Mercury in reply to R. M. Beverley, esq.* (Cambridge, 1836) p. 6 [not pubd].
19. *Report*, p. 21; ref. 3.
20. Ref. 10.
21. *Univs of Scotland, R. com., evidence*, III: *St Andrews*, p. 82; 1837 [94] xxxvii.
22. Ibid., I: *Edinburgh*, p. 436; 1837 [92] xxxv.
23. Ibid., pp. 483, [204–6]: II: *Glasgow*, pp. 196–8, 548–9; 1837 [93] xxxvi: III: *St Andrews*, pp. 83–7; 1837 [94] xxxvii: IV: *Aberdeen*, p. 308; 1837 [95] xxxviii.
24. *Cambridge Univ., R. com., rept*, p. 106; 1852–3 [1559] xliv.
25. See ref. 10; also evidence submitted to the royal commission of 1826.
26. *Univs of Scotland, R. com., rept*, p. 238; 1831 (310) xii; ibid., *evidence*, II: *Glasgow*, pp. 79–80, 139, 153; 1837 [93] xxxvi.
27. Percy Cradock, *Recollections of the Cambridge Union, 1815–1939* (Cambridge, 1953) pp. 7–10.
28. *Aberdeen Chronicle*, 8 Mar 1823, quoted in *Rectorial addresses delivered in the Universities of Aberdeen, 1835–1900*, ed. P. J. Anderson (Aberdeen, 1902) p. 348.
29. R. S. Rait, 'Joseph Hume and an academic rebellion', *Scottish Antiquary*, XIII no. 49 (July 1898) 24–6.
30. *Aberdeen rectorial addresses*, p. 350.
31. *Univs of Scotland, R. com., evidence*, IV: *Aberdeen*, p. 87; 1837 [95] xxxviii.
32. Evidence of Principal Brown, ibid., p. 80.
33. Ref. 30, p. 339.
34. R. G. Cant, *The University of St Andrews: a short history* (Edinburgh, 1946) p. 103; *Univs of Scotland, R. com., evidence*, III: *St Andrews*, p. 267; 1837 [94] xxxvii.
35. D. B. Horn, *A short history of the University of Edinburgh* (Edinburgh, 1967) p. 136.
36. Ibid., p. 141.
37. Bellot, *University College, London*, p. 191.
38. Ibid., pp. 197–8.

39. *London Medical Gazette*, VII (1830–1) 117–18.
40. *Lancet*, 1829–30, ii, 623 (17 July 1830).
41. Ibid., p. 847 (16 Aug 1830).
42. Ref. 39.
43. *Lancet*, 1830–1, i, 751.
44. *U. Coll. Gazette*, I (1887) 123.
45. *Lancet*, 1830–1, i, 749–53 (22 Feb 1831).
46. Ibid., 1830–1, ii, 16.
47. Ibid., p. 17.
48. *Univs of Scotland, R. com.*, rept, 1831 (310) xii; evidence, I: *Edinburgh*, 1837 [92] xxxv, II: *Glasgow*, 1837 [93] xxxvi, III: *St Andrews*, 1837 [94] xxxvii, IV: *Aberdeen*, 1837 [95] xxxviii.
49. *Oxford Univ., R. com.*, rept, 1852 [1482] xxii; *Cambridge Univ.*, *R. com.*, rept, 1852–3 [1559] xliv.
50. *Univs of Scotland, R. com.*, evidence, II: *Glasgow*, p. 548.
51. Ibid., I: *Edinburgh*, p. [203].
52. Ibid., p. [206].
53. Ref. 51.
54. *Municipal corporations in Scotland, R. com.*, local repts, p. 393; 1835 [31] xxix.

Chapter 2   The Scottish Example

1. *Aberdeen rectorial addresses*, pp. 365–9.
2. G. Foulkes (ed.), *Eighty years on: a chronicle of student activity in the University of Edinburgh* (Edinburgh, 1964); also Grant, *Story of the University of Edinburgh*, and Horn, *A short history*.
3. J. I. Macpherson, *Twenty-one years of corporate life at Edinburgh University: being a short history of the Students' Representative Council* (Edinburgh, 1905) p. 88.
4. *Constitution, laws, and bye-laws of the Students' Representative Council of the University of Edinburgh* (Edinburgh, 1894).
5. *The Student*, II no. 2 (1 Nov 1889).
6. Ref. 3, p. 88.
7. *The Student*, I no. 11 (25 May 1888).
8. Ibid., I no. 4 (19 Dec 1887).
9. Ibid., I no. 8 (28 June 1889).
10. Foulkes, *Eighty years on*, p. 28.
11. *The Student*, I no. 3 (2 Dec 1887); I no. 10 (20 Mar 1888).

12. P. 157.
13. *The Student*, 1 no. 12 (27 June 1888); Macpherson, *Twenty-one years*, p. 33.
14. P. 162.
15. D. B. Horn, 'The Universities (Scotland) Act of 1858', *University of Edinburgh Journal*, XIX no. 3 (1959) 178–9.
16. *H. C. Debs*, 28 June 1858, cols 507–23.
17. Ibid., 5 July 1858, cols 945–67.
18. Ibid., 29 July 1858, col. 2243.
19. *Rectorial addresses delivered before the University of Edinburgh, 1859–1899*, ed. A. Stodart-Walker (1900) p. 3.
20. *Univs of Scotland, R. com., rept etc.;* 1878 [C. 1935–C. 1935–iii] xxxii–v.
21. Professor Pirie, ibid., xxxiii, 339.
22. Professor Black, ibid., 783.
23. Professor Struthers, ibid., xxxiv, 30.
24. Ibid., 533–7.
25. Ibid., xxxii, 90–2.
26. Ref. 3, p. 32.
27. *The Times*, 10 Mar 1888.
28. Ibid., 30 Mar 1888.
29. *H. L. Debs*, 3 May 1888, cols 1193–4.
30. Ibid., 7 June 1888, col. 1336.
31. Ibid., cols 1340–1.
32. Ibid., 19 June 1888, cols 564–5.
33. Ibid., 7 June 1888, col. 1341.
34. *H. C. Debs*, 20 June 1889, cols 352–3.
35. W. A. Hunter (N. Aberdeen). Ibid., 27 June 1889, cols 918–19; 17 July 1889, cols 605–8.
36. *Univs (Scotland) bill [H.L.]*; 1888 (476) iii.
37. Documents, p. 157.
38. *The Student*, 1 no. 12 (27 June 1888).
39. See above, p. 33.
40. J. Donaldson, *Addresses delivered in the University of St Andrews from 1886 to 1910* (Edinburgh, 1911) p. 108.
41. Ibid., p. 123.
42. Ref. 3, p. 36.
43. *Univs of Scotland, com., rept etc.*, pp. 54–8; 1900 [Cd 276] xxv. Similar regulations were made for the other Scottish universities.
44. Ibid., pp. 101–2.

Chapter 3   Student Awakening in the South

1. *The Student*, II no. 2 (1 Nov 1889).
2. W. Macdonald, 'The SRC', *University Review*, II (1905–6) 287–90.
3. Macpherson, *Twenty-one years*, p. 74.
4. Quoted in Bellot, *University College, London*, p. 361.
5. Ibid., p. 362.
6. Hearnshaw, *Centenary history of King's College*, p. 184.
7. Ibid., p. 384.
8. David Taylor, *The godless students of Gower Street* (1968) p. 16.
9. R. Muir, *Ramsay Muir: an autobiography and some essays*, ed. S. Hodgson (1943) p. 24.
10. J. M. Mackay, *A new university* (Liverpool, 1914) p. 28.
11. Ref. 9, p. 29.
12. Ramsay Muir, 'The rise of student life', in *The making of the University* (Liverpool, 1907) pp. 37–50. [Reprinted from *The Sphinx*.]
13. Ref. 8, pp. 18–19.
14. A. N. Shimmin, *The University of Leeds: the first half-century* (Leeds, 1954) p. 85.
15. *Durham University Journal*, XII no. 11 (27 Feb 1897) 255, 259, 269; XIII no. 13 (13 May 1899) 269.
16. T. W. Moody and J. C. Beckett, *Queen's Belfast, 1845–1949* (1959) I, 365–6.
17. J. L. Garvin and J. Amery, *The life of Joseph Chamberlain* (1932–69) IV, 209–21.
18. Eric Ashby, *Universities: British, Indian, African* (1966) pp. 300–1.
19. J. M. Mackay, *The relations and functions and work of senate and faculty of the modern university in France and England, together with an account of the faculty of arts in Liverpool* (Liverpool, 1897).
20. E. A. Sonnenschein, 'Birmingham University and Mackay', in *A miscellany presented to J. M. Mackay . . . July 1914* (Liverpool, 1914) pp. 77–9.
21. E. J. Somerset, *The birth of a university: a passage in the life of E. A. Sonnenschein* (Oxford, 1934) pp. 14–15.
22. *The Times*, 31 May 1900.
23. Charter, 24 Mar 1900: University of Birmingham, *Calendar, 1900–1* (1900).
24. Ibid., *Calendar, 1903–4* (1903).

25. Ibid., *Calendar, 1902–3* (1902).
26. University of Manchester, *Calendar, 1904–5* (1904).
27. Charter, 15 July 1903: ibid.
28. Charter, 15 July 1903: University of Liverpool, *Calendar, 1903–4* (1903); ref. 9, p. 171.
29. *Durham University Journal*, XIII no. 13 (13 May 1899) 358.
30. Ibid., XVII no. 18 (27 Dec 1907) 205.
31. Ibid., XVIII no. 7 (4 Nov 1908) 84.
32. *Univ. education in Ireland, R. com., appx to 3rd rept*, pp. 116–17; 1902 [Cd 1229] xxxii.
33. *Univ. education in London, R. com., appx to 3rd rept*, p. 196; 1911 [Cd 5911] xx.
34. Ibid., *final rept*, pp. 157–60; 1913 [Cd 6717] xl.
35. *Univ. education in Wales, R. com., appx to 2nd rept*, pp. 103–6; 1917–18 [Cd 8699] xii.
36. Ibid.
37. Ibid., *final rept*, p. 31; 1918 [Cd 8991] xiv.
38. Ref. 16, p. 368.
39. *U.C.L. Union Magazine*, I i (Dec 1904) 14–16.
40. *University Review*, I (1905) 209, 528–31.
41. Ibid., III (1906) 509–14.
42. The following articles in *The University Review* dealt with this topic: T. B. Whitson, 'The case for self-governing residential halls', A. C. Ward, 'The residence of students in our new universities', J. W. Graham, 'Residential halls', W. W. Seton, 'Residential halls: some general considerations', II (1905–6) 255–63, 373–83, 464–9, 558–68; P. Geddes, 'University studies and university residence', T. B. Whitson, 'Self-governing residential halls', III (1906) 297–313, 346–51.
43. *Durham University Journal*, XVIII no. 7 (4 Nov 1908) 84–5.
44. *Glasgow University Magazine*, XXIII no. 1 (2 Nov 1910) 21.
45. Ref. 43, XVIII no. 13 (15 May 1909) 161.
46. *The Student*, IX (1911–12) 234.

Chapter 4   National Co-ordination

1. A. J. P. Taylor, *English history 1914–1945* (Oxford, 1965) p. 120.
2. I. S. Macadam, *Youth in the universities* [1922]; N.U.S. council and executive minutes, 1922–5.

3. Executive minutes, 12–15 July 1926.
4. Council minutes, 21–4 Oct 1927.
5. Ibid., 2–5 Nov 1928.
6. Executive minutes, 23–6 Jan 1931.
7. Ibid., 8–11 July 1932.
8. Council minutes, 3–6 Nov 1933.
9. Foulkes, *Eighty years on; N.U.S. annual reports, 1941–2, 1942–3, 1943–4* (1942–4); council minutes, 3–4 Feb 1945.
10. Executive minutes, 28–30 Sept 1922.
11. Ibid., 8–11 July 1927; H. Perkin, *Key profession: the history of the Association of University Teachers* (1969) p. 91.
12. Executive minutes, 4–5 Jan 1936.
13. Ibid., 11–14 Feb 1927.
14. Ibid., 11–15 July 1930.
15. Council minutes, 3–6 Nov 1933.
16. *N.U.S. annual report, 1925–6* (1926).
17. N.U.S., *Report of the annual congress . . . 1939* [1939].
18. *N.U.S annual report, 1927–8* (1928).
19. Council minutes, 5–7 Nov 1932.
20. Executive minutes, 27–8 Jan 1934.
21. Ibid., 20–1 Feb 1937.
22. Council minutes, July 1937.
23. Ibid., July 1938.
24. N.U.S., *The challenge to the university: a report of the 1938 congress* [1938].
25. N.U.S., *Graduate employment: a report of the 1937 congress* [1937].
26. Ref. 24.
27. Ref. 17.
28. Council minutes, 1–4 Nov 1929.
29. Ibid., 5–7 Nov 1932.
30. Ibid., 12–13 Nov 1938.
31. A.U.T., 'Report on university developments, 1944', *Universitie Review*, 16 no. 2 (May, 1944) 52–65.
32. N.U.S., *The future of university and higher education* [1944].
33. Ref. 24.
34. Ref. 17.
35. Council minutes, 14–15 Nov 1936.
36. Ibid., July 1938.
37. Executive minutes, 14–17 July 1933.
38. Ref. 24.

39. Council minutes, July 1938.
40. Ref. 17.
41. C. Grant Robertson, *The British universities* (1930) 72–5.
42. Ref. 17.
43. Council minutes, July 1938.
44. N.U.S., *The National Parliament of Youth: an education bill prepared by the National Union of Students* [1939].
45. N.U.S., *Defend the universities* [1940].
46. N.U.S., *Report of the British Student Congress, 1940* [1940].
47. *TES*, 13 April 1940, p. 136.
48. Council minutes, 12 May 1940 (extraordinary meeting).
49. Ibid., 6–7 July 1940.
50. Ibid., 9–10 Nov 1940 (extraordinary meeting).
51. Ibid., 9–10 Nov 1940.
52. N.U.S., *Students face the future: N.U.S. congress, Cambridge 1941* [1941].
53. B. Simon, *A student's view of the universities* (1943) p. 107.
54. Kingsley Martin, *Father figures* (1966) p. 158.
55. This incident and its consequences are described in *Clare Market Review*, n.s. XIV no. 2 (1934), no. 3 (1934); XV no. 1 (1934), no. 3 (1935); o.s. XXXII no. 1 (1936).
56. Ibid., XIV no. 3 (1934).
57. N.U.S. executive minutes, 13–16 July 1934.
58. Council minutes, 2 April 1940 (extraordinary meeting).

Chapter 5   The Flowering of the Student Estate

1. *NUS executive report* (1969) p. 98.
2. N.U.S. council minutes, 18–20 Feb 1949.
3. Ibid., 8–9 Feb 1947.
4. Ref. 2.
5. Ibid., 21–3 Nov 1952.
6. Ibid., 20–2 Nov 1953.
7. *NUS Year book, 1953–4*.
8. Council minutes, 25–7 Nov 1960.
9. Ibid., 20–2 Nov 1954.
10. Ibid., 12–14 Nov 1955.
11. Ibid. 6–9 April 1956.

12. Western European Union, *Report of the conference of European university rectors and vice-chancellors . . . 1955* (1955) pp. 114–16, 141, 184.
13. N.U.S. council minutes, 12–15 April 1957.
14. Ibid., 11–14 April 1958.
15. *Universities Quarterly*, 13 (1958–9) 9–22; G. C. Moodie, *The universities: a royal commission?* (Fabian Society Research Series, 209, 1959).
16. N.U.S., 'Report of a conference on the University Grants Committee and the 1962–1967 quinquennium . . . 22nd–23rd January 1960' (mimeo.).
17. Report of executive, 1957–8; appx to council minutes, 22–4 Nov 1958.
18. U.G.C., *Report of the Committee on university teaching methods* (H.M.S.O., 1964). The memorandum from the N.U.S., submitted to the committee in 1961, is reproduced on pp. 124–31.
19. *Higher education, dept. cttee, rept;* 1962–3, Cmnd 2154, xi. The evidence, written and oral, from the N.U.S. is in *Evidence*, pt I, vol. A, pp. 216–48; 1962–3, Cmnd 2154–VI, xiii.
20. N.U.S., 'Memorandum to the University Grants Committee' (1960, mimeo. draft).
21. University of Nottingham Union, *Report of the development and planning special committee, 1 March 1965* (1965) pp. 14–15.
22. 'Outline of a proposal for reorganising university education', in Committee on manpower resources for science and technology, *The flow into employment of scientists, engineers and technologists,* Cmnd 3760 (1968) p. 106.
23. Ref. 19.
24. Labour Party Study Group on higher education, *The years of crisis* [1962].
25. N.U.S. council minutes, 11–14 April 1958.
26. Ibid., 25–7 Nov 1960.
27. Ibid., 7–11 April 1961.
28. Ibid., 16–20 April 1963.
29. N.U.S., *Higher education – the future: executive statement on the Robbins committee report* [1964].
30. N.U.S., *Statement on education and welfare policy* (Oct 1964).
31. Ref. 18.
32. Ref. 29.
33. See the remarkable series of notes entitled 'Politics in the world of

science and learning' by Edward Shils in issues of *Minerva* since 1963; also: . . . *And scholars* by Eric Ashby, an oration delivered at the London School of Economics, 4 Dec 1964 (1965); and an essay by Richard Hoggart: 'Higher education and personal life: changing attitudes', in *Higher education: demand and response*, ed. W. R. Niblett (1969).

34. N.U.S. council minutes, 11–15 April 1965.

35. N.U.S., *Recommendations for the amendment of the charter of the University of Surrey* (18 May 1965); subsequently reprinted with correspondence between the secretary of state for education and science and the secretary of the N.U.S. under the title of *Outside the law* (24 Jan 1966).

36. Council minutes, 13–17 April 1966.

37. N.U.S., *Student participation in college government* (Oct 1966).

38. N.U.S., 'Memorandum submitted to the University Grants Committee on University development 1967/72'(Dec 1966, mimeo.).

39. *NUS Year book 1967*, p. 36.

40. Martin Lipset (ed.), 'Student politics', *Comparative Education Review*, 10 (1966) 129–376; and 'Students and politics', *Daedalus*, 97 (1968).

41. Council minutes, 24–7 Nov 1967, 5–9 April 1968, 22–5 Nov 1968. For a tendentious account of the episode, see D. Triesman, 'The CIA and student politics', in *Student power*, ed. A. Cockburn and R. Blackburn (1969) pp. 141–59.

42. This deliberate campaign is described by one of its partisans in *Student power* (ref. 41): D. Widgery, 'NUS – the student's muffler', pp. 119–40.

43. The statement is reproduced in *Minerva*, VI (1967–8) 559–60.

44. *Report of the Committee on the age of majority*, Cmnd 3342 (1967); *NUS Year book 1969*, p. 33.

45. G. and D. Cohn-Bendit, *Obsolete communism: the left wing alternative* (1968) p. 29.

46. The statement is reproduced in *Minerva*, VII (1968–9) 67–72.

47. P. Hartog and E. C. Rhodes, *An examination of examinations* (1935); and 'Examining in universities', *Universities Quarterly*, 21 (1966–7) 269–372.

48. Conference minutes, 8–12 April 1969, pp. 124–5.

49. Ibid., p. 124.

50. Ibid., pp. 125–36.

51. Ibid., p. 122.

Chapter 6   The Conscience of the Student Estate

1. N.U.S., 'The rights and responsibilities of students' (1967, draft).
2. C. Jencks and D. Riesman, *The academic revolution* (New York, 1968).
3. E. Shils, 'Of plenitude and scarcity', *Encounter* (May 1969) 37–57.
4. University of Oxford, 'Report of the Committee on relations with junior members' (the Hart report): supplement no. 7 to the *University Gazette*, XVIX (1969) 154.
5. N.U.S., *Report of the British Student Congress, 1940* [1940].
6. *New Left Review*, 50 (1968) 59.
7. Widgery, in *Student power*, p. 140.
8. S. Kelman, 'A slightly sceptical view', *Dialogue* (n.d.) 48.
9. D. Martin, 'The dissolution of the monasteries', in *Anarchy and culture*, ed. D. Martin (1969) p. 8.
10. R. Hoggart, 'Higher education and personal life: changing attitudes', in *Higher education: demand and response*, p. 211.
11. N. Spurway, *Authority in higher education* (1968) p. 62.
12. F. Rudolph, *The American college and university* (New York, 1965) p. 97.
13. H. S. Tremenheere, *I was there*, ed. E. L. and O. P. Edmonds (Windsor, 1965) p. 2.
14. P. C. Altbach (ed.), *Turmoil and transition: higher education and student politics in India* (New York, 1968).
15. Columbia University, *Crisis at Columbia: the Cox report* (New York, 1968); S. M. Lipset and S. S. Wolin (eds), *The Berkeley student revolt* (New York, 1965); R. Aron, *The elusive revolution* (1969); F. Mager and U. Spinnarke, *Was wollen die Studenten?* (Frankfurt, 1967); J. Habermas, *Protestbewegung und Hochschul-Reform* (Frankfurt, 1969); H. Kidd, *The trouble at L.S.E.* (1969).
16. Aron, *The elusive revolution*.
17. Ché Guevara, *Reminiscences of the Cuban revolutionary war* (1969) p. 157.
18. Ref. 9, p. 9.
19. A calm and accurate description of the attitude of the press at a sit-in at Bristol University is given by E. Wright: 'Bristol sit-in, through press eyes', *Universities Quarterly*, 23 (1968–9) 183–8.

20. It has been suggested by J. Searle ('The anatomy of student revolt', *Spectator*, 7 Mar 1969, p. 303) that it is television which selects and creates the charismatic leader and that the real leaders, unless they make an impression on television, are passed over.

21. J. J. Schwab, *College curriculum and student protest* (Chicago, 1969) p. 30.

22. This account is based on a full set of unpublished documents covering the whole episode.

23. Herve Bourges (ed.), *The student revolt* (1968) p. 16.

24. *University Affairs*, 10 (2 Oct 1968) 16.

25. R. Atkinson, 'Student power: why we want it', in *Teach yourself student power*, ed. Radical Student Alliance (1968, mimeo.).

26. Conference minutes, 8–12 April 1969.

27. J. Straw, 'Student participation in higher education' (Granada Guildhall lecture, 6 Oct 1969, mimeo.).

28. A selection is: University of York, *The role of students in the government of the university* (1968, mimeo.); Committee of presidents of universities of Ontario, *Student participation in university government* (Ottawa, 1968); University of Cambridge, 'First report on participation by junior members in the educational business of the university', *Cambridge University Reporter*, XCIX no. 2 (5 Feb 1969) 974–82 and the Hart report (ref. 4).

29. J. E. Eatwell, 'Some reflections on the Harvard strike', *Cambridge Review*, 91 (1969) 20; and (in much more sophisticated form) see the essays in T. Roszak (ed.), *The dissenting academy* (1967).

30. Ref. 16.

31. For the quotations and some of the ideas in the next few paragraphs we are indebted to Mr Charles Parkin, fellow of Clare College, who prepared for us a perceptive paper on authority and participation in universities.

32. The resolution mandating the N.U.S., which we quote on p. 119 proposes one-third student membership on central bodies and 50 per cent cn departmental committees with decision-making powers.

33. The theme is discussed by E. Ashby in 'The future of the nineteenth century idea of a university', *Minerva* VI (1967–8) 3–17.

34. Detailed evidence for the assertion is to be found in E. Ashby: 'Hands off the universities?', *Minerva*, VI (1967–8) 244–56.

35. N. Frye, 'The university and personal life: student anarchism and

the educational contract', in *Higher education: demand and response*, p. 35.

36. W. Moberly, *The crisis in the university* (1949).
37. N. Frye, 'The knowledge of good and evil', in *The morality of scholarship*, ed. M. Black (Ithaca, 1967) p. 1.
38. *Guardian*, 14 Nov 1969.

Index

Page numbers in italics refer to the documentary appendix.

Aberdeen, King's College and University of: rectorship at, 9, 18; student protest at (1834), 13. *See also* Universities, Scottish

Aberdeen, Marischal College and University of: rectorship at, 9, 11–13, 18; student protest at (1820s), 11–13. *See also* Universities, Scottish

Aberdeen, University of: rectorship at, 20, 30–1; student protest at (1861), 20–1; formation of S.R.C., 25, and memorial to H.M.G. (1888), 26, *156–62*

Acts relating to universities, *see* University legislation

Argyll (George Campbell),8th duke of,33–4

Aron, Raymond, 128, 131, 151

Association of University Teachers (A.U.T.): overture of, to N.U.S. (1927), 66–7; report of, on post-war university development (1944–5), 67, 74–5, 86, 88; attitude to student participation in university government, 74–5, 88; contribution to staff–student consultative committee, 74; joint public conference with N.U.S. (1945), 90, 93, and co-operation on call-up and demobilisation, 93

Astor, Nancy, viscountess, 64

Atkinson, Richard, 139

Balfour, Arthur James, 1st earl of, 63

Barker, Ernest, 64

Battersea College of Technology, *see* Surrey, University of

Bell, R. Fitzroy, 22, 23, 35

Beveridge, Sir William, 83–5

Birkbeck College: student representation on governing body of, 74

Birmingham,University of: statutory provision for guild of undergraduates at, and student representation on court of (1900), 49–50; staff–student conferences at, 67; abortive attempts at student representation on council of, 74; staff–student consultative committees at, 74; student submission of, to U.G.C., 101; mentioned, 73

Bristed, C. A., 6

Bristol, University of: statutory provision

for student representation on court of (1909), 51; staff–student lunches at, 74; student participation at, 74; student protest at, 131

British Inter-Universities Students' Congress (1905 etc.), *see* Inter-Universities Students' Congress

Brodetsky, Selig, 90

Button, Miss, 77

Caird, John, 30

Cambridge, University of: student membership of, ix; student life at, in early 19th century, 1–2, 6, paternalism at, 4–8, and student response, 10–11; absence of student evidence to commission of 1850, 9, 10; absence of student participation in government of, 43; tardy formation of S.R.C. in, 50; absence of student estate in, 57; influence of, on student residence in England, 59; ineligibility of, for full membership of N.U.S., 62, and consequence, 66; student protest against wearing of gowns, 108; mentioned, 19

Camperdown (Robert Haldane), 3rd earl of, 34

Chamberlain, Joseph, 47–8, 49, 58

Chicago, University of: technique of, in treating student turbulence, 136–8

Clare Market Review, The, 85

Cockburn, Henry, 18–19, 22

Cohn-Bendit, D., 116

Commission on Universities of Scotland (1826): appointment of, 16; character and purpose of, 17; student submissions to, 9, 17–18; and rectorship, 10, 18, 27–8; report and recommendations of, 11, 16, 18, 27–8

— (1876): appointment and membership of, 30; and rectorship, 30–1; absence of student submissions to, 31; recommendation of, 31

— (1889): appointment of, 35; student submissions to, 26–7, 36–7, *126–6*; its responsiveness to student opinion, 35–9

— on University education in Ireland (1901): student submissions to, 52–3, and response from, 53

Commision on University education in London (1909): student submissions to, 54–5; recommendations of, 55
— on University education in Wales (1916): student submissions to, 55–6; recommendations of, 57
— on University of Cambridge (1850): appointment of, 16; absence of student submissions to, 9, 10; report of, 9
— on University of Oxford (1850): appointment of, 16; absence of student submissions to, 9, 10; report of, 9
Committee of Vice-Chancellors and Principals: tentative contacts of N.U.S. with, 78, 86; tardy cognisance of N.U.S. by, 90, 96, 99, 108, 113; first meeting of, with N.U.S., 112–13; and statement of June 1968, 115; and concordat with N.U.S. (Oct 1968), ix, 116–17, 119, 143
Committee on higher education (1961), see Robbins Committee
Committee on the age of majority, see Latey report
Confédération internationale des étudiants (C.I.E.): formation of (1919), 61; first congress of (Prague, 1921), 61; early cracks in, 61–2; meeting of, in England, 64; attempts by N.U.S. to resolve political conflict in, 65; N.U.S. withdrawal from, 65, 92–3
Conference of European university rectors and vice-chancellors (1955), 97
Costelloe, B., 31
Curtis, Lionel, 64

Darvall, F. O., 68, 69, 70
David, Illtyd, 56
Dawson, G., 64
Department of education and science: and charters of technological universities, 109–10
Donaldson, Sir James, 36
Dunlop, A. Murray, 29
Durham, University of: early union in, 50; formation of collegiate and university S.R.C.s at, 47, 50; motion of Inter-Universities Students' Congress for student representation at, 60; absence of provision for student representation in Act of 1908, 60; withdrawal of S.R.C. from Inter-Universities Students' Congress, 60

East Anglia, University of, ix–x

Eccles, Sir David, 96, 97, 98, 107
Edinburgh, University of: rectorship at, 9, 18, 29–31, 36, 40; student attempt to influences taff appointment at (1833), 13; student petitions to commission of 1826, 17; student societies at, 21–2, and formation of Associated Societies, 22; S.R.C. at: genesis, 22–3, achievements (1884–1905), 23, memorials to H.M.G. (1887), 25–6, (1888), 26, 32, *156–62* and university commissioners (1890), 26–7, *162–166*, influence on Lord Lothian, 36, 21st birthday, 22, 40, 41, mode of effectiveness, 40; deputation of general council of, to H.M.G. (1888), 32; University Hall, 59–60; mentioned, 3, 8. *See also* Universities, Scottish
Ellis, E., jnr, 29
English Inter-Universities Students' Congress (1904), *see* Inter-Universities Students' Congress
Essex, University of: student protest at, 131

Family Law Reform Act, 1969, x
Foster, T. Gregory, 47
Froude, J. A., 30
Frye, Northrop, 140, 152
Fyvel, T. R., 107

Garvin, J. L., 64
Geddes, Patrick, 59
Gladstone, W. E., 30
Glasgow, University of: student membership of, ix; student submissions to commission of 1826, 9, 17; rectorship at, 9–10, 18, 20, 30, 31; formation of S.R.C., 25, and memorial to H.M.G. (1888), 26, 32, *156–62*; deputation of general council of, to H.M.G. (1888), 32; mentioned, 48. *See also* Universities, Scottish
Gower Street, battle of, 13–15
Grant, Sir Alexander, 23, 30
Grey of Fallodon, Edward, 1st viscount, 64

Haldane, Richard Burdon, 1st viscount, 32, 35, 54, 56, 63
Hale Committee on university teaching methods: N.U.S. submission to, 99, 101, 106; report of, 106
Hart, H. L. A., 124–5
Hart report, 124–5
Hawker, Bertram, 63
Hay, Sir Andrew Leith, 20

Henderson, Francis, 12
Herklots, H. G. G., 69, 70–1, 78, 88
Hermes, May, 64
Hoggart, Richard, 127
Horsbrugh, Florence, 94–5, 96
Hume, Joseph, 11–13
Hunter, W. A., 35
Huxley, T. H., 30

In loco parentis: concepts of, in early 19th century, 4–10; student rejection of, in 20th century, 102, 117
Inglis, John, 29
International Student Conference (I.S.C.): N.U.S. affiliation to, 93, and withdrawal from, 114
International Students' Bureau, 61
International Union of Students (I.U.S.): formation of (1946), 93; N.U.S. affiliation to, and withdrawal from, 93
Inter-Universities Students' Congress: at Manchester (1904), London (1905), and Edinburgh (1906), 58; reports of, on halls of residence (1905, 6), 58; motions of, in support of student representation at Durham and London (1908, 10), 60; disenchantment over, 60
Inter-Varsity Association: formation of (1919), 62; conference organised by (1921), 62
Irwin, Samuel, 52–3

Jardine, George, 5, 8, 9
Jarvis, James, 9

Kerr, Philip, 64
King's College, London: student life at, in early 19th century, 4; transitory students' union at, 41; weakness of corporate student life at, 41–2; provides first president of N.U.S., 63; principal of, supports nascent N.U.S., 64; mentioned, 95

Labour Party Study Group on higher education: report of, 103
Lamond, William, 9
Latey report, 115, 117
Leeds, University of (formerly Yorkshire College): merger of student societies at, and formation of S.R.C., 47; absence of recognition for S.R.C. in charter of (1904), 50; mentioned, 68
Lister, W. H., 54–5

Liverpool, University of (formerly University College): as pace-maker for student representative government in England, 43; formation of S.R.C. at, 45; student demonstration at (1892), 45–6; statutory provision for guild of undergraduates at, and for student representation on court of (1903), 50; role of guild in reshaping policy of N.U.S., 72; staff–student lunches at, 74
Lockhart, J. G., 1, 9
London, University of: weakness of corporate student life in, 41–2; evidence of S.R.C. to commission of 1909, 54–5, and response, 55
London School of Economics: student protest at (1934), 83–5, (1966), 114–15, 131; mode of government of student union at, 145
London Student, The, 42
Lorimer, James, 28
Lothian (Schomberg Henry Kerr), 9th marquis of, 32, 33, 34, 36, *156–7*

Macadam, Sir Ivison, vii, 63–4, 72, 82
MacArthur, B., 104, 106
Macaulay, T. B., 2
Macdonald, Sir J. H. A., 26, 32
Mackay, J. M., 44–5, 48–9
Maitland, E. F., 20–1
Manchester, University of (formerly Owens College): early students' unions at, 43; statutory provision for S.R.C. at (1903), but not for student representation on court of, 50; first Inter-Universities Students' Congress at (1904), 58; Dalton Hall, 59; University Life Group at, 72; mentioned, 95
Mansbridge, Albert, 64
Marcuse, Herbert, 125
Martin, Geoffrey, vii, 115, 116
Martin, Kingsley, 83
May, Ralph N., 64, 69
Meyer, F. S., 84–5
Milligan, F. S., 62
Ministry of education: attitude of, to N.U.S., 94–5, 96, 97, 98, 107
Moberly, Sir Walter, 153–4
Morley, Henry, 41, 42
Muir, Ramsay, 43–5, 46, 50, 75–7
Murray, Sir Keith, 98–9

Napier, Francis, 9th baron, and Ettrick, 1st baron, 34–5

National Union of Students (N.U.S.):
origins and formation of, 61–4; 1922–32:
international activities, 65, domestic fortunes, 65–7, annual congresses of, 64, 68,
student criticism of, 68–9, reappraises its
role, (1927) 70, 71–2, (1932) 72; 1933–45:
growing interest in reform of universities, 72–7, and of society, 77–86, annual
congresses of, 73, (1937) 67, 73, (1938)
73–4, 75, 78, (1939) 75–7, 78, (1940) 80–2,
(1941) 82–3, 86, (1942, 3) 86, co-operates
with Establishment, 77, 86, early militancy in, 77, politics in, 79, 80–3, 113,
charter of student rights and responsibilities (1940), 74, 81–2, 166–7, crisis in
leadership (1940), 82, position on 21st
birthday, 86, blueprint for post-war
university development, 86–90; 1945–
1954: international activities, 92–3,
domestic preoccupations, 93–4, politics
in, 93–4, 95, student charter (1949), 94,
restraint of, 94, 95, 96, and growing
sophistication, 95, waning interest in
congresses of, 95, malaise in, 95–6, reappraises its role (1954), 96; 1955–64:
growing interest in education, 97–103,
and pressure for participation, 103–8,
politics in, 113, policy statement (1964),
105, change of mood in, 105–8; 1965–9:
champions student rights in charters of
technological universities, 108–12, pur-
sues campaign for student participation,
112ff., draft statement of student rights
and responsibilities (1967), 122, politics
in, 113–14, 119, tactics of, 114–15, 119,
10-point programme for educational reform (1968), 115, concordat with Committee of V.C.s (1968), 116–17, 119, 143,
and with Association of Education Committees (1968), 118, 119, developing
social concern, 155; as spokesman for
student estate, ix, 92, 121–2, 126–7. See
also Student participation
New Left: challenges leadership and policy
of N.U.S., 114, 118–19; forms R.S.A.
and R.S.S.F., 114; as category of student
conscience, 123ff.; techniques of, 125,
130–36; rejects authority of university,
151
New Left Review, 125
Newcastle, University of: student submission of, to U.G.C., 101
Nottingham, University of: abortive attempts at student representation on

council of, 74; student submission of, to
U.G.C., 101–2

Oxford, University of: student life at, in
early 19th century, 1–2, paternalism at,
4, 6, 7, and student response, 10–11; absence of student evidence to commission
of 1850, 9, 10; absence of student participation in government of, 43; tardy
formation of S.R.C. in, 50; absence of
student estate in, 57; influence of, on
student residence in England, 59; ineligibility of, for full membership of
N.U.S., 62, and consequence, 66; alleged prohibition of Labour Club at, 83;
student protest at, 108; report of Committee on relations with junior members
[Hart report], 124–5

Pares, Sir Bernard, 75
Parkin, Charles, vii, 145 ff.
Pascal, Roy, 90
Pattison, G. S., 14–16
Pattison, Mark, 7
Pearson, C. H., 42
Pillans, James, 8
Piper, D., 104–5
Playfair, Lyon, 30
Privateer, The, 46
Privy Council: and charters of techno-
logical universities, 108–12, 113

Queen's University, Belfast (formerly
Queen's College): formation of S.R.C.
at, 47; evidence of S.R.C. to commission
of 1901, 52–3, and response, 53; pro-
jected student congress at (1902), 58;
statutory provision for student representation on senate of (1908), 53–4

Radical Socialist Students' Federation
(R.S.S.F.), 114
Radical Student Alliance (R.S.A.), 114
Ralphs, F. Lincoln, 69, 75
Rashdall, Hastings, 49
Reading, University of, 68
Rectorship, office of, in Scottish universi-
ties: traditional concept of, 29, 111–12;
character of, in 1826, 9–10; and com-
mission of 1826, 10, 18, 27–8; and act of
1858, 10, 20, 29; and commission of
1876, 30–1; and bill of 1888, 32–4; and
act of 1889, 27
Robbins Committee: N.U.S. submission

to, ix, 99–100, 102–3; N.U.S. debate and commentary on report of, 105

Robertson, Sir Charles Grant, 78

Robertson, James Patrick Bannerman, baron, 35, 52

Rosebery (Archibald Philip Primrose), 5th earl of, 33, 35, 36

Rosebourne, Cyril, 56

Royal Commission, *see* Commission

St Andrews, University of: student evidence to commission of 1826, 9, 17; rectorship at, 9, 13, 18; student protest at (1826), 13; S.R.C. at: formation, 25, memorial to H.M.G. (1888), 26, *156–62*, initiative over S.R.C.S., 25; mentioned, 8. *See also* Universities, Scottish

Schafer, Edward, 42, 47

Schairer, Reinhold, 78

Schlapp, Otto, 22–3

Schuster, Arthur, 58

Schwab, J. J., 135

Scott, C. P., 63

Scott, Sir Walter, 13

Scottish National Union of Students (S.N.U.S.): formation of, 25; relations of, with N.U.S., 66

Scottish Union of Students (S.U.S.), 100

Sedgwick, Adam, 7

Seeley, J. R., 41, 42, 48, 60

Sheffield, University of: absence of provision for S.R.C. in charter of (1905), 50; student representation on governing body of, 74; student submission of, to U.G.C., 101; mentioned, 69, 77

Simon, Brian, 69, 79–80, 81–2, 86, 89, 125

Simons, H. J., 84–5

Sit-in, characteristic features of, 134–5. *See also* Student protest

Soar, Marion, 56

Sonnenschein, E. A., 48–9

Sphinx, The, 46

Strassburg (*later* Strasbourg), University of: and S.R.C. in Britain, 22, 64; and genesis of N.U.S., 61, 64

Straw, Jack, 139–40, 142

Student, The (Edinburgh), 23–4, 40

Student apathy: in late 19th century, 23, 41–3, 44, 45, 47, 50; in early 20th century, 40, 51, 60; in 1920s and early 1930s, 66, 68–9, 70, 71–2; in later 1930s, 69, 75–6; in 1940s and early 1950s, 95–6; still a chronic infirmity, 69; sometimes preferable to participation, 146

Student charters: (1940), 74, 81–2, 122, *166–7*, (1949), 94, (1967 draft), 89, 122

Student conferences and congresses in Britain, *see* Inter-Universities Students' Congress, Inter-Varsity Association, National Union of Students, Students' Representative Councils of Scotland

Student congresses in Britain, *see* Student conferences

Student conscience, categories of, 123 ff.

Student membership of universities: constitutional provision for, ix–x; assumptions behind, 111; character and consequences of, 143–4; ambivalent attitude of N.U.S. to, 110–12; contrasting view of Scottish students in 1888, 111

Student numbers: contrast between, in England and Scotland, in early 19th century, 3; growth of, in 20th century, 91, 92

Student participation in university government: medieval origin of, 143; tradition of, in Scotland, 9–10, but not in England, 9; development of, in 19th century, in Scotland, 20, 27–39; provision for, in charters of Birmingham (1900), 49, Liverpool (1903), 50, Queen's, Belfast (1908), 53–4 and Bristol (1909), 51; absence of provision in charters of Manchester (1903), Leeds (1903), Sheffield (1905), 50, and in University of Durham Act, 1908, 60; an issue before commissions on university education in Ireland (1901), 52, 53, London (1909), 54–5, and Wales (1916), 55–7; plea for, by Durham students (1908), 50; motions for, by Inter-Universities Students' Congress (1908, 10), 50, 60; early discussion of, in N.U.S., 67, 74–5; claim to, in N.U.S. charter of 1940, 74, *167*; modified view on, in N.U.S. blue-print for university development (1944), 75, 88–9; growth in demand for (1957–64), 103–8; intensified pressure for (1966–8), 112–13; welcomed in V.C.s' statement (June 1968), 115; urged in N.U.S. 10-point programme (1968), 115–16; provision for, in concordat between Committee of V.C.s and N.U.S. (Oct 1968), 116–17; student objectives sought by, 117–18; N.U.S. policy on (Apr 1969), 119, 139; need for clarification of university attitude to, 136; wide-ranging definitions of, 138–9; lecture by Straw on, 139–40;

lessons to be learnt about, 139–42; case for, 143–4; rules to be observed in, 144–148; policy to be adopted on, 149. *See also* Rectorship

Student power, *see* Student participation

Student protest: long history of, 129; early examples of, in Scotland, 11–13, 20–1 and England, 13–16, 45–6, 83–6; recent phase of, in British universities, 108, 114–16, 131, and causes, 123, 129; exploitation of, by some student groups, 130ff.; modern techniques of, 125, 130–135; reflections on treatment of, 135–6, 136ff.

Students' representative council: genesis of, 22ff.; statutory recognition of, 32–5; spread of, from Scotland to the south, 41ff. *See also particular universities*

Students' Representative Councils of Scotland (S.R.C.S.): formation of, 25; annual conferences of, 25; representations of, on university legislation (1888), 26, 32, 111, *156–62*; withdrawal of, from Inter-Universities Students' Congress, 60; and student congress at Strasbourg, 61; relations of, with N.U.S., 66

Students' unions: N.U.S. claim to autonomy of, 89, 109, 110–12. *See also particular universities*

Student Vanguard, 84

Surrey, University of (formerly Battersea College of Technology): student influence on charter of, 109–12

Swindlehurst, A. A., 106

Thompson, L. F., 54

Thomson, Dr A., 14–15

Thomson, Malcolm, 61

Thorp, Thomas, 6

Times, The, 33, 49, 63, 99, 107

Times Educational Supplement, The, 82, 83

Truscot, Bruce, *pseud*. [i.e. Edgar Allison Peers], 73

Universities: misconceptions about power in, 139–42, 148; nature of authority in, 143–4, 149–55; unsolved problem concerning, 153–5

—, continental, in early 19th century, 5, 9, 13

—, English, in early 19th century: purpose of, and student life in, 1–2; paternalism

in, 4–8, 9, 10, and student response, 10–11

—, Scottish, in early 19th century: purpose of, and student life in, 2–3, paternalism in, 4, 5, 8, and student response, 11–13 *See also particular universities*

Universities Review, The, 67

University, The (N.U.S.), 68

University College London: student life at, in early 19th century, 4; battle of Gower Street at, 13–16; weakness of corporate student life at, 41–3; founding of *U.C. London Gazette* and U.C. Society, 42, and of students' union, 46–7

University College London Gazette, The, 42

University College Magazine (Liverpool), 45

University Grants Committee (U.G.C.): early reserve of, towards N.U.S., 96; invites student views on quinquennium of 1962–7, 98–9; student response, 100–2, and influence, 102; and charters of technological universities, 36, 109; and submission of N.U.S. for quinquennium of 1967–72, 112. *See also* Hale Committee

University legislation, for England: University of Durham Act, 1908, 60

—, for Ireland: Irish Universities Act, 1908, 53–4

—, for Scotland: Universities (Scotland) bill, 1857, 28; Universities (Scotland) Act, 1858, 10, 20, 28–9; Universities (Scotland) bills, 1883–7, 31–2; Universities (Scotland) bill, 1888, 24, 26, 32–5, 36; Universities (Scotland) Act, 1889, 24, 26, 27, 35

University Review, The, 59–60

Venn, J., 6–7

Vosper, Dennis, 96

Wales, University of: evidence of S.R.C. to commission of 1916, 55–6; and response, 57

Wall, Henry, 7

Wells, H. G., 81

Wemyss and March (Francis Wemyss-Charteris–Douglas), 10th earl of, 32

Whewell, William, 5–6, 10, 13, 16

Whytehead, Thomas, 6

Winchester College: pupil protest in, 129